# Britain's

# Best**Hotels**

**AA**

This product includes mapping data licensed from Ordnance Survey® with the permission of the Controller of Her Majesty's Stationery Office. © Crown copyright 2008. All rights reserved. Licence number 100021153.

Maps prepared by the Mapping Services Department of The Automobile Association.

Maps © Automobile Association Developments Limited 2008.

Advertising Sales:
advertisementsales@theAA.com

Editorial:
lifestyleguides@theAA.com

Assessments of AA inspected establishments are based on the experience of the hotel and restaurant inspectors on the occasion of their visit(s) and therefore descripti[on]... guide necessarily dictate an ele[ment of] opinion which may not reflect or d[isagree with your] own opinion on another occasion. W[e have tried] to ensure accuracy in this guide but th[ings] change and we would be grateful if read[ers would] advise us of any inaccuracies they may en[counter].

Typeset by AA Lifestyle Guides

Printed and bound by Graficas Estella, Spain

Editorial contributors: Phil Bryant, Penny Phenix and Julia Hynard

Cover credits
Front cover: Mandarin Oriental Hyde Park, London
Back cover: Luton Hoo, Golf and Spa, Bedfordshire

A CIP catalogue record for this book is available from the British Library

ISBN-13: 978-0-7495-5626-6

Published by AA Publishing, which is a trading name of Automobile Association Developments Limited, whose registered office is:
Fanum House, Basing View
Basingstoke
Hampshire RG21 4EA

www.theAA.com

Registered number 1878835

A03525

# Britain's
# Best**Hotels**

# Contents

| | | | |
|---|---|---|---|
| **Welcome** | 4 | **Useful Information** | 10 |
| **Using the guide** | 5 | **Inspectors' Choice** | 12 |
| **Best Quality** | 8 | | |

| | | | |
|---|---|---|---|
| **England** | 18 | Merseyside | 166 |
| Bedfordshire | 20 | Norfolk | 170 |
| Berkshire | 22 | Northamptonshire | 176 |
| Bristol | 27 | Northumberland | 178 |
| Buckinghamshire | 29 | Nottinghamshire | 181 |
| Cambridgeshire | 33 | Oxfordshire | 185 |
| Cheshire | 40 | Rutland | 190 |
| Cornwall & Isles of Scilly | 43 | Shropshire | 192 |
| Cumbria | 55 | Somerset | 196 |
| Derbyshire | 71 | Staffordshire | 205 |
| Devon | 75 | Suffolk | 209 |
| Dorset | 89 | Surrey | 214 |
| County Durham | 95 | East Sussex | 218 |
| Essex | 98 | West Sussex | 224 |
| Gloucestershire | 100 | Tyne & Wear | 230 |
| Greater Manchester | 108 | Warwickshire | 232 |
| Hampshire | 111 | West Midlands | 237 |
| Herefordshire | 122 | Wiltshire | 239 |
| Hertfordshire | 124 | Worcestershire | 241 |
| Isle of Wight | 127 | North Yorkshire | 246 |
| Kent | 130 | South & West Yorkshire | 252 |
| Lancashire | 136 | **Channel Islands** | 260 |
| Leicestershire | 141 | **Scotland** | 268 |
| Lincolnshire | 144 | **Wales** | 310 |
| London | 146 | | |

| | | | |
|---|---|---|---|
| **Maps** | 331 | **Index** | 346 |
| Maps 1-13 | 332 | Location Index | 346 |
| County Map | 345 | Hotel Index | 349 |

# Welcome

Britain's Best Hotels covers a selection of the very best hotels in England, Scotland, Wales and the Channel Islands. All establishments are professionally inspected by the AA to ensure the highest standards of hospitality, accommodation and food.

## The Best Hotels

This guide covers more than 280 town and country houses, small and metro hotels. Every establishment has received a star rating and percentage merit score following a visit by an AA inspector. This will help ensure that you will have a friendly welcome, comfortable surroundings, excellent food and a good service. Further details about the AA scheme, inspections and awards and rating system can be found on pages 8–9 of this guide.

## Before You Travel

Some places may offer special breaks and facilities not available at the time of going to press. If in doubt, it's always worth calling the hotel before you book. See also the useful information provided on pages 10–11, and visit www.theAA.com for up-to-date establishment and travel information.

# Using the Guide

Britain's Best Hotels has been designed to enable you to find an establishment quickly and efficiently. Each entry provides clear information about the type of accommodation, the facilities available and the local area.

Use the contents (page 3) to browse the main gazetteer section by county and the index to find either a location (page 346) or a specific hotel (page 349) by name.

**Finding Your Way**

The main section of the guide is divided into four main parts covering England, Channel Islands, Scotland and Wales. The counties within each of these sections are ordered alphabetically as are the town or village locations (shown in capital letters as part of the address) within each county. Finally, the establishments are listed alphabetically under each location name. Town names featured in the guide can also be located in the map section (page 331 onwards).

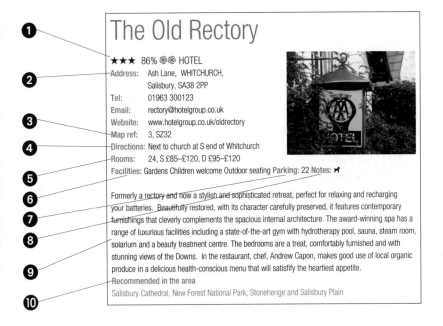

## The Old Rectory

① ★★★ 86% ◉◉ HOTEL
② Address:    Ash Lane, WHITCHURCH,
              Salisbury, SA38 2PP
   Tel:        01963 300123
   Email:      rectory@hotelgroup.co.uk
   Website:    www.hotelgroup.co.uk/oldrectory
③ Map ref:    3, SZ32
④ Directions: Next to church at S end of Whitchurch
⑤ Rooms:      24, S £85–£120, D £95–£120
⑥ Facilities: Gardens Children welcome Outdoor seating Parking: 22 Notes: ✈

⑦ Formerly a rectory and now a stylish and sophisticated retreat, perfect for relaxing and recharging
⑧ your batteries. Beautifully restored, with its character carefully preserved, it features contemporary furnishings that cleverly complements the spacious internal architecture. The award-winning spa has a range of luxurious facilities including a state-of-the-art gym with hydrotherapy pool, sauna, steam room, solarium and a beauty treatment centre. The bedrooms are a treat, comfortably furnished and with stunning views of the Downs. In the restaurant, chef, Andrew Capon, makes good use of local organic produce in a delicious health-conscious menu that will satisfify the heartiest appetite.
⑨ Recommended in the area
⑩ Salisbury Cathedral, New Forest National Park; Stonehenge and Salisbury Plain

### ① Stars and symbols

All entries in the guide have been inspected by the AA and, at the time of going to press, belong to the AA hotel scheme. Every establishment in the scheme is classified for quality with a rating of one to five stars (★). Every establishment in Britain's Best Hotels has three, four or five stars and a high merit score (%). The very best hotels in each of these categories have been given red stars (★). Alongside a star rating, each establishment has also been given one of six descriptive categories:
HOTEL (HL), TOWN HOUSE HOTEL (TH), COUNTRY HOUSE HOTEL (CHH), SMALL HOTEL (SHL), METRO HOTEL (MET) and BUDGET HOTEL (BUD). See pages 8–10 for more information on the AA ratings and awards scheme.

Rosette Awards ❀: This is the AA's food award (see page 9 for further details).

## ❷ Contact Details

The establishment address includes a locator or place name in capitals (e.g. NORWICH). Within each county, entries are ordered alphabetically first by this place name and then by the name of the establishment.

Telephone and fax numbers, and e-mail and website addresses are given where available. See page 10 for information about booking online. The telephone and fax numbers are believed correct at the time of going to press but changes may occur. The latest establishment details are on the Hotel pages at www.theAA.com.

Website addresses have been supplied by the establishments and lead you to websites that are not under the control of Automobile Association Developments Ltd. AADL has no control over and accepts no responsibility or liability in respect of the material on any such websites. By including the addresses of third-party websites AADL does not intend to solicit business.

## ❸ Map reference

The map reference is composed of two parts. The first number shows the atlas map number (from 1–13) at the back of the guide (see page 331 onwards). The second part is a National Grid reference. To find the town or village location one of the maps, locate the lettered square and read the first figure across and the second figure vertically using the gridlines to help guide you. For example, a map reference of '3, TQ28' refers to map 3 in the atlas section, grid square TQ on the map and a location of two across the grid square, running east-west and eight in a north-south direction. The map section of this guide also provides road and county information.

Maps locating each establishment and a route planner are available at www.theAA.com.

## ❹ Directions

Where possible, directions have been given from the nearest motorway or A road. Distances are provided in miles (m) and yards (yds).

## ❺ Room Information

The entries show the number of en suite letting bedrooms available. Bedrooms that have a private bathroom adjacent may be included as en suite. Further details of facilities provided in the rooms are listed in the main entry description (see ❾). Always phone in advance to ensure that the hotel has the facilities you require.

**Prices:** Prices are per room per night (unless otherwise specified) and are provided by the hoteliers in good faith. These prices are indications and not firm quotations. Always check before booking.

## ❻ Facilities

This section lists a selection of facilities offered by the hotel. It includes sports facilities such as indoor and outdoor swimming pools, golf, tennis and gym, options for relaxation such as spa, jacuzzi and solarium, and services such as satellite TV and Wi-fi and Internet accessibility. Use the key to the symbols on page 7 to help identify what's available at a particular hotel.

Additional facilities, such as access for disabled people, or notes about other services may be listed here and it is by no means exhaustive. Some hotels have restricted service during quieter months, and at this time some of the listed facilities will not be available. If unsure, contact the hotel before your visit, using the details provided in this guide.

## Payment

As most hotels now accept credit or debit cards we only indicate if an establishment does not accept any cards for payment. Credit cards may be subject to a surcharge – check when booking if this is how you intend to pay. Not all hotels accept travellers' cheques.

### ➐ Parking

This shows the number of parking spaces available. Other types of parking (on road or Park and Ride) may also be possible; check the descriptions for further information. Phone the establishment in advance of your arrival to check.

### ➑ Notes

This section provides details specific details relating to:

**Smoking policy:** In 2007 smoking was banned in public areas in England, Wales and Northern Ireland, following a similar ban in Scotland in 2006.

The proprietor can designate one or more bedrooms with ventilation systems where the occupants can smoke, but communal areas must be smoke-free. Communal areas include interior bars, restaurants and other public rooms such as lounges or gym facilities.

**Dogs:** Establishments that state no dogs may accept assist/guide dogs. Some places that do accept dogs may restrict the size and breed of dog and the rooms into which they can be taken. Always check the conditions of the hotel when making a booking.

**Children:** No children means children cannot be accommodated, or a minimum age may be specified, e.g. No children under 4 means no children under four years old. The main description may also provide details about other facilities available.

Establishments with special facilities for children may include a babysitting service or baby-intercom system, playroom or playground, laundry facilities, drying and ironing facilities, cots, high chairs and special meals. If you have very young children, check before booking.

**Other notes:** Additional facilities, such as access for disabled people, or notes about other services. See the specific entries for details. Always contact the hotel beforehand if you are unsure.

### ➒ Description

This may include specific information about the various facilities offered in the rooms, a brief history of the establishment, notes about special features and descriptions of the food where an award has been given (see 1 above).

### ➓ Recommended in the Area

This listings gives places of interest, local sights to visit and potential day trips and activities. The hotel may also provide further info.

## Key to symbols

| | |
|---|---|
| ★ | Black stars (see page 8) |
| ★ | Red stars (see page 9) |
| % | Merit score |
| ◉ | AA Rosette (see page 9) |
| 3, TQ28 | Map reference (see pages 331–345) |
| S | Single room |
| D | Double room |
| T | Twin room |
| Triple | Triple room |
| Family | Family room |
| ⊘ | No smoking in area indicated |
| ⊗ | No dogs allowed in area indicated |
| 🐕 | Dogs allowed in area indicated |
| Wi-fi | Wireless network available where indicated |
| STV | Satellite television |
| ▣ | Indoor swimming pool |
| ⌇ | Outdoor swimming pool |

# Best Quality

All entries in Britain's Best Hotels have excelled in several categories set by the AA inspection team. Red stars are awarded to the very best establishments in each star category and signify that the hotel offers the finest accommodation available.

### High Standards

Hotels recognised by the AA should:

- have high standards of cleanliness
- keep proper records of booking
- give prompt and professional service to guests, assist with luggage on request, accept and deliver messages
- provide a designated area for breakfast and dinner, with drinks available in a bar or lounge
- provide an early morning call on request
- have good quality furniture and fittings
- provide adequate heating and lighting
- undertake proper maintenance

The hotels in Britain's Best Hotels all have a three, four or five black or red star rating. The following is brief guide to some of the general expectations for each star classification:

### ★★★ Three Star

- Management and staff smartly and professionally presented and usually wearing a recognisable uniform
- A dedicated receptionist on duty at peak times
- At least one restaurant or dining room open to residents and non-residents for breakfast and dinner whenever the hotel is open
- Last orders for dinner no earlier than 8pm
- Remote-control television, direct-dial phone
- En suite bath or shower and WC

### ★★★★ Four Star

- A formal, professional staffing structure with smartly presented, uniformed staff anticipating and responding to your needs or requests
- Usually spacious, well-appointed public areas
- Reception staffed 24 hours by well-trained staff
- Express checkout facilities where appropriate
- Porterage available on request
- Night porter available

- At least one restaurant open to residents and non-residents for breakfast and dinner seven days per week, and lunch to be available in a designated eating area
- Last orders for dinner no earlier than 9pm
- En suite bath with fixed overhead shower and WC

### ★★★★★ Five Star

- Luxurious accommodation and public areas with a range of extra facilities. First time guests shown to their bedroom
- Multilingual service
- Guest accounts well explained and clearly presented
- Porterage offered
- Guests greeted at hotel entrance, full concierge service provided

- At least one restaurant open to residents and non-residents for all meals seven days per week
- Last orders for dinner no earlier than 10pm
- High-quality menu and wine list
- Evening service to turn down the beds.
- Remote-control television, direct-dial telephone at bedside and desk, a range of luxury toiletries, bath sheets and robes.
- En suite bathroom incorporating fixed overhead shower and WC

### ★ Inspectors' Choice

Each year the AA selects the best hotels in each rating. These hotels stand out as the very best in the British Isles, regardless of style. The selected Inspectors' Choice hotels in the main section of this guide are identified by red stars.

### Types of hotel

The majority of establishments in this guide come under the category of Hotel; other categories are listed below:

**Town House Hotel (TH):** A small, individual city or town centre property, which provides a high degree or personal service and privacy.

**Country House Hotel (CHH):** These are quietly located in a rural area

**Small Hotel (SHL):** Has less than 20 bedrooms and is managed by the owner

**Metro Hotel (MET):** A hotel in an urban location that does not offer an evening meal

**Budget Hotel (BUD):** These are usually purpose built modern properties offering inexpensive accommodation. Often located near motorways and in town or city centres

A small number of hotels in the guide are not rated because their star classification was not confirmed at the time of going to press. Check the AA website www.theAA.com for current information and ratings.

# AA Rosette Awards

Out of the many thousands of restaurants in the UK, the AA identifies some 1,800 as the best. The following is an outline of what to expect from restaurants with AA Rosette Awards. For a more detailed explanation of Rosette criteria please see www.theAA.com

◉ Excellent local restaurants serving food prepared with care, understanding and skill, using good quality ingredients.

◉◉ The best local restaurants, which aim for and achieve higher standards, better consistency and where a greater precision is apparent in the cooking. There will be obvious attention to the selection of quality ingredients.

◉◉◉ Outstanding restaurants that demand recognition well beyond their local area.

◉◉◉◉ Amongst the very best restaurants in the British Isles, where the cooking demands national recognition.

◉◉◉◉◉ The finest restaurants in the British Isles, where the cooking stands comparison with the best in the world.

# Useful Information

If you're unsure about any of the facilities offered, always check with the establishment before you visit or book accommodation. Up-to-date information on contacting all hotels in this guide can be found in the travel section of the www.theAA.com

## Hints on booking your stay

It's always worth booking as early as possible, particularly for the peak holiday period from the beginning of June to the end of September. Bear in mind that Easter and other public holidays may be busy too, and in some parts of Scotland, the ski season is a peak holiday period.

Some hotels will ask for a deposit or full payment in advance, especially for one-night bookings. And some hotels charge half-board (bed, breakfast and dinner) whether you require the meals or not, while others may only accept full-board bookings. Not all hotels will accept advance bookings for bed and breakfast, overnight or short stays. Some will not take reservations from mid week.

Once a booking is confirmed, let the hotel know at once if you are unable to keep your reservation. If the hotel cannot re-let your room you may be liable to pay about two-thirds of the room price (a deposit will count towards this payment). In Britain a legally binding contract is made when you accept an offer of accommodation, either in writing or by telephone, and illness is not accepted as a release from this contract. You are advised to take out insurance against possible cancellation, for example AA Single Trip Insurance or visit www.theAA.com.

## Booking online

Booking a place to stay can be a very time-consuming process, but you can search quickly and easily online for a place that best suits your needs. Simply visit www.theAA.com/hotels to search from around 8,000 quality rated hotels and B&Bs in Great Britain and Ireland. Then either check availability and book online by clicking on the 'Booking' button, or contact the establishment for further information.

## Prices

The AA encourages the use of the Hotel Industry Voluntary Code of Booking Practice, which aims to ensure that guests know how much they will have to pay and what services and facilities are included, before entering a financially binding agreement. If the price has not previously been confirmed in writing, guests should be given a card stipulating the total obligatory charge when they register at reception.

The Tourism (Sleeping Accommodation Price Display) Order of 1977 compels hotels, travel accommodation, guest houses, farmhouses, inns and self-catering accommodation with four or more letting bedrooms, to display in entrance halls the minimum and maximum price for one or two persons but they may vary without warning.

## Facilities for disabled guests

The final stage (Part III) of the Disability Discrimination Act (access to Goods and Services) came into force in October 2004. This means that service providers may have to make permanent adjustments to their premises. For further information, see the government website www.disability.gov.uk

Please note: AA inspectors are not accredited to make inspections under the National Accessibility Scheme. We indicate in the descriptions if an establishment has ground floor rooms; and if a hotel tells us that they have disabled facilities this is also included in the text.

The establishments in this guide should all be aware of their responsibilities under the Act. We recommend that you always telephone in advance to ensure that the establishment you have chosen has appropriate facilities.

Other useful websites to visit include:
www.holidaycare.org.uk
www.dptac.gov.uk/door-to-door

## Licensing Laws

Licensing laws differ in England, Wales, Scotland, the Republic of Ireland, the Isle of Man, the Isles of Scilly and the Channel Islands. Public houses are generally open from mid morning to early afternoon, and from about 6 or 7pm until 11pm, although closing times may be earlier or later and some pubs are open all afternoon. Unless otherwise stated, establishments listed are licensed. Hotel residents can obtain alcoholic drinks at all times, if the licensee is prepared to serve them. Non-residents eating at the hotel restaurant can have drinks with meals. Children under 14 may be excluded from bars where no food is served. Those under 18 may not purchase or consume alcoholic drinks. Club license means that drinks are served to club members only, 48 hours must lapse between joining and ordering.

## Fire Safety

The Fire Precautions Act does not apply to the Channel Islands, Republic of Ireland, or the Isle of Man, which have their own rules. As far as we are aware, all hotels listed have applied for and not been refused a fire certificate.

### Bank and Public Holidays 2008

| | |
|---|---|
| **New Year's Day** | 1st January |
| **New Year's Holiday** | 2nd January (Scotland) |
| **Good Friday** | 21st March |
| **Easter Monday** | 24th March |
| **May Day Bank Holiday** | 5th May |
| **Spring Bank Holiday** | 26th May |
| **August Holiday** | 4th August (Scotland) |
| **Late Summer Holiday** | 25th August |
| **St Andrew's Day** | 1st December (Scotland) |
| **Christmas Day** | 25th December |
| **Boxing Day** | 26th December |

# www.theAA.com

Go to www.theAA.com to find more AA listed guest houses, hotels, pubs and restaurants – There are around 12,000 establishments on the site.

Routes & Traffic on the home page leads to a route planner. Simply enter your postcode and the establishment postcode given in this guide and click Confirm. Check your details and then click GET MY ROUTE and you will have a detailed route plan to take you from door-to-door.

Use the Travel section to search for Hotels & B&Bs or Restaurants & Pubs by location or establishment name. Scroll down the list of finds for the interactive map and local routes.

Postcode searches can also be done on www.ordnancesurvey.co.uk and www.multimap.com, which will also provide useful aerial views of your destination.

# Inspectors' Choice
# Red Star Hotels

Assessed and announced annually, the AA's Inspectors' Choice Awards recognise the very best hotels in Britain. These hotels offer consistently outstanding levels of quality, comfort, cleanliness and customer care. Hotels are listed in county order, showing their star classification, rosettes and telephone number.

## ENGLAND

### BERKSHIRE

Maidenhead — **Fredrick's Hotel**
★★★★  ⊛⊛⊛  ☎ 01628 581000

Newbury — **The Vineyard at Stockcross**
★★★★★  ⊛⊛⊛⊛  ☎ 01635 528770

### BUCKINGHAMSHIRE

Aylesbury — **Hartwell House Hotel**
★★★★  ⊛⊛⊛  ☎ 01296 747444

Taplow — **Cliveden**
★★★★★  ⊛⊛⊛  ☎ 01628 668561

### CHESHIRE

Chester — **The Chester Grosvenor & Spa**
★★★★★  ⊛⊛⊛  ☎ 01244 324024

### CORNWALL & ISLES OF SCILLY

Bryher — **Hell Bay Hotel**
★★★  ⊛⊛  ☎ 01720 422947

Fowey — **Marina Villa**
★★  ⊛⊛⊛  ☎ 01726 833315

Fowey — **The Old Quay House Hotel**
★★  ⊛⊛  ☎ 01726 833302

Portscatho — **Driftwood**
★★★  ⊛⊛⊛⊛  ☎ 01872 580644

St Martin's — **St Martin's on the Isle**
★★★  ⊛⊛⊛  ☎ 01720 422090

Tresco — **The Island Hotel**
★★★  ⊛⊛  ☎ 01720 422883

### CUMBRIA

Brampton — **Farlam Hall Hotel**
★★★  ⊛⊛  ☎ 016977 46234

Grange-over-Sands — **Clare House**
★  ⊛  ☎ 015395 33026

Howtown — **Sharrow Bay Country House Hotel**
★★★  ⊛⊛  ☎ 017684 86301

Keswick — **Swinside Lodge**
★★  ⊛⊛  ☎ 017687 72948

Watermillock — **Rampsbeck Country House Hotel**
★★★  ⊛⊛⊛  ☎ 017684 86442

Windermere — **Gilpin Lodge Country House Hotel**
★★★★  ⊛⊛⊛  ☎ 015394 88818

Windermere — **Holbeck Ghyll Country House Hotel**
★★★★  ⊛⊛⊛  ☎ 015394 32375

Windermere — **Linthwaite House Hotel**
★★★  ⊛⊛⊛  ☎ 015394 88600

Windermere — **The Samling**
★★★  ⊛⊛⊛  ☎ 015394 31922

### DERBYSHIRE

Baslow — **Fischer's Baslow Hall**
★★★  ⊛⊛⊛⊛  ☎ 01246 583259

Rowsey — **East Lodge Country House**
★★★  ⊛⊛  ☎ 01629 734474

### DEVON

Ashwater — **Blagdon Manor Hotel & Restaurant**
★★★  ⊛⊛  ☎ 01409 211224

Burrington — **Northcote Manor**
★★★  ⊛⊛  ☎ 01769 560501

Chagford — **Gidleigh Park**
★★★★  ⊛⊛⊛⊛  ☎ 01647 432367

| | | |
|---|---|---|
| Chagford | | **Mill End Hotel** |
| ★★ | ◉◉ | ☎ 01647 432282 |
| Honiton | | **Combe House Hotel & Restaurant** |
| ★★★ | ◉◉ | ☎ 01404 540400 |
| Lewdown | | **Lewtrenchard Manor** |
| ★★★ | ◉◉◉ | ☎ 01566 783256 |

## DORSET

| | | |
|---|---|---|
| Evershot | | **Summer Lodge Country House Hotel** |
| ★★★★ | ◉◉◉ | ☎ 01935 482000 |
| Gillingham | | **Stock Hill Country House** |
| ★★★ | ◉◉◉ | ☎ 01747 823626 |

## CO DURHAM

| | | |
|---|---|---|
| Romaldkirk | | **Rose & Crown Hotel** |
| ★★ | ◉◉ | ☎ 01833 650213 |
| Seaham | | **Seaham Hall Hotel** |
| ★★★★★ | ◉◉◉ | ☎ 0191 516 1400 |

## ESSEX

| | | |
|---|---|---|
| Dedham | | **Maison Talbooth** |
| ★★★ | ◉◉ | ☎ 01206 322367 |

## GLOUCESTERSHIRE

| | | |
|---|---|---|
| Buckland | | **Buckland Manor** |
| ★★★ | ◉◉ | ☎ 01386 852626 |
| Cheltenham | | **Hotel on the Park** |
| ★★★ | ◉◉ | ☎ 01242 518898 |
| Corse Lawn | | **Corse Lawn House Hotel** |
| ★★★ | ◉◉ | ☎ 01452 780771 |
| Lower Slaughter | | **Lower Slaughter Manor*** |
| ★★★ | | ☎ 01451 820456 |
| Tetbury | | **Calcot Manor** |
| ★★★★ | ◉◉ | ☎ 01666 890391 |
| Thornbury | | **Thornbury Castle** |
| ★★★ | ◉◉ | ☎ 01454 281182 |
| Upper Slaughter | | **Lords of the Manor** |
| ★★★ | ◉◉◉ | ☎ 01451 820243 |

## HAMPSHIRE

| | | |
|---|---|---|
| Beaulieu | | **Montagu Arms Hotel** |
| ★★★ | ◉◉ | ☎ 01590 612324 |
| Brockenhurst | | **Rhinefield House** |
| ★★★★ | ◉◉ | ☎ 01590 622922 |
| New Milton | | **Chewton Glen Hotel** |
| ★★★★★ | ◉◉◉ | ☎ 01425 275341 |
| Rotherwick | | **Tylney Hall Hotel** |
| ★★★★ | ◉◉ | ☎ 01256 764881 |
| Winchester | | **Lainston House Hotel** |
| ★★★★ | ◉◉◉ | ☎ 01962 863588 |

## ISLE OF WIGHT

| | | |
|---|---|---|
| Yarmouth | | **George Hotel** |
| ★★★ | ◉◉ | ☎ 01983 760331 |

## KENT

| | | |
|---|---|---|
| Ashford | | **Eastwell Manor** |
| ★★★★ | ◉◉ | ☎ 01233 213000 |
| Lenham | | **Chilston Park Hotel** |
| ★★★★ | ◉◉ | ☎ 01622 859803 |

## LEICESTERSHIRE

| | | |
|---|---|---|
| Melton Mowbray | | **Stapleford Park** |
| ★★★★ | ◉◉ | ☎ 01572 787000 |

## LONDON

| | | |
|---|---|---|
| E14 | | **Four Seasons Hotel Canary Wharf** |
| ★★★★★ | ◉ | ☎ 020 7510 1999 |
| NW1 | | **The Landmark London** |
| ★★★★★ | ◉◉ | ☎ 020 7631 8000 |
| SW1 | | **The Berkeley** |
| ★★★★★ | ◉◉◉◉ | ☎ 020 7235 6000 |
| SW1 | | **The Goring** |
| ★★★★★ | ◉◉ | ☎ 020 7396 9000 |
| SW1 | | **The Halkin Hotel** |
| ★★★★★ | ◉◉◉ | ☎ 020 7333 1000 |
| SW1 | | **Jumeirah Carlton Tower** |
| ★★★★★ | ◉◉ | ☎ 020 7235 1234 |
| SW1 | | **The Lanesborough** |
| ★★★★★ | ◉◉ | ☎ 020 7259 5599 |
| SW1 | | **Mandarin Oriental Hyde Park** |
| ★★★★★ | ◉◉◉◉ | ☎ 020 7235 2000 |
| SW1 | | **No 41*** |
| ★★★★★ | | ☎ 020 7300 0041 |
| SW1 | | **The Stafford** |
| ★★★★ | ◉◉ | ☎ 020 7493 0111 |
| SW3 | | **The Capital** |
| ★★★★★ | ◉◉◉◉ | ☎ 020 7589 5171 |
| SW7 | | **Baglioni Hotel** |
| ★★★★★ | ◉◉ | ☎ 020 7368 5700 |

| W1 | | | Athenaeum |
| ★★★★★ | ◉ | ☎ 020 7499 3464 | |
| W1 | | | Claridge's |
| ★★★★★ | ◉◉◉ | ☎ 020 7629 8860 | |
| W1 | | | The Connaught |
| ★★★★★ | | ☎ 020 7499 7070 | |
| W1 | | | The Dorchester |
| ★★★★★ | ◉◉◉ | ☎ 020 7629 8888 | |
| W1 | | | Four Seasons Hotel London |
| ★★★★★ | ◉ | ☎ 020 7499 0888 | |
| W1 | | | The Ritz |
| ★★★★★ | ◉◉ | ☎ 020 7493 8181 | |
| W8 | | | Royal Garden Hotel* |
| ★★★★★ | | ☎ 020 7937 8000 | |
| W8 | | | Milestone Hotel |
| ★★★★★ | ◉◉ | ☎ 020 7917 1000 | |
| WC2 | | | One Aldwych |
| ★★★★★ | ◉◉ | ☎ 020 7300 1000 | |

## NORFOLK

| Blakeney | | | Morston Hall |
| ★★★ | ◉◉◉ | ☎ 01263 741041 | |
| Grimston | | | Congham Hall Country House Hotel |
| ★★★ | ◉◉ | ☎ 01485 600250 | |
| North Walsham | | | Beechwood Hotel |
| ★★★ | ◉◉ | ☎ 01692 403231 | |
| Norwich | | | The Old Rectory |
| ★★ | ◉◉ | ☎ 01603 700772 | |

## NORTHAMPTONSHIRE

| Daventry | | | Fawsley Hall* |
| ★★★★ | | ☎ 01327 892000 | |

## NOTTINGHAMSHIRE

| Nottingham | | Restaurant Sat Bains with Rooms |
| ★★★ | ◉◉◉◉ | ☎ 0115 986 6566 | |

## OXFORDSHIRE

| Great Milton | | Le Manoir Aux Quat' Saisons |
| ★★★★★ | ◉◉◉◉◉ ☎ 01844 278881 | |

## RUTLAND

| Oakham | | | Hambleton Hall |
| ★★★★ | ◉◉◉◉ | ☎ 01572 756991 | |

## SHROPSHIRE

| Worfield | | | Old Vicarage Hotel |
| ★★★ | ◉◉◉ | ☎ 01746 716497 | |

## SOMERSET

| Bath | | | The Bath Priory Hotel |
| ★★★★ | ◉◉◉ | ☎ 01225 331922 | |
| Bath | | | The Queensberry Hotel |
| ★★★ | ◉◉ | ☎ 01225 447928 | |
| Porlock | | | The Oaks Hotel |
| ★★★ | ◉ | ☎ 01643 862265 | |
| Shepton Mallet | | | Charlton House Hotel |
| ★★★★ | ◉◉ | ☎ 01749 342008 | |
| Wellington | | | Bindon Country House Hotel & Restaurant |
| ★★★ | ◉◉ | ☎ 01823 400070 | |

## STAFFORDSHIRE

| Lichfield | | | Swinfen Hall Hotel |
| ★★★★ | ◉◉ | ☎ 01543 481494 | |

## SUFFOLK

| Hintlesham | | | Hintlesham Hall Hotel |
| ★★★★ | ◉◉◉ | ☎ 01473 652334 | |

## SURREY

| Bagshot | | Pennyhill Park Hotel & The Spa |
| ★★★★★ | ◉◉◉ | ☎ 01276 471774 | |

## SUSSEX, EAST

| Forest Row | | | Ashdown Park Hotel and Country Club |
| ★★★★ | ◉◉ | ☎ 01342 824988 | |
| Newick | | | Newick Park Hotel & Country Estate |
| ★★★ | ◉◉ | ☎ 01825 723633 | |
| Uckfield | | | Horsted Place |
| ★★★ | ◉◉ | ☎ 01825 750581 | |

## SUSSEX, WEST

| Amberley | | | Amberley Castle |
| ★★★★ | ◉◉◉ | ☎ 01798 831992 | |
| Cuckfield | | | Ockenden Manor |
| ★★★ | ◉◉◉ | ☎ 01444 416111 | |
| East Grinstead | | | Gravetye Manor Hotel |
| ★★★ | ◉◉◉ | ☎ 01342 810567 | |

| | | |
|---|---|---|
| Gatwick Airport | | **Langshott Manor** |
| ★★★ | @@ | ☎ 01293 786680 |
| Lower Beeding | | **South Lodge Hotel** |
| ★★★★ | @@@ | ☎ 01403 891711 |
| Turners Hill | | **Alexander House Hotel** |
| | | **& Utopia Spa** |
| ★★★★ | @@ | ☎ 01342 714914 |

## WARWICKSHIRE

| | | |
|---|---|---|
| Alderminster | | **Ettington Park Hotel** |
| ★★★★ | @@ | ☎ 01789 450123 |
| Royal Leamington Spa | | **Mallory Court Hotel** |
| ★★★ | @@@ | ☎ 01926 330214 |

## WILTSHIRE

| | | |
|---|---|---|
| Castle Combe | | **Manor House Hotel** |
| ★★★★ | @@@ | ☎ 01249 782206 |
| Colerne | | **Lucknam Park** |
| ★★★★★ | @@@ | ☎ 01225 742777 |
| Malmesbury | | **Whatley Manor** |
| ★★★★★ | @@@ | ☎ 01666 822888 |

## WORCESTERSHIRE

| | | |
|---|---|---|
| Chaddesley Corbett | | **Brockencote Hall** |
| | | **Country House Hotel** |
| ★★★ | @@ | ☎ 01562 777876 |

## YORKSHIRE, NORTH

| | | |
|---|---|---|
| Bolton Abbey | | **The Devonshire Arms** |
| | | **Country House Hotel*** |
| ★★★★ | | ☎ 01756 710441 |
| Crathorne | | **Crathorne Hall Hotel** |
| ★★★★ | @@ | ☎ 01642 700398 |
| Harrogate | | **Rudding Park Hotel & Golf** |
| ★★★★ | @@ | ☎ 01423 871350 |
| Masham | | **Swinton Park** |
| ★★★★ | @@@ | ☎ 01765 680900 |
| Yarm | | **Judges Country House Hotel** |
| ★★★ | @@@ | ☎ 01642 789000 |
| York | | **The Grange Hotel** |
| ★★★ | @@ | ☎ 01904 644744 |
| York | | **Middlethorpe Hall & Spa** |
| ★★★★ | @@ | ☎ 01904 641241 |

## YORKSHIRE, WEST

| | | |
|---|---|---|
| Wetherby | | **Wood Hall Hotel** |
| ★★★★ | @@ | ☎ 01937 587271 |

# CHANNEL ISLANDS

## JERSEY

| | | |
|---|---|---|
| Rozel | | **Château la Chaire** |
| ★★★ | @@ | ☎ 01534 863354 |
| St Brelade | | **The Atlantic Hotel** |
| ★★★★ | @@@ | ☎ 01534 744101 |
| St Helier | | **The Club Hotel & Spa** |
| ★★★★ | @@@@ | ☎ 01534 876500 |
| St Saviour | | **Longueville Manor Hotel** |
| ★★★★ | @@@ | ☎ 01534 725501 |

# SCOTLAND

## ABERDEENSHIRE

| | | |
|---|---|---|
| Ballater | | **Darroch Learg Hotel** |
| ★★★ | @@@ | ☎ 013397 55443 |

## ANGUS

| | | |
|---|---|---|
| Glamis | | **Castleton House Hotel** |
| ★★★ | @@ | ☎ 01307 840340 |

## ARGYLL & BUTE

| | | |
|---|---|---|
| Eriska | | **Isle of Eriska** |
| ★★★★★ | @@@ | ☎ 01631 720371 |
| Port Appin | | **Airds Hotel** |
| ★★★★ | @@@ | ☎ 01631 730236 |
| Tighnabruaich | | **An Lochan** |
| ★★★ | @@ | ☎ 01700 811239 |
| Tobermory (Isle of Mull) | | **Highland Cottage** |
| ★★★ | @@ | ☎ 01688 302030 |

## DUMFRIES & GALLOWAY

| | | |
|---|---|---|
| Newton Stewart | | **Kirroughtree House** |
| ★★★ | @@ | ☎ 01671 402141 |
| Portpatrick | | **Knockinaam Lodge** |
| ★★★ | @@@ | ☎ 01776 810471 |

## EAST LOTHIAN

| | | |
|---|---|---|
| Gullane | | **Greywalls Hotel** |
| ★★★ | @@@ | ☎ 01620 842144 |

## CITY OF EDINBURGH

| | | |
|---|---|---|
| Edinburgh | | **Channings** |
| ★★★★ | @@ | ☎ 0131 332 3232 |

| Edinburgh | | The Howard Hotel |
|---|---|---|
| ★★★★ | 🌹 | ☎ 0131 274 7402 |
| Edinburgh | | Prestonfield |
| ★★★★★★ | 🌹🌹 | ☎ 0131 225 7800 |

## FIFE

| Markinch | | Balbirnie House |
|---|---|---|
| ★★★★ | 🌹🌹 | ☎ 01592 610066 |
| St Andrews | | The Old Course Hotel, Golf Resort & Spa |
| ★★★★★★ | 🌹🌹🌹 | ☎ 01334 474371 |
| St Andrews | | Rufflets Country House & Garden Restaurant |
| ★★★★ | 🌹🌹 | ☎ 01334 472594 |
| St Andrews | | St Andrews Golf Hotel |
| ★★★ | 🌹🌹 | ☎ 01334 472611 |

## CITY OF GLASGOW

| Glasgow | | Hotel du Vin at One Devonshire Gardens |
|---|---|---|
| ★★★★ | 🌹🌹 | ☎ 0141 339 2001 |

## HIGHLAND

| Fort William | | Inverlochy Castle Hotel |
|---|---|---|
| ★★★★★★ | 🌹🌹🌹 | ☎ 01397 702177 |
| Lochinver | | Inver Lodge Hotel |
| ★★★★ | 🌹🌹 | ☎ 01571 844496 |
| Nairn | | Boath House |
| ★★★ | 🌹🌹🌹🌹 | ☎ 01667 454896 |
| Poolewe | | Pool House Hotel |
| ★★★ | 🌹🌹 | ☎ 01445 781272 |
| Shieldaig | | Tigh an Eilean |
| ★ | 🌹🌹 | ☎ 01520 755251 |
| Strontian | | Kilcamb Lodge Hotel |
| ★★★ | 🌹🌹 | ☎ 01967 402257 |
| Tain | | The Glenmorangie Highland Home at Cadboll |
| ★★ | 🌹🌹 | ☎ 01862 871671 |

## NORTH AYRSHIRE

| Brodick (Isle of Arran) | | Kilmichael Country House Hotel |
|---|---|---|
| ★★★ | 🌹🌹 | ☎ 01770 302219 |

## PERTH & KINROSS

| Aucheterarder | | The Gleneagles Hotel |
|---|---|---|
| ★★★★★ | 🌹🌹🌹🌹 | ☎ 01764 662231 |
| Dunkeld | | Kinnaird |
| ★★★★ | 🌹🌹 | ☎ 01796 482440 |

## SCOTTISH BORDERS

| Peebles | | Cringletie House |
|---|---|---|
| ★★★★ | 🌹🌹 | ☎ 01721 725750 |

## SOUTH AYRSHIRE

| Ballantrae | | Glenapp Castle |
|---|---|---|
| ★★★★★ | 🌹🌹🌹 | ☎ 01465 831212 |
| Troon | | Lochgreen House Hotel |
| ★★★★ | 🌹🌹🌹 | ☎ 01292 313343 |
| Turnberry | | The Westin Turnberry Resort |
| ★★★★★ | 🌹🌹 | ☎ 01655 331000 |

# WALES

## CEREDIGION

| Eglwysfach | | Ynyshir Hall |
|---|---|---|
| ★★★ | 🌹🌹🌹 | ☎ 01654 781209 |

## CONWY

| Llandudno | | Bodysgallen Hall & Spa |
|---|---|---|
| ★★★★ | 🌹🌹🌹 | ☎ 01492 584466 |
| Llandudno | | Osborne House |
| ★★★★ | 🌹 | ☎ 01492 860330 |
| Llandudno | St Tudno Hotel and Restaurant | |
| ★★★ | 🌹🌹 | ☎ 01492 874411 |

## GWYNEDD

| Caernarfon | | Seiont Manor Hotel |
|---|---|---|
| ★★★ | 🌹🌹 | ☎ 01286 673366 |

## POWYS

| Dolgellau | | Penmaenuchaf Hall Hotel |
|---|---|---|
| ★★★ | 🌹🌹 | ☎ 01341 422129 |
| Llangammarch Wells | The Lake Country House & Spa | |
| ★★★ | 🌹🌹 | ☎ 01591 620202 |

*Hotels marked with an asterisk\* had not yet had their Rosette rating confirmed at the time of going to press.*

# ENGLAND

Yorkshire Dales National Park

# BEDFORDSHIRE

Rolling hills of Bedfordshire near Ampthill

Melchbourne, Bedfordshire

# Luton Hoo Hotel, Golf & Spa

**Address:** The Mansion House, LUTON LU1 3TQ
**Tel:** 01582 734437
**Fax:** 01582 485438
**Email:** reservations@lutonhoo.com
**Website:** www.lutonhoo.com
**Map ref:** 3, TL02
**Directions:** Close to M1, Junction 10
**Rooms:** 144, S £235–£810 D 275–£850
**Facilities:** Spa Tennis Golf

This magnificent Grade I listed building opened as a hotel in 2007 after a massive restoration project. Set in extensive parkland, the palatial mansion retains all of its former grandeur, with expertly restored paintings, tapestries and bespoke interior design. Bedrooms and suites are spread between the mansion house, former Adam's coach house, Flower Garden and parklands, all as opulent as the price-tag would suggest. Exquisite fine dining is offered in the Wernher Restaurant, with less formality in Adam's Brasserie in the former stables. Leisure amenities include a golf course, spa, tennis court and field sports.

**Recommended in the area**

Whipsnade Wild Animal Park and Tree Cathedral; St Albans; Knebworth

# BERKSHIRE

The River Thames at Windsor Bridge

# Coppid Beech

★★★★  77% ◉◉ HL

Address:  John Nike Way, BRACKNELL  RG12 8TF
Tel:      01344 303333
Fax:      01344 301200
Email:    welcome@coppid-beech-hotel.co.uk
Website:  www.coppidbeech.com
Map ref:  3, SU36
Directions: M4 junct 10 take Wokingham/Bracknell onto A329. In 2m take B3408 to Binfield at rdbt. Hotel 200yds on right
Rooms: 205, S £65–£235 D £85–£255 Facilities: ⊗ Sauna Jacuzzi Solarium  Gym STV Wi-Fi in bedrooms Parking: 350

The setting on the edge of Bracknell's modern town centre might not excite, but this unusual hotel doesn't rely on its location to attract. It features a stunning three-story aquarium towering above its atrium and boasts a sophisticated nightclub, an Austrian Bier Keller, and a fully-equipped health club. Its Alpine-style architecture also fits well with the neighbouring dry ski slope and winter sports complex. With so much to offer, the Coppid Beech has become a popular meeting place for locals and an appealing venue for weddings and conferences. The bedrooms have all the facilities you would expect from its star rating, including mini bar, satellite TV, high-speed Wi-Fi (extra charge) and the possibility of viewing your bill and checking out. They even have two hairdryers rather than the usual one, and an ever-increasing number are having air-conditioning installed. There's an informal menu in the Bier Keller's Brasserie, light snacks all day in the Lounge Bar, and fine dining in Rowan's Restaurant, where a meal might start with Rowan's Gourmet Platter and continue with pan-fried red mullet with Cornish crab mash on a crayfish and truffle nage.

**Recommended in the area**

Windsor Castle and Windsor Great Park; Thorpe Park; Legoland

# Donnington Valley Hotel & Spa

★★★★  85% ◉◉ HL

Address:  Old Oxford Road, Donnington,
          NEWBURY  RG14 3AG
Tel:      01635 551199
Email:    general@donningtonvalley.co.uk
Website:  www.donningtonvalley.co.uk
Map ref:  3, SU46
Directions: M4 junct 13, take A34 signed Newbury.
Take exit signed Donnington/Services, at rdbt take
2nd exit signed Donnington. Left at next rdbt

Rooms: 111 Facilities: ⊕ Sauna Jacuzzi Gym STV Wi-Fi in bedrooms Parking: 150 Notes: ⊗

The AA's Hotel of the Year (England) 2007–2008 for consistently high standards of hospitality and service, this fine country hotel has recently had a £14 million redevelopment. Set in rolling Berkshire countryside, it boasts its own 18-hole golf course and a sumptuous state-of-the-art spa. The bedrooms are in elegant contemporary style with luxury linens, marble bathrooms and all kinds of little extras to enhance the experience.

Recommended in the area

Donnington Castle; The Watermill Theatre; Highclere Castle

# The Vineyard at Stockcross

★★★★★ ◉◉◉◉ HL

Address:  Stockcross, NEWBURY  RG20 8JU
Tel:      01635 528770
Fax:      01635 528398
Email:    general@the-vineyard.co.uk
Website:  www.the-vineyard.co.uk
Map ref:  3, SU46
Directions: From M4 take A34 towards Newbury, exit
at 3rd junct for Speen. Right at rdbt then right again
at 2nd rdbt

Rooms: 49, S £200 D £420–£617 Facilities: ⊕ Spa Sauna Jacuzzi Gym STV Parking: 100 Notes: ⊗

Owned by Sir Peter Michael, who also owns the Peter Michael Winery in California, this hotel offers the ultimate in indulgence, from the superb bedrooms and suites to the gourmet dining experience. Executive Chef John Campbell, author of Formulas for Flavour, has created here one of the finest restaurants in the country, with more than 2,000 international wines, including Peter Michael wines, of course. The hotel is also a showcase for works from the owner's personal art collection.

Recommended in the area

Highclere Castle; The Watermill Theatre; Newbury Racecourse

# Novotel Reading Centre

★★★★ 77% ⊕ HL
**Address:** 25b Friar Street, READING RG1 1DP
**Tel:** 0118 952 2600
**Fax:** 0118 952 2610
**Email:** h5432@accor.com
**Website:** www.novotel.com
**Map ref:** 3, SU77
**Directions:** M4 junct 11 or A33 towards Reading, exit on left for Garrard St car park, at rdbt take 3rd exit on Friar St
**Rooms:** 178, from £59 **Facilities:** ⊛ Sauna Gym STV Wi-fi available **Parking:** 15

The Novotel chain have come up with an exciting new brand style, and this one occupies a gleaming new building right in the heart of town. The location is perfect for business guests and shoppers who want to be right on the spot, and some of the most glorious Berkshire countryside is on the doorstep. The accommodation here is supremely stylish and each of the air-conditioned rooms has a queen-size bed with duvet, a sofa-bed or armchair, a swivel desk for working or dining, satellite flat-screen TV with movies and games, and high-speed internet access. Bathrooms are up-to-the-minute and have a bath and separate shower. Public areas are equally chic, with rich colours setting off the natural textures of wood and stone. One of the best developments here is the flexible approach to food service. Understanding the need to fit in with guests' busy schedules and preferences, the Novotel provides whatever you want, whenever you want it. Dishes all come in taster, starter and main course sizes and the same menu is available from 6am to midnight in the Elements Restaurant and Bar and round the clock as room service. On weekends a full English breakfast is served until noon. There are good conference facilities and a leisure suite with indoor pool.

**Recommended in the area**

The Oracle Shopping Centre; The Hexagon; riverside entertainment venues

# Sir Christopher Wren's House Hotel & Spa

★★★★  73% ⊚⊚ HL

Address: Thames Street, WINDSOR  SL4 1PX
Tel:      01753 861354
Fax:      01753 860172
Email:    reservations@wrensgroup.com
Website:  www.sirchristopherwren.co.uk
Map ref:  3, SU97
Directions: M4 junct 6, 1st exit from relief road,
follow signs to Windsor, 1st major exit on left, turn left at lights
Rooms: 96, S from £85 D from £97 Facilities: Sauna Jacuzzi Gym STV Wi-Fi throughout hotel
Conference and Meeting Facilities Parking: 10 Notes: No Pets

Sir Christopher's House Hotel & Spa is part of an elegant 17th Century town house with a privileged
location beside the River Thames between Eton Bridge and the walls of Windsor Castle. It offers
guests many high-class facilities including 58 ensuite bedrooms in the main house, 38 in adjacent
annexes, 18 rooms suitable for families and six ground floor rooms. There is also a range of function
and meeting rooms ideal for weddings, business or events, and Strok's two AA Rosette restaurant
serving modern British cuisine and featuring an al fresco riverside terrace perfect for relaxation during
the summer. The hotel also has its own dedicated health and fitness spa, the Wrens Club, featuring a
gymnasium, spa Jacuzzi and a number of treatment rooms offering a wide range of manicures, facials,
massage and relaxing body treatments. The hotel is conveniently located for Heathrow and central
London as well as being close to all of Windsor and Eton's attractions, including Legoland and Ascot
Race course.

Recommended in the area

Windsor Castle; Eton College; Legoland; Windsor Great Park

# BRISTOL

Clifton Suspension Bridge

# Mercure Brigstow Bristol

★★★★ 74% ◉ HL

Address: 5–7 Welsh Back, BRISTOL  BS1 4SP
Tel/Fax: 0117 929 1030
Email: H6548@accor.com
Website: www.mercure.com
Map ref: 2, ST57
Directions: Left at Baldwin St lights. Take first left into Queen Charlotte St
Rooms: 116 Facilities: Gym STV Wi-fi available
Notes: ⊗ in bedrooms

It would be hard to find a better Bristol location than this, overlooking the river and at the heart of the city-centre's lively shopping and entertainments district. The renowned Bristol Old Vic and Hippodrome theatres are a short stroll away and the motorway network and city airport are very close, making this a great weekend break destination. The air-conditioned bedrooms have an imaginative contemporary décor and the stylish modern bathrooms, with bath and separate shower, come complete with telephone and radio. The in-room facilities include high speed internet, voicemail, safe and minibar. Upgrade to one of the superior rooms and you will not only have a panoramic window and a balcony overlooking the river, but also the ultimate indulgence of a plasma-screen TV in the bathroom. The Ellipse restaurant is a spacious, open-plan area with windows overlooking the cobbled street and river. You can watch the world go by as you sample the accomplished modern international cuisine, with some regional specialities offered for good measure. A good selection of wines is offered at very good prices. The relaxing Ellipse bar has a less formal menu. Guests at the Mercure Brigstow have complimentary membership of the nearby Welsh Back Gym, which includes squash courts and a sauna.

Recommended in the area

SS Great Britain; City Museum and Art Gallery; Bristol Zoo Gardens

# BUCKINGHAMSHIRE

West Wycombe

# Villiers Hotel

★★★★ 74% ◉◉ HL
Address: 3 Castle Street, BUCKINGHAM MK18 1BS
Tel: 01280 822444
Fax: 01280 822113
Email: villiers@oxfordshire-hotels.co.uk
Website: www.oxfordshire-hotels.co.uk
Map ref: 3, SP36
Directions: M1 junct 13 (S) or junct 15A (N) or M40 junct 9 (S) or junct 10(N) follow signs to Buckingham. Castle St by Town Hall
Rooms: 46, S £105–£135 D £120–£165 Facilities: STV Wi-Fi available Parking: 40
Notes: ⊗ in bedrooms

Guests can enjoy a town centre location with a high degree of comfort at this 400-year-old former coaching inn. Relaxing public areas feature flagstone floors, oak panelling and real fires whilst bedrooms are modern, spacious and equipped to a high level. Diners can unwind in the atmopsheric bar before taking dinner in the award-winning restaurant.

**Recommended in the area**
Stowe Landscape Gardens; Silverstone motor racing circuit; Bicester Village designer outlet shopping

# Danesfield House Hotel & Spa

★★★★ 85% ◉◉◉ HL
Address: Henley Road, MARLOW SL7 2EY
Tel: 01628 891010
Fax: 01628 890408
Email: reservations@danesfieldhouse.co.uk
Website: www.danesfieldhouse.co.uk
Map ref: 3, SU38
Directions: 2m from Marlow on A4155 towards Henley
Rooms: 84, S £165–£355 D £175–£355
Facilities: ⓥ Sauna Jacuzzi Solarium Spa Swimming Pool Gym STV Wi-Fi throughout Parking: 100
Notes: ⊗ in bedrooms

A magnificent mansion set in 65 acres of elevated landscaped gardens, overlooking the River Thames and, beyond, the Chiltern Hills. Impressive public rooms include the cathedral-like Grand Hall – morning coffee here is an experience – the award-winning Oak Room restaurant and the Orangery, for less formal dining. Both restaurants and the extensive outside terrace are popular with local residents.

**Recommended in the area**
Henley River Cruises; Hambleden Valley; Marlow boutique shopping

# Macdonald Compleat Angler

★★★★  84% ◉◉◉ HL

**Address:** Marlow Bridge, MARLOW  SL7 1RG
**Tel:**  0870 400 8100
**Email:**  compleatangler@macdonald-hotels.co.uk
**Website:** www.macdonald-hotels.co.uk/
  compleatangler
**Map ref:** 3, SU88
**Directions:** M40 junct 4, A404(M) to rdbt, Bisham
exit,1m to Marlow Bridge, hotel on right
**Rooms:** 64 **Facilities:** 2 award-winning restaurants
**Parking:** 100

Named after Isaak Walton's world-famous book, the Compleat Angler overlooks the Thames as it cascades over Marlow weir and under the town's historic bridge. Fashionable for many decades, it has welcomed many famous people, including Dame Nellie Melba, F Scott Fitzgerald, Noël Coward, Tallulah Bankhead, Clint Eastwood, Princess Diana and even, in 1999, the Queen, eating in a public restaurant for the first time, albeit as the guest of the president of Hungary. Many of the 400-year-old, but now newly refurbished, bedrooms overlook the river and are all equipped with flat screen TVs, air conditioning, and six have four-posters. In an unusual touch, they all have door bells. A recent development was the creation of two restaurants: one is Dean Timpson at The Compleat Angler, a relaxed fine dining, three AA-Rosette restaurant which provides classic food with a modern twist. The other is Bowaters, named after Sir Ian and Lady Bowater who owned the hotel for almost 50 years, with two AA Rosettes and its own riverside terrace, where contemporary British food is served. The oak-panelled cocktail bar, with cosy alcoves and comfortable lounge, is an ideal place to meet friends, perhaps before taking a Champagne picnic aboard one of the hotel's private boats.

**Recommended in the area**

Hughenden Manor, Windsor Castle, Henley-on-Thames

All Saints Church, Marlow

# Cliveden

★★★★★ ⑯⑯⑯ CHH

**Address:** TAPLOW  SL6 0JF
**Tel:** 01628 668561
**Fax:** 01628 661837
**Email:** reservations@clivedenhouse.co.uk
**Website:** www.clivedonhouse.co.uk
**Map ref:** 3, SU98
**Directions:** M4 junct 7, follow A4 towards
Maidenhead for 1.5m, turn onto B476 towards
Taplow, 2.5m, hotel on left
**Rooms:** 39, D £423–£1169 **Facilities:** ⑲ ↿ Sauna Jacuzzi Tennis Gym STV Wi-fi **Parking:** 60

Three dukes, a former prince of Wales and the Astor family have called Cliveden home and guests have included many crowned heads, statesmen and celebrities. The palatial stately home, set in glorious Thames-side grounds, now offers the ultimate in luxurious accommodation within easy reach of London. In the care of the National Trust it maintains the standards of service and cuisine as well as the trappings of is elegant past. Guests can also dine royally in the two gourmet restaurants.
**Recommended in the area**
Windsor Castle and Windsor Great Park; Burnham Beeches; Ascot Racecourse

# CAMBRIDGESHIRE

The Mathematical Bridge, Cambridge

# The Cambridge Belfry

★★★★ 82% ◉◉ HL

Address: Back Street, CAMBOURNE CB23 6BW
Tel: 01954 714600
Fax: 01954 714610
Email: cambridgebelfryreservations@qhotels.co.uk
Website: www.qhotels.co.uk
Map ref: 3, TL35
Directions: M11 junct 13 take A428 towards Bedford,
follow signs to Cambourne. Exit at Cambourne
keeping left. Left at rdbt, hotel on left
Rooms: 120, S £80–£130 D £90–£140 Facilities: ⊗ Spa Sauna Jacuzzi Solarium Tennis Gym STV
Wi-fi available Parking: 200 Notes: ⊗

Set in a tranquil lakeside setting on the outskirts of Cambridge, this modern hotel offers the very highest standards of accommodation coupled with great service. The tastefully decorated en suite bedrooms include twins and doubles, some of which are interconnecting, executive bedrooms and suites. There are six individually-styled penthouse suites occupying the whole of the third floor. Original artwork adorns the lounge areas, creating a spacious, contemporary atmosphere that extends throughout. The award winning Bridge Restaurant offers an impressive menu complemented by an array of wines, whilst a more informal menu can be served in our lounge or terrace areas overlooking the lake, where you can enjoy morning coffee, afternoon tea or al fresco dining during the warmer months. Guests can relax in the hotel's Reflection Spa & Leisure Club or pamper themselves with an indulgent spa treatment from the wide selection of therapies and treatments available. Outside, for the more energetic, there is an all weather floodlit tennis court. The Cambridge Belfry is a good base for sightseeing and day trips around Cambridge and the surrounding countryside.

Recommended in the area

King's College Chapel; Milton Country Park; Linton Zoo

# Arundel House Hotel

★★★ 79% HL

Address: Chesterton Road, CAMBRIDGE CB4 3AN
Tel: 01223 367701
Fax: 01223 367721
Email: info@arundelhousehotels.co.uk
Website: www.arundelhousehotels.co.uk
Map ref: 3, TL45
Directions: City centre on A1303
Rooms: 103, S £75–£110 D £95–£140 Parking: 70
Notes: ⊗ in bedrooms

By definition, a fine location in the city of Cambridge would surely be one that overlooks the River Cam and open parkland. The Arundel House Hotel does just that. This privately owned hotel, once a row of Victorian townhouses, is only a short walk from the historic centre, and its shops, restaurants and pubs. All bedrooms are en suite, with either a bath, shower, or both. They also have tea and coffee making facilities, TV, radio, hair dryer and direct dial phone; irons, ironing boards and room safes are on the way. Relax in a comfortable armchair in the bar, then move into the adjacent restaurant, decorated in refreshing yellow, orange, gold and green, with upholstered chairs, crisp white and yellow linen, and oak dressers. A wide range of imaginative dishes features on its fixed price, carte, vegetarian and children's menus, all freshly prepared in the hotel's scrupulously clean, award-winning kitchens. Another time, try the all-day Conservatory Brasserie, which offers main meals, snacks and cream teas. The charming garden outside its doors is surprisingly tranquil, despite the proximity of the city centre. While retaining its original façade, the Coach House behind the main building has been completely rebuilt to provide three conference rooms and 22 bedrooms

Recommended in the area

Kings College Cambridge; Imperial War Museum Duxford; Anglesey Abbey (NT)

River Cam, Cambridge

# Best Western The Gonville Hotel

★★★ 78% HL

Address: Gonville Place,
         CAMBRIDGE CB1 1LY
Tel: 01223 366611
Fax: 01223 315470
Email: all@gonvillehotel.co.uk
Website: www.bw-gonvillehotel.co.uk
Map ref: 3, TL45
Directions: M11 junct 11, on A1309 follow city
centre signs. At 2nd mini rdbt right into Lensfield Rd,
over junct with lights. Hotel 25yds on right
Rooms: 73, S £89–£140 D £99–£160 Facilities: Wi-fi available Parking: 80

The hotel is centrally located on the eastern side of the city's historic centre, and overlooks a 25-acre open park. All rooms are en suite, and some are air-conditioned. The hotel's Chancellor's Restaurant and the more informal Atrium Restaurant offer local dishes and wide-ranging cuisine. The Abington Suite and the adjoining Gresham House gardens are a popular venue for social occasions.

Recommended in the area

Cambridge University; Imperial War Museum, Duxford; National Horseracing Museum, Newmarket

# Hotel Felix

★★★★ 81% ◉◉ HL

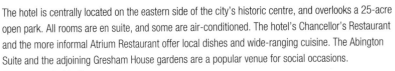

Address: Whitehouse Lane, CAMBRIDGE CB3 0LX
Tel: 01223 277977
Email: help@hotelfelix.co.uk
Website: www.hotelfelix.co.uk
Map ref: 3, TL45
Directions: N on A1307, right at The Travellers Rest
Rooms: 52, S £145–£199 D £180–£290
Facilities: STV Wi-fi in bedrooms Parking: 90

On the western edge of historic Cambridge, this charming hotel is most convenient for visitors driving to the city on the M11 or A14. Within the Victorian mansion, set in over a hectare of landscaped gardens, original features stand out against the clean and elegant modern décor and there are two new wings of bedrooms. These are elegantly minimalist, with silk curtains at the huge windows, duck-down duvets and Egyptian cotton on the beds and spacious bathrooms. In-room amenities include dataport and wireless internet, minibar, satellite TV and bathrobes. The restaurant, serving modern British cuisine with a Mediterranean influence, has well spaced tables and specially commissioned art works.

Recommended in the area

Fitzwilliam Museum; King's College Chapel; The Sedgwick Museum of Earth Sciences

# Bell Inn Hotel

★★★   78% ◎ HL

**Address:** Great North Road, STILTON  PE7 3RA
**Tel:**        01733 241066
**Fax:**       01733 245173
**Email:**     reception@thebellstilton.co.uk
**Website:** www.thebellstilton.co.uk
**Map ref:** 3, TL18
**Directions:** A1(M) junct 16, follow Stilton signs. Hotel in village
**Rooms:** 22, S £72.50–£109.50 D £99.50–£129.50
**Facilities:** STV Wi-Fi in bedrooms **Parking:** 30 **Notes:** ⊗ in
bedrooms

Just off the Great North Road, this lovely 17th-century coaching
inn has served the famous and infamous alike – film star Clark Gable, and highwayman Dick Turpin, for
example. The magnificent inn sign is an exact replica of the original and, together with its wrought-iron
bracket, weighs an astonishing two and three-quarter tons. Curiously, the famous blue cheese has
never been made in Stilton; in coaching days it was extensively sold in the local market and the village's
name stuck. Recently refurbished en suite bedrooms, including two with four-posters and several
with Jacuzzis, are ranged around the old courtyard. For dining, guests have a choice – the beamed
Galleried Restaurant, with its AA-Rosette-awarded menu of modern British cuisine; the softly lit Bistro,
offering internationally influenced dishes; and the stone-floored Village Bar, offering bar meals and
snacks. Browse over the menus in a comfortable leather armchair in the first-floor Dick Turpin's room,
so named because legend says he escaped to his horse, Black Bess, from the window. In favourable
weather eat, or just have a drink, in the courtyard. Byron's Room (another famous guest) adjoins the
Marlborough Suite, which can accommodate up to 100 business delegates theatre style.
**Recommended in the area**
Peterborough Cathedral; Imperial War Museum, Duxford; Flag Fen

King's College, Cambridge

# Crown Lodge Hotel

★★★ 77% ◉ HL

**Address:** Downham Rd, WISBECH PE14 8SE
**Tel:** 01945 773391
**Email:** office@thecrownlodgehotel.co.uk
**Website:** www.thecrownlodgehotel.co.uk
**Map ref:** 3, TF4P
**Directions:** On A1122/A1101 approx 5m from town
**Rooms:** 10, S £60–£66 D £80–£88
**Facilities:** Wi-Fi available **Parking:** 55

Off the beaten track in the Cambridgeshire fenlands, Crown Lodge is a friendly hotel with modern facilities and restful contemporary décor throughout the restaurant, bar and lounge areas. The bedrooms enjoy the same style, enlivened by modern art, and have the benefit of individual heating controls, modem points, trouser press and tea– and coffee-making trays. The food covers the culinary spectrum, from sophisticated creations such as roast wild rabbit wrapped in pancetta to traditional steak and kidney pie. Crown Lodge is also a mecca for squash players, with its own courts and a lively competition scene. Call a week ahead to book a court.

**Recommended in the area**

Ely Cathedral; Welney Wildfowl and Wetlands Trust; Wicken Fen National Nature Reserve

# CHESHIRE

Arley Hall garden

Wildboarclough, Peak District

# Alderley Edge Hotel

★★★ 83% ◉◉ HL

**Address:** Macclesfield Road,
ALDERLEY EDGE SK9 7BJ
**Tel:** 01625 583033
**Email:** sales@alderleyedgehotel.com
**Website:** www.alderleyedgehotel.com
**Map ref:** 6, SJ87
**Directions:** off A34 in Alderley Edge onto B5087
towards Macclesfield. Hotel 200yds on right
**Rooms:** 50, S £72.50–£205 D £110–£400
**Facilities:** STV Wi-fi in bedrooms **Parking:** 90 **Notes:** ⊗ in bedrooms

Built of local sandstone in 1850 by a Manchester cotton king, this well-furnished hotel in charming grounds has grand views over the Cheshire Plain at the front, and the lovely garden at the rear. Room goodies include bowls of fruit, bathrobes, trouser press, hairdryer and tea and coffee making facilities. Some even have sofa beds too – great for families. The bar and adjacent lounge lead into the split-level conservatory restaurant, where a combined carte and fixed price menu offers welcome flexibility.

**Recommended in the area**

Jodrell Bank; Quarry Bank Mill; Tatton Park

# The White House Manor Townhouse

★★★★ 76% ◉◉ TH

Address: New Road, PRESTBURY SK10 4HP
Tel:     01625 829376
Fax:     01625 827441
Email:   info@thewhitehouse.uk.com
Website: www.thewhitehouse.uk.com
Map ref: 7, SJ87
Directions: 2m N of Macclesfield on A538
Rooms: 12, S £50–£105 D £110–£150 Facilities: Jacuzzi STV
Wi-Fi in bedrooms Parking: 12 Notes: ⊗ in bedrooms

This restored Georgian House has been transformed into a luxurious private sanctuary of 21st-century sophistication that defies its quaint rural setting. Each of the 12 individual bedrooms exhibit an imagination, humour and laser-sharp sense of detail, and choices range from Crystal and Campion, with locally made four-poster beds, to Aphrodite, Minerva and Millennium, which have their own Turkish steam rooms. All have sumptuous bathrooms, fine towels, soft robes and The White Company Toiletries, while some have power showers, hydrotherapy baths or wet rooms. Every bedroom features a writing area with complimentary Wi-Fi, stationery, tea trays and home made biscuits, mini bars with fresh ice, flat screen satellite TV, DVD system, i-Pod docking stations, fresh flowers and more. Freshly prepared Cheshire breakfasts can be delivered to your room or enjoyed in the conservatory with views of the garden and village beyond. Recommended for its contemporary fine dining is the nearby White House Restaurant, which has two AA rosettes and is just a short walk away. Though it is under separate management, guests at the manor can charge meals to their hotel bill.

Recommended in the area

Lyme Park (NT); Jodrell Bank; Quarry Bank Mill and Styal Country Park (NT)

Sea Thrift growing on the Lizard Peninsula

# Hell Bay

★★★ ◉◉ HL

**Address:** BRYHER, Isles of Scilly
TR23 0PR
**Tel:** 01720 422947
**Fax:** 01720 423004
**Email:** contactus@hellbay.co.uk
**Website:** www.hellbay.co.uk
**Map ref:** 1, SV81
**Directions:** Island location means it is only accessible by
helicopter from Penzance, ship from Penzance or plane from
Southampton, Bristol, Exeter, Newquay or Land's End
**Rooms:** 25, S £195–£450 D £260–£600
**Facilities:** ⋌ Sauna Jacuzzi Gym STV

This is the ultimate gourmet escape and a perfect place to re-charge your batteries, Hell Bay provides plenty of peace and tranquillity as well as privacy and seclusion. An informal and relaxed hideaway the hotel is located in extensive private grounds on the south side of the remote island of Bryher in the Isles of Scilly. It's a place where New England and the Caribbean meets Cornwall. The rooms, all suites, are beautifully furnished in Lloyd Loom with Malabar Fabrics set against cool ocean blues and greens. The service is personal and the food is a delight – both in fact are award winning. Owners Robert and Lucy Dorrien-Smith have filled the hotel with original sculptures and paintings by artists with local connections; Barbara Hepworth, Ivon Hitchens, Julian Trevelyan and Richard Pearce from Bryher. One call can set up your entire holiday at Hell Bay – as staff are able to arrange return travel, accommodation, insurance and boating transfers. Fantastic short breaks available year round – contact the hotel for further details.

**Recommended in the area**

Tresco Abbey Garden; Gallery Tresco; Cromwell's Castle

# Falcon Hotel

★★★  78% HL

Address:   Breakwater Road, BUDE  EX23 8SD
Tel:          01288 352005
Fax:          01288 356359
Email:      reception@falconhotel.com
Website:  www.falconhotel.com
Map ref:  1, SS20
Directions: off A39 into Bude, follow road to
Widemouth Bay. Hotel on right over canal bridge
Rooms: 29, S £58–£63 D £116–£126
Facilities: STV Wi-Fi in bedrooms **Parking:** 40 **Notes:** ⊗ in bedrooms

This hotel has been welcoming guests for more than 200 years. The bedrooms and en suite bathrooms
are all furnished and decorated to a very high standard. The air-conditioned restaurant and the
Coachman's Bar both provide modern English cuisine with international twists, fully complemented
by an extensive range of beers and wines. The Beer Terrace has wonderful views over the canal and
harbour and the hotel's walled gardens are a delight. Private functions can be held in the Acland Suite.
**Recommended in the area**
Clovelly; Tintagel; Boscastle

# Falmouth Hotel

★★★  75% ◉ HL

Address:   Castle Beach, FALMOUTH  TR11 4NZ
Tel:          01326 312671
Email:      reservations@falmouthhotel.com
Website:  www.falmouthhotel.com
Map ref:  1, SW83
Directions: Take A30 to Truro then A390 to
Falmouth. Follow signs for beaches, hotel on seafront
near Pendennis Castle
Rooms: 69, S £65–£75 D £98–£210 **Facilities:** ⊗
Sauna Jacuzzi Solarium Gym STV Wi-fi available **Parking:** 120

Falmouth's first Victorian-era hotel has five acres of beautiful gardens, and is opposite a sandy beach.
Many of its comfortable bedrooms, some with balconies, look across Falmouth Bay to Pendennis Point.
Roomy public areas include the bar/lounge, an outdoor terrace and the grand Trelawney Restaurant.
The Falmouth offers a choice of dining experiences, including gourmet dishes, showcasing the full
talents of the chef and his team, along with plenty for those who enjoy the simpler things in life.
**Recommended in the area**
Pendennis Castle; National Maritime Museum of Cornwall; Gweek Seal Sanctuary

# Green Lawns Hotel

★★★ 77% HL

Address: Western Terrace,
FALMOUTH TR11 4QJ
Tel: 01326 312734
Fax: 01326 211427
Email: info@greenlawnshotel.com
Website: www.greenlawnshotel.com
Map ref: 1, SW83
Directions: On A39
Rooms: 39, S £60–£105 D £70–£190
Facilities: ⊗ Sauna Jacuzzi Solarium Tennis Gym Wi-Fi in bedrooms Parking: 60

The lawns that give this ivy-clad hotel its name are long-matured grounds that take full advantage of the subtropical climate of the region. In summer they blaze with a profusion of flowers and shrubs, and have won prizes for the hotel in garden competitions over many years. Among the hotel's top-of-the-range rooms are some that are equipped with four-poster beds, Jacuzzis, and Victorian roll-top baths. All rooms are equipped with colour television, radio, hairdriers, irons and trouser presses, and room service is available 24 hours a day. Residents can enjoy free use of a large heated indoor swimming pool, a sauna, a Jacuzzi spa, a solarium and a small gymnasium. There are further facilities for such sports as squash, tennis and snooker at the Falmouth Club, which is adjacent to the hotel. The Garras Restaurant complements its fine cuisine with a wide range of vintage wines. A range of special offers for stays of two nights or more are available throughout the year. The hotel caters for wedding parties, conferences and other functions, and on-site car parking can accommodate 60 cars. A short walk brings the visitor to Gyllynvase Beach on Falmouth Bay.

Recommended in the area

National Maritime Museum, Cornwall; Tate St Ives; The Eden Project, St Austell; Pendennis Castle; Gweek Seal Sanctuary

# The Greenbank

★★★ 80% ◉ HL

**Address:** Harbourside, FALMOUTH TR11 2SR
**Tel:** 01326 312440
**Email:** reception@greenbank-hotel.co.uk
**Website:** www.greenbank-hotel.co.uk
**Map ref:** 1, SW83
**Directions:** 500yds past Marina on Penryn River
**Rooms:** 58, S £70–£80 D £105–£260
**Facilities:** Wi-Fi in bedrooms **Parking:** 44

Located by the marina, and with its own 17th-century quay and private beach, this smart hotel's enviable waterside position may well have motivated one-time regular guest Kenneth Grahame to write *The Wind in the Willows* – his letters about Mole, Ratty and Toad are on display. All rooms are en suite, with deluge showers, direct dial phone, TV, hairdryer and beverage tray, while most have splendid views across the estuary to the Roseland Peninsula. The Riverbank restaurant provides a season-inspired Modern British menu featuring freshly caught fish and seafood, meats from Redruth's appropriately named Angus Trotter, and locally foraged herbs and berries.

**Recommended in the area**

National Maritime Museum Cornwall, Pendennis Castle, Eden Project

# Bedruthan Steps Hotel

★★★★ 76% ◉ HL

**Address:** MAWGAN PORTH TR8 4BU
**Tel:** 01637 860555
**Email:** office@bedruthan.com
**Website:** www.bedruthan.com
**Map ref:** 1, SW86
**Directions:** From A39/A30 follow signs to Newquay Airport. Past the airport turn right at T-junct to Mawgan Porth. Hotel at top of hill on left
**Rooms:** 101 en suite, from £67 **Facilities:** ⊕ ⌇
Sauna Jacuzzi Tennis Snooker Gym Wi-fi available **Parking:** 100 **Notes:** ⊗ in bedrooms

Eco-friendly Bedruthan is set above the award-winning Mawgan Porth beach on the dramatic North Cornwall Coast. The new Ocean Spa at Bedruthan offers a place to relax and unwind with an infinity spa pool, a traditional Hammam room, aroma and steam rooms. Described as 'comfortable contemporary', experience deep squashy sofas, big comfortable beds and stylish surroundings. The award winning Indigo Bay Restaurant creates mouthwatering dishes from the finest of Cornwall's local produce.

**Recommended in the area**

Eden Project; Padstow Harbour; Cornish Gardens

# Meudon Hotel

★★★ 85%  CHH

| | |
|---|---|
| Address: | MAWNAN SMITH  TR11 5HT |
| Tel: | 01326 250541 |
| Fax: | 01326 250543 |
| Email: | wecare@meudon.co.uk |
| Website: | www.meudon.co.uk |
| Map ref: | 1, SW72 |

Directions: From Truro A39 towards Falmouth at Hillhead (anchor & cannons) rdbt, follow signs to Maenporth Beach. Hotel on left 1m after beach

Rooms: 29, S £75–£125 D £150–£250 Facilities: Wi-fi available Parking: 50

There's good reason for the hotel not sounding Cornish. It takes its name from the nearby farmhouse, which Napoleonic prisoners of war named after Meudon, their French village. The private mansion, incorporating two 17th–century coastguard's cottages, which forms the basis of this family-owned hotel came many years later. It stands in a sub-tropical valley leading to private Bream Cove, from where the coastal path leads round Rosemullion Head to the Helford River. Surrounded by its own 'hanging gardens'and National Trust land, it houses a reception area, comfortable lounges, cocktail bar and restaurant, with antiques, oil paintings, log fires, Wilton carpets and fresh flowers everywhere. All guest rooms are in quiet new wings overlooking the gardens, each one with private bathroom (many with bidet), as well as TV, radio, and tea and coffee facilities. Nowhere, says the hotel, will you hear canned music. The restaurant, which harbours a fruiting vine, offers 'English at its best' cooking, with the accent on fresh fish and seafood, game, vegetables and other produce grown to Meudon's requirements by local producers. A judicial list of fine wines from the old and new world will complement your evening's pleasure. In summer months many guests spend their time relaxing in the exotic gardens.

**Recommended in the area**

Eden Project; National Maritime Museum, Cornwall; Trebah Gardens

# Headland Hotel

★★★★ 77% ◉ HL

**Address:** Fistral Beach,
NEWQUAY TR7 1EW
**Tel:** 01637 872211
**Fax:** 01637 872212
**Email:** office@headlandhotel.co.uk
**Website:** www.headlandhotel.co.uk
**Map ref:** 1, SW86
**Directions:** Off A30 onto A392 at Indian Queens, approaching
Newquay follow signs for Fistral Beach, hotel adjacent
**Rooms:** 104, S £81–£148 D £83–£326 **Facilities:** ⓧ ⤻
Sauna Tennis STV Wi-Fi in bedrooms **Parking:** 400

Take the laid back beauty of the surfing paradise of Fistral Beach, mix it with the splendour of the imposing Headland, and you have the perfect location. Once inside, the range of public rooms include quiet sitting rooms and the impressive Ballroom and Front Lounge with stunning views over the ocean. The bedrooms range from Budget to Best, all tastefully furnished to a high standard of comfort. The Headland Restaurant is open for breakfast and dinner daily, and also Sunday Lunch, serving top quality local produce prepared imaginatively in elegant surroundings. A more informal style of dining can be found in the Sand Brasserie with its expansive views over Fistral Beach. Here you can enjoy a delicious cappuccino with homemade cakes or a full meal including local lobster thermidor. With a range of short breaks available, from Sheer Indulgence for a touch of romance and relaxation, to Adrenaline Adventures and Storm Watching Breaks for a more active break, there is something for most people throughout the year. On site, guests can enjoy a game of tennis, a round of pitch and putt, a game of croquet or just relax beside the outdoor pool topping up the tan.

**Recommended in the area**

Eden Project; Lanhydrock (NT); Tate St Ives

# Talland Bay Hotel

★★★   83% ⚘⚘ CHH

Address:  Porthallow,
          PORTHALLOW, Looe PL13 2JB
Tel:      01503 272667
Email:    reception@tallandbayhotel.co.uk
Website:  www.tallandbayhotel.co.uk
Map ref:  1, SX25
Directions: Signed from x-rds on A387 Looe to Polperro road
Rooms:    23, S £30–£105 D £95–£225
Facilities: ⚓ Parking: 23

Tucked into an unspoiled corner of Cornwall, this hotel is
perfectly placed for those who enjoy lovely beaches, spectacular
coastlines and glorious gardens. And after a full day of exploring the delights of the Lizard Peninsula,
the Talland Bay is a perfect place to unwind. It is set in delightful sub-tropical gardens overlooking the
sea, a view shared by the excellent Terrace restaurant, with its crisp white linen, upholstered chairs
and interesting menus of traditional and contemporary dishes. Featuring the best local ingredients,
including seafood brought ashore at Looe, the quality of the cooking has earned the restaurant two
AA rosettes. You could start the meal with seared hand-dived scallops with apple and ginger purée,
continue with a main course of Cornish lamb with fondant potato, flageolet beans, salsify, tomato and
balsamic dressing, then round it all off with light-as-a-feather rhubarb mille-feuille, with crème vanille
and rhubarb sorbet. Sunday lunch is deservedly popular here too. Each of the spacious bedrooms has
an individual style and décor, but all share the country-house theme. Some rooms have sea views and
some also feature a balcony or private garden terrace. Dog-lovers will be glad to learn that their four-
legged friends are welcome here too.

**Recommended in the area**

South West Coast Path; Glendurgan (NT); Seal Sanctuary

# Driftwood

★★★ 86% ◉◉◉ HL

Address: Rosevine, PORTSCATHO  TR2 5EW
Tel:       01872 580644
Fax:       01872 580801
Email:     info@driftwoodhotel.co.uk
Website:   www.driftwoodhotel.co.uk
Map ref: 1, SW83
Directions: A390 towards St Mawes. On A3078 turn left to
Rosevine at Trewithian
Rooms: 15, S £127.50–£165 D £180–£220 Facilities: Wi-fi in
bedrooms Parking: 30 Notes: ⊗ on premises

In seven acres of cliffside gardens, with panoramic views of
Gerrans Bay, stands this peaceful and secluded hotel. Walk down a wooded path to your own little
cove and look out across the very waters that will provide your dinner lobster or crab. Head indoors to
find stylishly contemporary sitting rooms stocked with books, magazines and board games. There's
even a small games room for the children. Comfortable, uncluttered bedrooms are decorated in soft
shades reminiscent of the seashore. Ground floor rooms have their own decked terrace, while tucked
away, overlooking the sea, is a restored weatherboarded cabin with two bedrooms and a sitting room.
A large deck in the sheltered terraced garden is strewn with steamer chairs for taking in the unbroken
sea view. On warm evenings hurricane lamps are lit for pre-dinner drinks and after-dinner coffee. The
three-AA Rosette award restaurant (from which, no surprise, you can again see the sea) serves fresh,
locally sourced food – and not just fish. Yes, there's John Dory or monkfish, for example, but the menu
will also feature dishes such as roasted Terras Farm duck breast, pastilla of duck leg, endives and
orange and port jus.

Recommended in the area

Falmouth Maritime Museum; Lost Gardens of Heligan; Tate Gallery St Ives

# Penventon Park Hotel

★★★  78%  HL

**Address:** REDRUTH  TR15 1TE
**Tel:**      01209 203000
**Fax:**      01209 203001
**Email:**    hello@penventon.com
**Website:**  www.penventon.com
**Map ref:**  1, SW64
**Directions:** Off A30 at Redruth. Follow signs for Redruth West, hotel 1m S
**Rooms:** 65, S £65–£110 D £95–£175 **Facilities:** ℞ Sauna Jacuzzi Solarium Gym Wi-Fi in bedrooms **Parking:** 100

The Penventon Park Hotel is a splendid Georgian mansion, now adapted to the highest standards of modern convenience and luxury. Although large – it sits in 10 acres of private grounds – it is a private hotel run by the Pascoe family. Its accommodation includes 20 newly built garden suites, two of which are equipped with four-poster beds. All rooms have en suite facilities, and television, including satellite TV, direct-dial telephone and drinks-making facilities. The hotel has a health and leisure spa, which includes a heated indoor swimming pool, a sauna, a gymnasium and a sunroom. A staff beautician and a masseuse are available. The Dining Galleries Restaurant features Cornish dishes in addition to its English, French and Italian cuisines. The restaurant also offers vegetarian menus and a wide range of fish dishes. Four function rooms are available for private parties, conferences, civil ceremonies and wedding receptions. Special breaks are available at Christmas, New Year and St Valentine's Day, and at other times of year. Being located centrally in the county, it is within an hour of all of Cornwall's attractions. The hotel is conveniently situated close to the A30 road, giving easy access to Truro, St Ives and other locations. Children of all ages are welcome at the hotel.

**Recommended in the area**

St Michael's Mount; National Maritime Museum, Falmouth; Tate Gallery.

# The Island Hotel

★★★ ◎◎ HL

**Address:** TRESCO, Isles of Scilly TR24 0PU
**Tel:** 01720 422883
**Fax:** 01720 423008
**Email:** islandhotel@tresco.co.uk
**Website:** www.tresco.co.uk
**Map ref:** 1, SV81
**Directions:** Helicopter service Penzance to Tresco, hotel on NE of island
**Rooms:** 48, S £130–£225 D £260–£720 Half Board
**Facilities:** ⚲ Tennis STV Wi-fi available
**Notes:** ⊗ in bedrooms

Set in its own manicured gardens and private beach with a seasonal sailing school, the Island Hotel overlooks Old Grimsby Sound and the Cromwellian fort known as 'the Blockhouse'. All rooms are brightly furnished and many benefit from lounge areas, balconies or terraces. Both the spacious and comfortable bar and lounge areas and the award winning restaurant all enjoy stunning seascapes. The first-floor, balconied Garden Wing looks towards Crow Sound and the Eastern Isles. The carefully prepared, imaginative cuisine at the AA-Rosetted restaurant makes an excellent showcase for locally caught fish, island vegetables and Tresco reared beef. Activities and facilities include a tennis court, croquet lawn, heated outdoor swimming pool, kite flying as well as shrimping or fishing. Special Activity Holidays are available in 2008 and include a wide range of pursuits such as art, walking, photography, birding and yoga. One telephone call can set up your entire holiday at The Island Hotel – as staff are able to arrange return travel, accommodation, insurance and boating transfers. Fantastic short breaks available year round – contact the hotel for further details.

**Recommended in the area**

Tresco Abbey Garden; Gallery Tresco; Cromwell's Castle

# Trenython Manor Hotel

★★★   80% ⊛ CHH

Address:   Castle Dore Road, TYWARDREATH,
           Fowey PL24 2TS
Tel:       01726 814797
Fax:       01726 817030
Email:     trenython@clublacosta.com
Website:   www.trenython.co.uk
Map ref:   1, SX05
Directions: A390/B3269 towards Fowey, after 2m
right into Castledore. Hotel 100mtrs on left
Rooms: 23 Facilities: ⊛ Sauna Jacuzzi Solarium Tennis Gym STV Wi-fi available Parking: 50
Notes: ⊗ in bedrooms

Trenython, a successful marriage of Italian style and English charm, stands in 25 acres overlooking
St Austell Bay. The 17th-century hotel retains its original staircases and colonnades and many of the
bedrooms have sea views. Trenython Manor's Restaurant serves a range of meats and fish, including
fresh lobster.
Recommended in the area
Eden Project; Pine Lodge Gardens; Lanhydrock House

# The Nare Hotel

★★★★   85% ⊛ CHH

Address:   Carne Beach, VERYAN TR2 5PF
Tel:       01872 501111
Fax:       01872 501856
Email:     office@narehotel.co.uk
Website:   www.narehotel.co.uk
Map ref:   1, SW93
Directions: From Tregony follow A3078 for approx
1.5m. Left at Veryan sign, through village towards
sea & hotel Rooms: 39, S £109–£223 D £206–
£410 Facilities: ⊛ ⅄ Sauna Jacuzzi Tennis Gym STV Steam room Hot tub Parking: 80

Overlooking Carne beach on the beautiful Roseland Peninsula and surrounded by subtropical gardens
and National Trust land, The Nare offers the comfort and elegance of a country house by the sea in a
secluded tranquil setting. Considered by many to be the most comfortable hotel in Cornwall, the caring
staff give an increasingly rare and unobtrusive traditional service. The hotel also enjoys a well-earned
reputation for delicious food – seafood a speciality – as well as a comprehensive wine cellar.
Recommended in the area
The Eden Project; The National Maritime Museum; Falmouth

# CUMBRIA

Kendal, Cumbria

Wast Water, Lake District National Park

# Rothay Manor

★★★  82% ◉ HL

Address: Rothay Bridge, AMBLESIDE  LA22 0EH
Tel:      015394 33605
Email:    hotel@rothaymanor.co.uk
Website:  www.rothaymanor.co.uk/aa
Map ref:  5, NY30
Directions: In Ambleside follow signs for Coniston (A593). Hotel 0.25 mile SW of Ambleside
Rooms: 19, S £85–£130 D £135–£210
Facilities: Wi-Fi available Parking: 45 Notes: ⊗

For 40 years the same family has run this hotel, a Regency house built in 1825 and set in its own landscaped gardens, a quarter of a mile from Lake Windermere. The bedrooms are individually designed, with en suite facilities, telephone, television, hairdryer and tea- and coffee-making facilities. Several of the highest-quality rooms have balconies and a view of the fells. Flowers and antiques create the atmosphere of a traditional country house. Meals are prepared from local produce and complemented by a wine list selected with unusual care.

**Recommended in the area**

Lake Windermere; Dove Cottage (Wordsworth); Hill Top (Beatrix Potter).

# Armathwaite Hall

★★★★  80% ◉ CHH

Address: BASSENTHWAITE CA12 4RE
Tel:     017687 76551
Fax:     017687 76220
Email:   reservations@armathwaite-hall.com
Website: www.armathwaite-hall.com
Map ref: 5, NY23
Directions: M6 junct 40/A66 to Keswick rdbt then
A591 signed Carlisle. 8m to Castle Inn junct, turn
left. Hotel 300yds

Rooms: 42, S £130–£160 D £210–£350 Facilities: ⊗ Sauna Jacuzzi Solarium Tennis Gym STV
Wi-Fi available Parking: 100

Enjoying fine views over Bassenthwaite Lake, this impressive 17th-century mansion is peacefully
situated in 400 acres of deer park, surrounded by wooded valleys against the dramatic backdrop of
Skiddaw, one of England's highest mountains. Public areas, such as the elegant Lake Room, feature
splendid panelling and stonework, and roaring log fires on cooler days. Most of the individually
designed bedrooms, including the Hartley Tower Suite, with its private roof terrace, look across either
gardens, parkland or the lake. Each has a private bathroom, radio, satellite TV, in-house video, direct
dial phone, hairdryer and hospitality tray. In the AA Rosette-awarded Lake View restaurant traditional
English and classic French dishes, refined to reflect today's healthier lifestyle, make full use of
Cumbrian seasonal produce. Over traditional afternoon tea in the conservatory you might be able to
spot England's only breeding pair of osprey. Spa Leisure features an indoor swimming pool, sauna,
gym, croquet and tennis, as well as an holistic beauty salon. During weekends and school holidays the
children's Freebee Club offers a programme of fun and entertainment.

Receommended in the area

Wordsworth House; Derwentwater Lake Cruises; Ravenglass and Eskdale Railway

# The Pheasant

★★★ 81% ◉ HL

Address: BASSENTHWAITE,
          Cockermouth CA13 9YE
Tel:      017687 76234
Fax:      017687 76002
Email:    info@the-pheasant.co.uk
Website:  www.the-pheasant.co.uk
Map ref:  5, NY23
Directions: Midway between Keswick &
Cockermouth, signed from A66
Rooms: 15, S £75–£90 D £150–£186 Parking: 40

A charming old coaching inn in well-tended gardens, at the unspoilt northern end of the Lake District, this is a good example of a traditional Cumbrian hostelry. Its history stretches back over 500 years to its origins as a farmhouse, then from 1778 an alehouse. One of its 19th-century regulars was the famous huntsman John ('With his hounds and his horn in the morning') Peel who would often celebrate and recount his exploits in the tap room. Now the hotel bar, this mellow, oak-panelled room with exposed beams, wooden settles, polished parquet flooring and log fires remains more or less unchanged, although there's probably been quite a turnover in its great selection of malt whiskies. The individually decorated bedrooms have been sympathetically refurbished to a high standard with en suite bathrooms offering both bath and power shower, and all equipped with phone, tea tray and flat-screen TV. On the daily changing menu in the attractive beamed restaurant might be roast rack of Cumbrian lamb with shepherds pie and minted mash potato, or grilled fillet of sea bass with roast lobster cream sauce. Lighter lunches are available in the lounges or bar. Traditional Cumbrian afternoon tea means homemade scones with rum butter.

Recoommended in the area

Rheged Discovery Centre; Muncaster Castle; Skiddaw

Wordsworth's birthplace (NT), Cockermouth

# Borrowdale Gates Country House Hotel

★★★ 80% ⊛ CHH

**Address:** BORROWDALE, Keswick CA12 5UQ
**Tel:** 017687 77204
**Fax:** 017687 77254
**Email:** hotel@borrowdale-gates.com
**Website:** www.borrowdale-gates.com
**Map ref:** 5, NY21

**Directions:** From A66 follow B5289 for approx 4m.
Turn right over bridge, hotel 0.25m beyond village.

**Rooms:** 27, S £65–£90 D £130–£200 **Facilities:** STV **Parking:** 29 **Notes:** ⊗ in bedrooms

An attractive, well-maintained and friendly hotel in a woodland location with a backdrop of rugged fells.
The public rooms include a choice of antique furnished lounges with welcoming open fires. Bedrooms,
many with glorious views, come in a variety of styles and sizes and all are well equipped. The restaurant
provides a modern interpretation of classic French and British dishes, using the best local produce.

**Recoommended in the area**

Derwentwater Lake Cruises; Beatrix Potter Gallery; Wordsworth House

# Farlam Hall Hotel

★★★ ◎◎ HL

Address: BRAMPTON  CA8 2NG
Tel: 016977 46234
Fax: 016977 46683
Email: farlam@relaischateaux.com
Website: www.farlamhall.co.uk
Map ref: 6, NY56
Directions: On A689 (Brampton to Alston). Hotel 2m on left, (not in Farlam village)
Rooms: 12, S £150–£175 D £280–£330
Facilities: Wi-Fi available Parking: 35

This large, creeper-clad manor house is set in 12 acres of lovely grounds amid beautiful and wild Cumbrian countryside. Dating back to the 16th century, it is mostly a creation of the 1800s, when the Thompson family were in residence, and steam railway enthusiasts will revel in its connection with George Stephenson and his Rocket locomotive (its experimental track once ran through the grounds here). Today it offers warm hospitality from the family owners and 12 luxurious bedrooms, each with an ultra-modern bathroom. Two are ground-floor rooms, and another room in the converted stables which is reached by an external stone staircase. After a day exploring the fells, there's nothing nicer than to relax in one of the two large drawing rooms, where open fires add to the ambience in cooler weather. The restaurant, also open to non-residents in the evenings, offers a high standard of modern cuisine based on the sound traditional skills of the team of chefs. Dinner is served at 8pm, with a small, daily-changing menu, and guests usually congregate for pre-dinner drinks and canapes in one of the drawing rooms. A smart style of dress is requested. Residents who are around during the day can also get a light lunch. No children under five years.

Recommended in the area

Northern Pennines Area of Outstanding Natural Beauty; Hadrian's Wall; Eden Valley

Stock Ghyll Force, Ambleside

# Clare House

★ ◎ HL

**Address:** Park Road, GRANGE-OVER-SANDS
LA11 7HQ
**Tel:** 015395 33026
**Fax:** 015395 34310
**Email:** info@clarehousehotel.co.uk
**Website:** www.clarehousehotel.co.uk
**Map ref:** 5, SD47
**Directions:** Off A590 onto B5277, through Lindale into Grange, keep left, hotel 0.5m on left

**Rooms:** 18, S £76 D 152 **Facilities:** Wi-Fi available **Parking:** 18 **Notes:** ⊗ in bedrooms

A family-run hotel, with Morecambe Bay to the south and the Lake District to the north; most rooms enjoy a view over the bay. They are all centrally heated, well equipped, and some have balconies. A full English breakfast is the ideal start to the day, before setting off along the mile-long promenade at the foot of the garden. Return for a light lunch or skilfully prepared dinner chosen from a menu of English and French traditional and speciality dishes.
**Recommended in the area**
Holker Hall; Windermere Steamboat Centre; Cumberland Pencil Museum

**61**

# Best Western Castle Green Hotel in Kendal

★★★   83% ◉◉ HL

Address: KENDAL  LA9 6RG
Tel:       01539 734000
Email:    reception@castlegreen.co.uk
Website: www.castlegreen.co.uk
Map ref: 6, SD59
Directions: M6 junct 37/A684 towards Kendal. Hotel on right after 5m
Rooms: 100, S £79–£99 D £98–£138 Facilities: ⊗ Solarium Gym STV Wi-Fi throughout
Parking: 200 Notes: ⊗

The Castle Green, with Kendal on its doorstep, is well placed for exploring the southern end of the beautiful Lake District. Standing in 14 acres of woodlands and gardens, this smart modern hotel offers comfort and convenience in all its en suite rooms. They all look bright and fresh with soft duvets, satellite TV and a tempting room service menu. Those wanting more space and a little more luxury might opt for an Executive room, while the two rooms with a four-poster will appeal to those after something different or a litle more romantic. The bustling Greenhouse restaurant offers a choice of things to look at – in one direction, through huge panoramic windows, are the landscaped gardens and Kendal Castle; in the other, the chefs at work in the theatre-style kitchen. The produce is the best the region can provide – try Cumbrian lamb, for example, or Morecambe Bay shrimps. Alexander's, in the grounds, is the hotel's genuine real-ale pub, serving hearty meals and snacks. Work out in the leisure club's gym, swim in the indoor pool, or relax in the steam room. In addition there are large conference and training centre facilities available.

Recommended in the area

Abbot Hall Art Gallery; Lake District National Park; Levens Hall & Topiary Gardens

# Dale Head Hall Lakeside Hotel

★★★ 78% ◉◉ CHH

**Address:** Lake Thirlmere, KESWICK CA12 4TN
**Tel:** 017687 72478
**Fax:** 017687 71070
**Email:** onthelakeside@daleheadhall.co.uk
**Website:** www.daleheadhall.co.uk
**Map ref:** 5, NY22
**Directions:** Between Keswick & Grasmere. Off A591 onto private drive
**Rooms:** 12, S £127.5–£135 D £205–£260
**Parking:** 30 **Notes:** ⊗ in bedrooms

The oldest part of the main house dates from the early 16th century, although it has been much extended over the centuries. It stands alone on the edge of Thirlmere with Helvellyn, England's third highest mountain, rising behind. For much of the 20th century it was the summer residence of the Mayor of Manchester until, in 1990, the city council sold the property and the long process of restoration and transformation into a private hotel began. Comfortable and inviting public areas include a choice of lounges, but no bar, and an atmospheric beamed restaurant. There are three styles of bedroom – the Fellside in the original house, the Lakeside in the Victorian wing, and, in a new extension, the particularly spacious Superior Lakeside, some with hand-crafted four-posters. Whichever style you choose, the gardens can be seen sloping gently towards the shore of the lake which, incidentally, supplies Manchester with 50 million gallons of water a day. The restaurant has two AA Rosettes awarded for excellence of cuisine and service for seven years running, and features a short, daily-changing menu based on fresh local produce, such as Borrowdale trout, and salt marsh lamb. The stable block at the rear has been converted into self-catering accommodation.

**Recommended in the area**

Lake District National Park; Ravenglass and Eskdale Railway; Cumberland Pencil Museum

# Swinside Lodge

★★ ◉◉ CHH

Address: Grange Rd, Newlands,
KESWICK CA12 5UE
Tel: 017687 72948
Fax: 017687 73312
Email: info@swinsidelodge-hotel.co.uk
Website: www.swinsidelodge-hotel.co.uk
Map ref: 5, NY22
Directions: off A66 left at Portinscale. Follow road to Grange for 2m ignoring signs to Swinside & Newlands Valley
Rooms: 7, S £108 D £176–£216 Facilities: Wi-Fi in bedrooms Parking: 12 Notes: ⊗ in bedrooms

Swinside Lodge is a Georgian country house hotel in the Newlands Valley, just west of Derwentwater, known as the Queen of the Northern Lakes. It stands alone, surrounded by hills, valleys and woodlands, at the foot of a mountain called Cat Bells, in one of the most unspoilt areas of the Lake District National Park. A short stroll takes you to the lakeside and the regular boat service by the Keswick launch. Pastel blues and yellows in the reception rooms give them a fresh, clean look, while the sitting rooms offer books, maps and fresh flowers. Seven attractively decorated bedrooms offer a high degree of comfort and good views. All have a private bath and/or shower, TV, radio, hair dryer, hospitality tray and other extras. In the restaurant, candlelight accentuates the richness of the red walls and ceiling. Very much a Lake District favourite, with fresh, local produce used as much as possible in everything, from the home-baked breads, soups and puddings to the petits fours served with coffee. A four-course dinner is served at 7.30 each evening, preceded by aperitifs and canapés. Those who enjoy sailing, bird watching and fell walking will certainly be in their element at Swinside Lodge.

Recommended in the area

Ospreys at Whinlatter Forest; Castlerigg Stone Circle; Borrowdale

# Rampsbeck Country House Hotel

★★★ ◉◉◉ HL

Address: WATERMILLOCK,
           Penrith CA11 0LP
Tel:       017684 86442
Fax:       017684 86688
Email:    enquiries@rampsbeck.co.uk
Website: www.rampsbeck.co.uk
Map ref: 6, NY42
Directions: M6 junct 40, signs for A592 to Ullswater,
at T-junct with lake in front, turn right, hotel is 1.5m
along lake's edge

Rooms: 19, S £80–£135 D £130–£260 Facilities: Wi-Fi available Parking: 30

Rampsbeck is an idyllic 18th century Country House on the shores of Lake Ullswater. This beautifully situated hotel, has spectacular views of the lake and fells, it stands in 18 acres of parkland and gardens including plenty of lake frontage. Privately owned and managed it offers peace, pleasure and privacy. Guests can relax in style on comfortable settees in a choice of elegant reception rooms which offer afternoon teas and, in the evenings during winter, log fires. The individually decorated bedrooms, many with special features, offer a comfort and standard you would expect from a luxury country house. The enjoyment of good food is an integral part of any stay at the Rampsbeck providing superb cuisine and breathtaking views; the hotel boasts an award winning 3 AA-Rosetted restaurant. The attractive, candlelit dining room has superb lake views and here guests can enjoy the very best of modern French and English cuisine. Less than 15 minutes from the M6 motorway, Lake Ullswater provides a relaxing and tranquil place to stay and it makes an ideal base for enjoying the peace and serenity of the Northern Lakes.

Recommended in the area

Windermere; Grasmere; Ambleside; Keswick; Coniston

# Beech Hill Hotel

★★★ 81% ◉◉ HL

**Address:** Newby Bridge Road,
WINDERMERE LA23 3LR
**Tel:** 015394 42137
**Fax:** 015394 43745
**Email:** reservations@beechhillhotel.co.uk
**Website:** www.beechhillhotel.co.uk
**Map ref:** 6, SD49
**Directions:** Follow A592 from Bowness to Newby
Bridge, hotel 4m on right
**Rooms:** 57, S £50–£110 D £70–£170 **Facilities:** ◉ Solarium **Parking:** 70

This stylish, terraced, country house hotel is set on high ground leading down to the shores of Lake Windermere. Across the water the fells are in full view – and splendidly so – from the spacious, open-plan lounge where, in winter, a fire burns cheerily in the antique fireplace. All bedrooms are en suite and come with hospitality tray, direct dial phone, TV, radio alarm clock and hairdryer. Some have patio doors that open on to a garden terrace or private balcony, others have king-size or four-poster beds, while the rooms whose style is described as 'city chic' include plasma TV and air conditioning. The Wordsworth Suite, with a seven-foot oak bed, even has its own private garden with a hot tub. Burlington's Restaurant, with two long-standing AA Rosettes to its credit, also overlooks the water, as does the lounge. Its Gourmet menu is a five-course affair, which features French-English fusion dishes prepared from the best Cumbrian produce, while the Simple Taste menu is shorter and, indeed, simpler. The hotel has a private lakeside beach and jetty, indoor pool and, as well as ample parking. The many attractions of the Lake District National Park, both natural and man-made, are conveniently within easy reach.

**Recommended in the area**

Aquarium of the Lakes; Beatrix Potter Gallery; Lakeland Motor Museum

# Gilpin Lodge Country House Hotel & Restaurant

★★★★ ◉◉◉ HL

Address: Crook Road, WINDERMERE  LA23 3NE
Tel:      015394 88818
Email:    hotel@gilpinlodge.co.uk
Website:  www.gilpinlodge.co.uk
Map ref:  6, SD49
Directions: M6 junct 36, take A590/A591 to rdbt
north of Kendal, take B5284, hotel 5m on right

Rooms: 20, S £175 D £250–£360 Facilities: Wi-Fi in bedrooms Parking: 40 Notes: ⊗ in bedrooms

An elegant, friendly hotel in 20 tranquil acres of gardens, moors and woodland, owned and run by two generations of the Cunliffe family. The en suite bedrooms all have bath and shower, Molton Brown toiletries and bath robes. Individually and stylishly decorated to a high standard, they are quiet, with delightful views. Each room has a sitting area, TV, direct-dial phone, radio, hair dryer, and beverage tray with home-made biscuits; some rooms also have a trouser press. The Garden Suites have enormous beds, walk-in dressing areas, large sofas, modern fireplaces, flatscreen TVs and sensual bathrooms. Glass-fronted lounge areas lead to individual gardens with cedarwood hot tubs. Food is important at Gilpin Lodge. The nine chefs are passionate about using the finest local, organic ingredients as extensively as possible. It's hard to put a label on the food - classically based, yes, yet thoroughly modern and imaginative, without being too experimental. Tables have fresh flowers, candles at night, crisp white linen, fine china and glass, and gleaming silver. The wine list, featuring over 300 wines from 13 countries, reflects real interest rather than a desire to sell high priced vintages. Residents have free use of a local leisure club, although on-call spa therapists will visit guest rooms.

Recommended in the area

Lake Windermere; Beatrix Potter Gallery; Dove Cottage and Wordsworth Museum

# Lindeth Howe Country House Hotel & Restaurant

★★★   86% ◉◉ HL

**Address:** Lindeth Drive, Longtail Hill,
WINDERMERE LA23 3JF
**Tel:** 015394 45759
**Fax:** 015394 46368
**Email:** hotel@lindeth-howe.co.uk
**Website:** www.lindeth-howe.co.uk
**Map ref:** 6, SD49
**Directions:** Turn off A592, 1m S of Bowness onto B5284 (Longtail Hill) signed Kendal & Lancaster, hotel last driveway on right
**Rooms:** 36, S £60–£85 D £120–£250 **Facilities:** ⊗ Sauna Gym STV **Notes:** ⊗ in bedrooms

Once owned by Beatrix Potter, Lindeth Howe enjoys views across Lake Windermere. There is a delightful Terrace and Library and the bedrooms are furnished to a high standard. Canapés and drinks in the lounge may be followed by a five-course dinner in the Dining Room.
**Recommended in the area**
World of Beatrix Potter; Windermere Lake Cruises; Mountain Goat mini-coach tours

# Linthwaite House Hotel & Restaurant

★★★   ◉◉◉ CHH

**Address:** Crook Road, WINDERMERE LA23 3JA
**Tel:** 015394 88600
**Fax:** 015394 88601
**Email:** stay@linthwaite.com
**Website:** www.linthwaite.com
**Map ref:** 6, SD49
**Directions:** A591 towards The Lakes for 8m to large rdbt, take 1st exit (B5284), 6m, hotel on left. 1m past Windermere golf club
**Rooms:** 27, S £120–£170 D £170–£320 **Facilities:** STV Wi-Fi in bedrooms **Parking:** 40 **Notes:** ⊗ in bedrooms

A beautiful country house hotel in a sublime hilltop setting overlooking Lake Windermere and the fells. Inviting public rooms include an attractive conservatory, veranda, adjoining lounge and bar. Individually decorated en suite bedrooms combine contemporary furnishings with classical styles. The restaurant serves modern British food, using top quality local produce. Voted the 'most romantic' hotel by the AA.
**Recommended in the area**
Lake District National Park; Dove Cottage; Scafell Pike

Lake Windermere

# The Samling

★★★ ◉◉◉ HL

Address: Ambleside Road, WINDERMERE
          LA23 1LR
Tel:      015394 31922
Fax:      015394 30400
Email:    info@thesamling.com
Website:  www.thesamling.com
Map ref:  6, SD49
Directions: turn right off A591,
            300mtrs after Low Wood Hotel

Rooms: 11, S £290–£520 D £290–£520 Facilities: Hot tub STV Parking: 15 Notes: ⊗ in bedrooms

This three-gabled gem is situated in 67 acres of grounds, high above Lake Windermere. The spacious, beautifully furnished bedrooms and suites are split between the main house and some converted cottages, and all but two overlook the lake. Public rooms include an award-winning dining room where the food, made from the best local ingredients, is light and imaginative and the wine selection can more than hold its own. Outdoor activities include water-skiing, paragliding, canoeing and croquet.

**Recommended in the area**

Sailing on Lake Windermere; Dove Cottage; Jenkins Crag

# Washington Central Hotel

★★★   85% ◉ HL

**Address:** Washington Street, WORKINGTON  CA14 3AY
**Tel:**      01900 65772
**Fax:**      01900 68770
**Email:**    kawildwchotel@aol.com
**Website:** www.washingtoncentralhotelworkington.com
**Map ref:**  5, NY02
**Rooms:** 46, S £85–£105 D £125–£195 **Facilities:** ⊗ Sauna
Jacuzzi Solarium  Gym STV Wi-Fi available **Parking:** 10
**Notes:** ⊗ in bedrooms

Enjoying a prominent town-centre location, this distinctive
red-brick hotel is within walking distance of most amenities,
including shops, cinema and parks, while only a little further afield are the delights of the Lake District
National Park. Its eminently laudable claim is that staff here are 'memorably friendly and hospitable'.
Public areas include several lounges, a spacious bar, a popular coffee shop and Caesar's leisure club,
which has a 20-metre swimming pool surrounded by frescoes. The well-maintained and comfortable
en suite bedrooms are equipped with satellite TV, in-house entertainment, hairdryer, trouser press,
work desk, direct-dial phones and modem point, as well as fresh coffee- and tea- making facilities. The
executive accommodation includes a four-poster suite with hi-fi system and luxurious lounge. In the
wood-panelled Carlton Restaurant, recently awarded an AA Rosette, only the best local ingredients will
do for dishes such as walnut-crusted seabass with roasted pancetta, and seared Barbary duck breast.
For special occasions, book the eight-cover Clock Tower Restaurant, not just for the food, but for
outstanding views towards Scotland, the Isle of Man and the Lakes. Bar meals are available lunchtimes
and evenings in the lounge bar, snug or conservatory.

**Recommended in the area**

Western Lakes; Grasmere; Solway Firth

Haddon House gardens

# Riverside House Hotel

★★★  88% ◉◉ HL

Address:  Fennel Street, ASHFORD IN THE WATER,
          Bakewell DE45 1QF
Tel:      01629 814275
Fax:      01629 812873
Email:    riversidehouse@enta.net
Website:  www.riversidehousehotel.co.uk
Map ref:  7, SK16
Directions: Turn right off A6 Bakewell/Buxton road
2m from Bakewell, hotel at end of main street
Rooms: 14, S £155–£200 D £230–£295 Facilities: STV Parking: 40 Notes: ⊗ in bedrooms

A graceful, creeper-clad Georgian mansion in peaceful landscaped gardens by the River Wye, a major tributary of the Derwent. Its high quality accommodation, fine dining and outstanding service have ensured the hotel a place in the pantheon of Peak District retreats. Individually styled en suite bedrooms are furnished with rich fabrics and antiques, and are equipped with satellite TV, tea- and coffee-making tray and direct-dial phone. The smart public rooms include a drawing room, two dining rooms, a bright conservatory and, in the original 17th-century part of the house, an oak-panelled lounge. The huge inglenook fireplace here once served the original kitchen, now part of the charming two-AA Rosette Riverside Rooms restaurant. Tastefully designed with soft décor and chic antique tables and chairs, and artwork depicting local scenes and places of interest, the menus here combine modern English, international and local cuisine, typical dishes at dinner being pan-roasted fillet of Derbyshire beef, or roasted vegetable strudel. Alternatively, there is the Conservatory Room, open daily for lunch and dinner, offering fresh seafood, deli sandwiches and a wide variety of healthy options, such as chargrilled chicken salad. On a summer's afternoon you can play croquet on the lawn.

Recommended in the area

Dovedale; Chatsworth House; Haddon Hall

# Best Western George Hotel

★★★  80% ◉◉ HL

**Address:** Main Road, HATHERSAGE S32 1BB
**Tel:**  01433 650436
**Fax:**  01433 650099
**Email:**  info@george-hotel.net
**Website:**  www.george-hotel.net
**Map ref:**  7, SK28
**Directions:** In village centre on A6187 SW of Sheffield. Also 20 miles from the M1 junction 29
**Rooms:** 22, S £88–£99 D £97–£175
**Facilities:** Free Wi-Fi in bedrooms **Parking:** 40 **Notes:** ⊗ in bedrooms

With its 500 year history, the George occupies a prominent position at the heart of the picturesque Peak District village of Hathersage. Under the ownership of Eric Marsh since 1996, the George has undergone a continual transformation to a 'smart' hotel offering every modern facility to the guest, whilst retaining many key original features. Sympathetic modernisation offers simple décor in the bedrooms, a light and contemporary feel in the Restaurant combined with much original artwork and antiques throughout the building. Renowned for it's friendly, informal and attentive service, George's Restaurant is a key feature of the Hotel. A strong local following makes pre-booking essential. Executive Chef Ben Handley is now in his eleventh year at the George and continues to show a flair and passion for his cooking; a philosophy of using the best produce possible, much locally sourced, remains central to his popular following. A modern approach to cooking is matched by a 'compact' wine list, featuring an eclectic mix of styles, grape varieties and countries of origin; eight wines are offered by the glass and the bar boasts a surprising range of malt whiskies. Other facilities include private dining and conference facilities for up to eighty guests, a wedding licence and inclusive car parking.

**Recommended in the area**

Peak National Park; Chatsworth House; Haddon Hall

# The Peacock at Rowsley

★★★  88% ◉◉ HL

**Address:** Bakewell Road, ROWSLEY,
Bakewell DE4 2EB
**Tel:** 01629 733518
**Fax:** 01629 732671
**Email:** reception@thepeacockatrowsley.com
**Website:** www.thepeacockatrowsley.com
**Map ref:** 7, SK26
**Directions:** A6, 3m before Bakewell, 6m from
Matlock towards Bakewell
**Rooms:** 16, S £75–£100 D £145–£210 **Facilities:** STV Wi-Fi in bedrooms **Parking:** 25

Within Britain's oldest national park, this is a perfect base for taking exhilarating walks across lonely moorland, for exploring beautiful secluded valleys and pretty villages, and for fishing – the hotel owns fly fishing rights on the Wye and Derwent, the latter flowing through the garden. In 2004 Keira Knightley, Matthew Macfadyen and other actors and crew stayed here while filming *Pride and Prejudice* at Haddon Hall. The bedrooms are luxurious, most with king- or super king-size beds, and each has been styled by the international designer, India Mahdavi, who has blended antique furniture with contemporary décor. One room has a four-poster bed, another has an antique bed from Belvoir Castle. Modern facilities include modem ports, and there are soft drinks as well as tea- and coffee-making supplies. The main restaurant overlooks the garden and has an interesting menu that might include starters like duck liver ballotine with hazelnuts and figs, or smoked eel with apple purée, celeriac remoulade and a quail's egg. Main courses are equally imaginative, with recent offerings including shoulder of lamb with roast sweetbread, black olive gnocchi, fennel and goat's cheese. There's also a cosy bar, with an open fire and stone walls, serving real ales, cocktails and simple dishes.

**Recommended in the area**

Haddon Hall; Chatsworth House; Peak District National Park

# DEVON

Clovelly harbour

Torquay

# Northcote Manor

★★★ ◉◉ CHH

**Address:** BURRINGTON, Umberleigh EX37 9LZ
**Tel:** 01769 560501
**Fax:** 01769 560770
**Email:** rest@northcotemanor.co.uk
**Website:** www.northcotemanor.co.uk
**Map ref:** 2, SS61
**Directions:** off A377 opposite Portsmouth Arms, into
hotel drive. NB. Do not enter Burrington village
**Rooms:** 11, S  D £155–£255 **Facilities:** Tennis STV
Wi-Fi available **Parking:** 30

This beautiful, early 18th-century hotel stands surrounded by 20 acres of woodlands and lawns, including a newly reinstated Victorian water garden, much to the delight of local dragonflies. Suites and bedrooms are all very appealing, while no two are identical in size, decor or furnishings. The restaurant's seasonal gourmet menu offers well-prepared, locally sourced dishes such as Exmoor lamb or rod-caught Cornish turbot, with exceptional wines to accompany each course.

**Recommended in the area**

Exmoor Bird Gardens; Rosemoor RHS Garden; Marshall Falcons

# Gidleigh Park

★★★★ ◎◎◎◎ CHH

Address: CHAGFORD TQ13 8HH
Tel: 01647 432367
Fax: 01647 432574
Email: gidleighpark@gidleigh.com
Website: www.gidleigh.com
Map ref: 2, SX78
Directions: from Chagford, right at Lloyds Bank (with it on your right)into Mill St. After 150yds fork right, follow lane 2m to end. Do not use satellite navigation
Rooms: 24, S £380–£520 D £480–£620 Facilities: Tennis STV Wi-Fi in bedrooms Parking: 25

In 45 acres of lovingly tended grounds within Dartmoor National Park, this world-renowned hotel emerged rejuvenated from a multi-million pound refurbishment in 2006. Its many Arts and Crafts features help to explain its comfortable atmosphere and its timeless charm. Spacious public areas feature antique furniture, works of art and beautiful flowers. There are more antiques and artwork in the individually styled, beautifully decorated bedrooms, some with separate seating areas, some with balconies and many with panoramic views of the river Teign, moorland or forest. The beds are huge, the marble bathrooms stunning and the wet-rooms imaginative. All rooms come with Wi-Fi and flat-screen TVs. As if staying here wouldn't be memorable enough, Michael Caines MBE's modern British cuisine, together with a fine wine list, could only enhance the experience. Oak-panelled Meldon is the most elegant dining room; Teign, with Lloyd Loom furniture, is lighter and more informal; while Nattadon, with banquette seating and a wine wall, is the contemporary one. Typically appearing at dinner might be slow-roast Hatherleigh venison with braised pork belly, while a tasting menu could offer John Dory with tomato and langoustine bisque. Spa and beauty treatments are available in all rooms.

Recommended in the area

Castle Drogo; Canonteign Country Park; Dartington Crystal; Rosemoor Garden; Widecombe in the Moor

Dartmoor National Park

# Mill End Hotel

★★  ◎◎ HL

Address:  Dartmoor National Park,
          CHAGFORD TQ13 8JN
Tel:      01647 432282
Email:    info@millendhotel.com
Website:  www.millendhotel.com
Map ref:  2, SX78
Directions: From A30 at Whiddon Down follow A382
to Moretonhampstead. After 3.5m hump back bridge
at Sandy Park, hotel on right by river
Rooms: 14, S £90 D £90–£155 Facilities: Wi-Fi available Parking: 25

Situated on a river bank and lulled by the sound of a working waterwheel, this former flour mill provides
classic comfort for its residents. The upstairs rooms enjoy fine views, while the downstairs rooms have
private patios. The restaurant offers award-winning food, with continually changing menus making the
most of local and seasonal ingredients. There are three meeting rooms for up to 40 people. Guests can
play croquet on the lawns, and anglers can use the hotel's private fishing licence.
Recommended in the area
Castle Drogo; Chagford; Dartmoor National Park

# Langstone Cliff Hotel

★★★ 77% HL

| | |
|---|---|
| Address: | Dawlish Warren, |
| | DAWLISH EX7 0NA |
| Tel: | 01626 868000 |
| Fax: | 01626 868006 |
| Email: | reception@langstone-hotel.co.uk |
| Website: | www.langstone-hotel.co.uk |
| Map ref: | 2, SX97 |

Directions: 1.5m NE off A379 Exeter road to Dawlish Warren
Rooms: 66, S £71–£88 D £112–£136 Facilities: ⊕ ⊀ Tennis
Gym STV Wi-Fi in bedrooms Parking: 200

It was the Rogers family who welcomed the first guests here
in 1947. They're still here, although it's generations two and three now, and still welcoming some of
those pioneering visitors. Such loyalty is understandable: the views of the sea from the lawn, veranda
and lounges are breathtaking, and a two-mile stretch of beach is five-minutes' walk away. The service
is attentive, the public rooms spacious, the lounges are comfortable and the bars friendly. Bedrooms
undergo frequent updating to reflect changing expectations of comfort and convenience. Many are
designed as family rooms, some have balconies, and all are en suite, with TV, radio, baby-listening,
phone and other amenities. The extensive breakfast menu in the Lincoln Restaurant gets guests off to
a good start. Coffee shop-style service offers anything from a sandwich, baguette or Danish pastry to
a selection of hot and cold meals, with dinner chosen from a fixed price menu or the carvery. Many of
the sensibly priced wines are available by the glass. There are indoor and outdoor heated pools, a hard
tennis court, compact leisure centre and full-size snooker table. An 18-hole golf course is nearby, but
you can practise your swing beforehand in the hotel grounds.

Recommended in the area

Paignton Zoo; Powderham Castle; Miniature Pony Centre

# The Horn of Plenty

★★★   85% ®®® HL

Address: GULWORTHY  PL19 8JD
Tel:       01822 832528
Fax:      01822 834390
Email:   enquiries@thehornofplenty.co.uk
Website: www.thehornofplenty.co.uk
Map ref:  1, SX47
Directions: from Tavistock take A390 W for 3m. Right at
Gulworthy Cross. After 400yds turn left and after 400yds hotel
on right
Rooms: 10, S £150–£240 D £160–£250 Parking: 25

A former AA Hotel of the Year, the Horn of Plenty continues
to provide first rate food and accommodation in a glorious location. Surrounded by a designated
Area of Outstanding Natural Beauty, it has fine grounds of its own and is just off the western edge of
Dartmoor. Joint proprietor (with Paul Roston) is master chef Peter Gorton, who trained at some of the
finest restaurants in the UK and abroad and provides the culinary highlight to any stay here. The dinner
menu might include such starters as roast pigeon wrapped in potato on a foie gras salad with a port
and red wine dressing, or steamed red mullet on a crab cake with ginger and spring onions. Recent
main courses have featured spiced duck breast with a cherry compote and port sauce, and pan-fried
sea bass with a white wine saffron sauce. Remember to look up from the food occasionally to enjoy
the view of the Tamar Valley out of the glass-fronted dining room. The hotel's bedrooms are luxurious
and include fresh flowers, bottled water, home-made shortbread biscuits and towelling robes, and
bathrooms have a range of beauty products. Some rooms are in the coach house, and these have
balconies overlooking the walled gardens.

Recommended in the area

Morwelham Quay; Buckland Abbey (NT); Plymouth

# Combe House Hotel & Restaurant

★★★  ◉◉ HL

Address: Gittisham, HONITON  EX14 3AD
Tel:      01404 540400
Fax:      01404 46004
Email:    stay@thishotel.com
Website:  www.thishotel.com
Map ref:  2, ST10
Directions: off A30 1m S of Honiton, follow Gittisham Heathpark signs
Rooms: 16, S £139–£340 D £168–£450
Facilities:  Wi-Fi available Parking: 38

This Elizabethan manor stands on high ground, enjoying views over 3,500 acres of estate land. The interior is richly adorned with carved oak panelling and family portraits of those who have owned the house. Some of the local produce that features in the award-winning restaurant's meals comes from the hotel's own gardens. The extensive and interesting wine list includes a fine range of Chablis. Wedding vows can be made at Combe Hall, and, if wished, the House can also be booked for use.

Recommended in the area

World Heritage Coast; Exmouth to Lyme Regis; Dartmoor National Park; Honiton; Exeter

# Ilsington Country House Hotel

★★★   85% ◉◉ HL

Address: Ilsington Village, ILSINGTON,
         Newton Abbot TQ13 9RR
Tel:      01364 661452
Email:    hotel@ilsington.co.uk
Website:  www.ilsington.co.uk
Map ref:  2, SX77
Directions: M5 onto A38 to Plymouth. Exit at Bovey Tracey. 3rd exit from rdbt to 'Ilsington', then 1st right. Hotel in 5m by Post Office
Rooms: 25, S £92–£98 D £136–£144 Facilities: Sauna Jacuzzi Gym Wi-Fi in bedrooms
Parking: 100

Ilsington Country House Hotel is a friendly, family-owned hotel in 10 acres of Dartmoor's southern slopes, offering tranquillity and far-reaching views. The air-conditioned restaurant serves local fare and classic dishes featuring fresh market produce. Scrumptious Devonshire cream teas are served in the conservatory or garden.

Recommended in the area

Castle Drogo; Buckfast Abbey; Dartmoor National Park

# Buckland-Tout-Saints

★★★ 85% ◉◉ CHH

Address: Goveton, KINGSBRIDGE TQ7 2DS
Tel:     01548 853055
Fax:     01548 856261
Email:   buckland@tout-saints.co.uk
Website: www.tout-saints.co.uk
Map ref: 2, SX74
Directions: Turn off A381 to Goveton. Follow brown tourism signs to St Peter's Church. Hotel 2nd right after church

Rooms: 16, S £79–£135 D £99–£199 Facilities: STV Wi-Fi in bedrooms Parking: 40 Notes: ⊗

In a tiny village that takes its name from the Toutsaints family who held the manor in 1238, this delightful William & Mary house is only a short drive from the international sailing centre of Salcombe. You might, however, need the sat-nav, or just a trusty old Ordnance Survey map, to guide you there through winding country lanes. Surrounded by over four acres of beautifully tended gardens and woodland, this peaceful retreat's bedrooms are tastefully furnished and attractively decorated. Eight original rooms, some with four-poster beds, and two luxurious suites have been updated in a traditional Devon country-house style, while the six new ones have been given a strikingly modern appearance, and offer stunning views across the valley. All have flat-screen TVs. Holder of two AA Rosettes for many years, the Queen Anne Restaurant is acknowledged as one of the finest in the area. Its original Russian pine panelling creates an elegant environment for dining on head chef Callum Kier's largely locally sourced dishes. The Blue Room, with its Adam-style fireplace and décor, is the perfect venue for intimate private dinners for up to 12 guests, while the Kestrel Suite is popular for larger functions and perfect for weddings.

**Recommended in the area**

Salcombe; Dartmouth; The Eden Project

# Riviera Hotel

★★★★　80% ◉◉ HL

**Address:** The Esplanade, SIDMOUTH  EX10 8AY
**Tel:** 01395 515201
**Fax:** 01395 577775
**Email:** enquiries@hotelriviera.co.uk
**Website:** www.hotelriviera.co.uk
**Map ref:** 2, SY18
**Directions:** M5 junct 30 & follow A3052
**Rooms:** 26, S £114–£170 D £228–£318 (prices inclusive of dinner and breakfast)
**Facilities:** STV  **Parking:** 26

This superb Regency building on Sidmouth's Esplanade dates from the age when the town grew to prominence as a fashionable resort. The hotel overlooks Lyme Bay, yet is close to the town centre. Many of the bedrooms enjoy fine views over the sea, and all have en suite facilities and colour television, radio, direct-dial telephones and hairdryers. The dining room too has fine views over the sea, and emphasizes local seafood in its wide-ranging menus, which are both à la carte and fixed-price. Cream teas can be enjoyed in the lounge or, in summer, on the patio. Light refreshments are always available at any time of the year. A resident pianist enhances the ambience of the Regency Bar on many evenings. Private functions including wedding parties and business conferences can be accommodated. The hotel can arrange sporting activities in the area: golfing at concessionary fees at the nearby Sidmouth Golf Club and Woodbury Park Golf and County Club; riding; and pheasant- and duck-shooting on local estates. The Heritage Coast Trail passes nearby. The hotel offers packages of weekend and three-day breaks. All the sights of Devon can be reached within a short journey time, and the M5 motorway lies only 13 miles from the hotel. Children of all ages are welcomed.

**Recommended in the area**

Bicton Gardens; Killerton House and Gardens; Exeter Cathedral.

# Westcliff Hotel

★★★  85%  HL

Address: Manor Road, SIDMOUTH
EX10 8RU
Tel: 01395 513252
Fax: 01395 578203
Email: stay@westcliffhotel.co.uk
Website: www.westcliffhotel.co.uk
Map ref: 2, SY18
Directions: Turn off A3052 to Sidmouth then to
seafront and esplanade, turn r, hotel directly ahead
Rooms: 40, S £66–£132 D £132–£236
Facilities: ⅄ STV Wi-Fi available Parking: 40

The privately owned Westcliff Hotel is set in two beautiful acres of lawns and gardens, right in the middle of the Jurassic Coast, a World Heritage Site since 2001. In fact, the Westcliff's position gives it a natural advantage sheltering it from every wind but the south. Regency Sidmouth is known as the 'Jewel of the West Country' and its town centre, promenade and beaches are a just a short walk away. Locally renowned for excellent food and courteous and efficient service, the Westcliff Hotel offers elegant lounges and a cocktail bar open on to the heated outdoor swimming pool (June to September). The different types of bedroom are well proportioned, tastefully furnished and equipped with all the usual amenities. Most have sea views, some from their own private balconies. In fact, it is only a few of the single and standard rooms that do not face the sea. The Harding's restaurant offers a tempting choice of both carte and fixed price menus, and views of the red cliffs for which this part of Devon is famous. The Westcliff Hotel is open all year round.

Recommended in the area

Bicton Gardens; Crealy Adventure Park; Otterton Mill; Jurassic Coast (World Heritage Site); Sidmouth; red cliffs of Devon

# Corbyn Head Hotel & Orchid Restaurant

★★★   77% ◉◉◉ HL

**Address:** Torbay Road, Sea Front, TORQUAY
TQ2 6RH
**Tel:** 01803 213611
**Fax:** 01803 296152
**Email:** info@corbynhead.com
**Website:** www.corbynhead.com
**Map ref:** 2, SX96
**Directions:** Follow signs to Torquay seafront, turn right on
seafront. Hotel on right with green canopies
**Rooms:** 45, S £60–£70 D £120–£140 **Facilities:** ⟋ Sauna
Solarium Gym  Wi-Fi available **Parking:** 50

This establishment is sited in a magnificent setting on Torbay's waterfront just a minute's leisurely
walk to Livermead Beach. The rooms are all en suite; most have sea views, and many have
private balconies. Guests staying seven nights on the standard tariff receive a free extra night's
accommodation, and there are accommodation packages at Christmas, New Year and throughout
the year. The three AA Rosette air-conditioned Orchid Restaurant offers fine dining on the top floor of
the hotel, with magnificent views over Torbay. Smart casual wear is requested here. The traditional
English cuisine of the Harbour View Restaurant, made with only the finest local produce, is constantly
changing. The Regency Lounge and the Continental Coffee Bar open onto the Poolside Terrace and
offer wonderful views to guests enjoying morning coffee and afternoon tea. The Corbyn Head Hotel also
offers free onsite parking.

**Recommended in the area**

Paignton Zoo; Kent's Cavern, Torquay; Babbacombe Model Village

Exeter Cathedral

# Orestone Manor Hotel & Restaurant

★★★  87% ◉ HL

| | |
|---|---|
| Address: | Rockhouse Lane, Maidencombe, |
| | TORQUAY  TQ1 4SX |
| Tel: | 01803 328098 |
| Fax: | 01803 328336 |
| Email: | info@orestonemanor.com |
| Website: | www.orestonemanor.com |
| Map ref: | 2, SX96 |

Directions: Follow A38 off motorway to A380 then B3192 coast road Teignmouth to Torquay
Rooms: 12, S £99–£149 D £135–£225 Facilities: ⚡ Wi-Fi in bedrooms Parking: 40

All rooms at the Orestone have en suite bathrooms and are beautifully decorated. Skilfully prepared contemporary English cuisine makes full use of the superb local produce. Diners have a choice of where to enjoy pre and post-dinner drinks, gazing out at the fine views over the English Channel.
Recommended in the area
Kent's Cavern; Babbacombe Model Village; Dart Valley Railway

# Woodbury Park Hotel Golf & Country Club

★★★★ 72% ◉ HL

**Address:** Woodbury Castle, WOODBURY,
Exeter EX5 1JJ
**Tel:** 01395 233382
**Fax:** 01395 234701
**Email:** enquiries@woodburypark.co.uk
**Website:** www.woodburypark.co.uk
**Map ref:** 2, SY08
**Directions:** M5 junct 30, A376 then A3052 towards Sidmouth, onto B3180, hotel signed
**Rooms:** 60, S £60–£150 D £75–£200 **Facilities:** ⑨ Sauna Jacuzzi Tennis Gym STV Wi-Fi in
bedrooms **Parking:** 400 **Notes:** ⊗ in bedrooms

Woodbury Park stands in 500 acres of Devon's most beautiful countryside, and provides the ultimate
in sport and leisure facilities, as well as spacious, luxuriously appointed en suite bedrooms, suites and
individual Swiss-style lodges. Many have balconies, with sweeping views across the surrounding greens
of the two parkland golf courses and rolling countryside of the Exe Valley. The glass-roofed Atrium
Restaurant is flooded with natural light by day and, on clear nights, a canopy of stars encourages a
romantic mood. The carte offers a mouth-watering array of freshly cooked seasonal fish, meat and
game dishes, and the wine list is impressive. Private dining facilities are available, while light snacks,
tea and coffee are served in the Conservatory in the Clubhouse. You can also re-live the thrills of
Formula One in the unique 'The Nigel Mansell World of Racing', then stand alongside the actual
Formula One racing cars he drove to victory. Enjoy a game of football on the Premier-standard pitch, or
a swim in the leisure centre.

**Recommended in the area**

Woodbury Castle; Exeter Cathedral; World of Country Life

# Woolacombe Bay Hotel

★★★  78%  HL

Address:  South Street, WOOLACOMBE  EX34 7BN
Tel:       01271 870388
Fax:       01271 870613
Email:     woolacombe.bayhotel@btinternet.com
Website:  www.woolacombebayhotel.co.uk
Map ref:  1, SS44
Directions: From A361 take B3343 to Woolacombe. Hotel in centre on left
Rooms: 63, S £75–£102 D £150–£204 Facilities: ⊗ ⚲
Sauna Solarium Tennis Gym STV Wi-Fi available Parking: 150
Notes: ⊗ in bedrooms

This family hotel, built in the late 1880s, is set in 6-acre grounds leading to Woolacombe's three-mile stretch of Blue Flag golden sands. The village is in an Area of Outstanding Natural Beauty, surrounded by National Trust headlands with many little coves. Barricane Beach is world renowned for its variety of exotic sea shells and is a true delight for the serious shell-seeker. The hotel has been sensitively taken into the 21st century with superb leisure facilities and amenities of which guests have unlimited use. In addition there is a 9-hole approach golf and a health suite. Golf and Health spa breaks are available. There is also a fully-equipped gymnasium, aerobics studio, billiard room, table tennis and squash court as well as a drying room for wetsuits and weather gear. For children there is an adventure playground, paddling pools, crèche and baby monitoring. Doyle's restaurant has unbroken views to Lundy Island and, as befits its Edwardian origins, features chandeliers and high ceilings. It is renowned for its fine dining, ambience and the quality of its English and French cusine. The Bay Brasserie is a popular venue for morning coffee, lunches, Devon cream teas and dinner using local Devon produce.

Recommended in the area

Mortehoe Heritage Centre; Marwood Hill Gardens; Arlington Court (NT)

# DORSET

Lyme Regis

Bournemouth

# Chine Hotel

★★★   80% ◉ HL

Address: Boscombe Spa Rd,
         BOURNEMOUTH BH5 1AX
Tel:     0845 337 1550 (/1570 Fax)
Email:   reservations@fjbhotels.co.uk
Website: www.fjbhotels.co.uk
Map ref: 1, SZ19
Directions: Follow A35 to St Pauls rdbt. Take exit
onto St Pauls Rd to Christchurch Rd. Boscombe Spa
Rd 3rd on right
Rooms: 87, S £50–£85 D £60–£100 Facilities: ⊗ ⃗ Sauna Jacuzzi Solarium Gym STV Wi-Fi
available Parking: 50

Attention to detail is a hallmark in the well-appointed en suite bedrooms, many with a sea-facing
balcony. The charming SeaView Restaurant's mouth-watering menu presents freshly caught fish,
carefully selected meats, vegetarian options and a very good wine list. The hotel also caters for
conferences, meetings and functions. The beach is just a short walk through the three acre-gardens.
Recommended in the area
Bournemouth Shopping Centre; Poole Quay; New Forest National Park

# Best Western Waterford Lodge Hotel

★★★ 75% HL

| | |
|---|---|
| **Address:** | 87 Bure Lane, Friars Cliff, |
| | CHRISTCHURCH  BH23 4DN |
| **Tel:** | 01425 282100 |
| **Fax:** | 01425 278396 |
| **Email:** | waterfordlodgehotel@yahoo.co.uk |
| **Website:** | www.waterfordlodge.co.uk |
| **Map ref:** | 3, SZ19 |

**Directions:** A35 onto A337 towards Highcliffe. Turn right from rdbt signed Mudeford. Hotel 0.5m on left

**Rooms:** 18, S £68–£99 D £90–£150 **Facilities:** STV Wi-Fi available **Parking:** 38 **Notes:** ⊗

Just a five-minute stroll from a stretch of unspoiled beaches, Waterford Lodge is also within a short drive of glorious countryside, historic towns and cities and the lively resort of Bournemouth. Set in charming gardens, the stylish hotel is based on the former mansion of the Duchess of Waterford, and has recently been extended and sympathetically refurbished. Quality fabrics and restful décor define the bedrooms, including ground floor rooms for those who prefer not to tackle the stairs – there is no lift, but none of the rooms is higher than first floor level. All of the bedrooms are spacious and comfortable, and include cosy armchairs and a well-lit desk with dataport. Some of the rooms also have free wireless internet access, which is available to all in the lounge and reception area. Fine dining is another attraction here, with modern English cuisine served in the stately restaurant. Dishes on the good-value set price dinner menus might inlude pan-seared scallops with tarragon butter and spinach, followed, perhaps, by paillard of chicken flavoured with basil and rosemary, and accompanied by pommes mousseline and courgettes. There is also a less formal menu available in the lounge bar.

**Recommended in the area**

Red House Museum; Highcliffe Castle; New Forest National Park

# Stock Hill Country House Hotel & Restaurant

★★★  ◉◉◉ CHH

**Address:** Stock Hill, GILLINGHAM  SP8 5NR
**Tel:**  01747 823626
**Fax:**  01747 825628
**Email:**  reception@stockhillhouse.co.uk
**Website:** www.stockhillhouse.co.uk
**Map ref:** 2, ST82
**Directions:** 3m E on B3081, off A303
**Rooms:** 9, S £145–£165 D £280–£320 (prices include dinner, bed and breakfast) **Facilities:** Sauna
Tennis **Parking:** 20 **Notes:** ⊗ in bedrooms

This lovely Victorian mansion, approached along a beech-lined driveway, is set in 11 acres of wooded grounds and landscaped gardens on the borders of Dorset, Somerset and Wiltshire. The gracious period décor has a very welcoming feel and guests are enchanted by the array of antiques, including an original Osbert Lancaster cartoon (his grandfather once lived here). The bedrooms are equally sumptuous in their furnishings, and some of the comfortable beds have interesting designs. Each room is individually styled and has an ensuite bathroom. Hospitality here is top notch, including the welcome offer of a pot of tea when guests return from their day of sightseeing. The highlight of any stay here, though, is the exciting food in the three-AA Rosette restaurant, where chef Peter Hausner offers a dramatic and highly individual choice of dishes based on a blend of classic French and English cuisine, with influence of his native Austria. The menus change on a daily basis, and make good use of fresh local produce, and the fixed-price Sunday lunch and 'Lazy Lunches' (Tuesday to Friday only) offer exceptionally good value. Children over seven years are welcome.

**Recommended in the area**

Stourhead House and Garden; Stonehenge; Kingston Lacy Country House;

# Harbour Heights Hotel

★★★★  81% ◉◉ HL

**Address:** 73 Haven Road, Sandbanks,
POOLE  BH13 7LW
**Tel:** 0845 337 1550
**Fax:** 0845 337 1570
**Email:** reservations@fjbhotels.co.uk
**Website:** www.fjbhotels.co.uk
**Map ref:** 3, SZ09
**Directions:** Follow signs for Sandbanks, hotel on left after Canford Cliffs
**Rooms:** 38, S £125–£210 D £250–£420 **Facilities:** STV Wi-Fi available **Parking:** 50
**Notes:** ⊗ in bedrooms

Comfort is clearly the priority in the luxuriously designed bedrooms of this contemporary boutique hotel, many directly overlooking Poole Harbour. The Harbour Brasserie offers an impressive menu, relaxing music, funky furniture and myriad cocktails. Hytes is available for private and corporate hire. The bar and restaurant extend onto tiered, landscaped terraces with panoramic views towards the Purbeck Hills.

**Recommended in the area**

Tank Museum; Swanage Railway; Purbeck Heritage Coast

# Haven Hotel

★★★★  73% ◉◉ HL

**Address:** Banks Road, Sandbanks, POOLE BH13 7QL
**Tel:** 0845 337 1550
**Fax:** 0845 337 1570
**Email:** reservations@fjbhotels.co.uk
**Website:** www.fjbhotels.co.uk
**Map ref:** 3, SZ09
**Directions:** B3965 towards Poole Bay, left onto the Peninsula. Hotel 1.5m on left next to Swanage Toll Ferry point
**Rooms:** 78, S £99.50–£210 D £190–£390
**Facilities:** ⊗ ⤳ Sauna Jacuzzi Solarium Tennis STV  **Parking:** 160 **Notes:** ⊗ in bedrooms

For more than 100 years, the Haven has graced the southernmost point of Sandbanks peninsula. Its five lounges are all different, so there's always one to meet the needs of the moment. Guest rooms are exceedingly comfortable, most having balconies overlooking the sea or harbour. The water's edge La Roche restaurant offers a seasonal menu. The informal Seaview Restaurant is no less impressive.

**Recommended in the area**

Brownsea Island; Compton Acres; Corfe Castle

Sandbanks beach

# Sandbanks Hotel

★★★★  74% ◉ HL

**Address:** 15 Banks Road, Sandbanks,
POOLE  BH13 7PS
**Tel:** 0845 337 1550 (/1570 Fax)
**Email:** reservations@fjbhotels.co.uk
**Website:** www.fjbhotels.co.uk
**Map ref:** 3, SZ09
**Directions:** A338 from Bournemouth onto Wessex
Way, to Liverpool Victoria rdbt. Left and take 2nd exit
onto B3965. Hotel on left

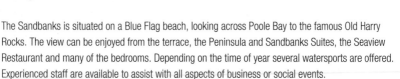

**Rooms:** 110, S £75–£150 D £150–£310 **Facilities:** ⊗ Sauna Jacuzzi Gym STV Wi-Fi available
**Parking:** 120 **Notes:** ⊗ in bedrooms

The Sandbanks is situated on a Blue Flag beach, looking across Poole Bay to the famous Old Harry
Rocks. The view can be enjoyed from the terrace, the Peninsula and Sandbanks Suites, the Seaview
Restaurant and many of the bedrooms. Depending on the time of year several watersports are offered.
Experienced staff are available to assist with all aspects of business or social events.
**Recommended in the area**
Poole Quay; Alice in Wonderland Park; Jurassic Coastal Path

# CO DURHAM

Barnard Castle bridge

# Headlam Hall

★★★   80% ⊛ HL

Address: Headlam, Gainford, DARLINGTON
DL2 3HA
Tel:      01325 730238
Fax:     01325 730790
Email:   admin@headlamhall.co.uk
Website: www.headlamhall.co.uk
Map ref: 7, NZ21
Directions: 2m N of A67 between Piercebridge
and Gainford

Rooms: 40, S £85–£150 D £110–£175 Facilities: ⊗ Sauna Jacuzzi Tennis Gym STV Wi-Fi in bedrooms Parking: 80

Headlam Hall is a fine 17th-century mansion amid beautiful grounds and gardens in a tranquil part of Teesdale. A glorious haven for anyone conducting business in the Middlesbrough-Stockton-Darlington conurbation to the east, it is also perfect for leisure travellers wanting to explore rural Co Durham and the Yorkshire Dales. There is also the option of taking in a round of golf on the hotel's own nine-hole course, a dip in its spacious indoor pool with water-jet feature, a work-out in the gym or a pampering spa treatment. The spa also has a sauna, steam room and air-conditioned exercise studio. Not surprisingly, the hotel is a popular venue for functions and conferences.The bedrooms come in a variety of sizes, some with elegant period furniture, others in cosy cottage style. All have contemporary touches and facilities including satellite TV and modem points. The public areas are richly decorated and include a cocktail bar and the elegant drawing room overlooking the main lawn. The restaurant, with four different areas, serves modern British cuisine such as roast lamb with a goats cheese crust, confit of garlic, ratatouille and rosemary jus, or slow-roased belly pork with root vegetables, parsnip purée and sage cream.

Recommended in the area

Raby Castle; Bowest Museum; High Force

Durham Cathedral

# Seaham Hall Hotel

★★★★★ ◎◎◎ HL

**Address:** Lord Byron's Walk, SEAHAM  SR7 7AG
**Tel:** 0191 516 1400
**Fax:** 0191 516 1410
**Email:** reservations@seaham-hall.com
**Website:** www.seaham-hall.com
**Map ref:** 8, NZ44
**Directions:** from A19 take B1404 to Seaham, over level crossing at lights. Hotel approx 0.25m on right
**Rooms:** 19, S £225–£575 D £225–£575 **Facilities:**
🕲 Sauna Jacuzzi Solarium  Gym STV Wi-Fi available **Parking:** 120 **Notes:** ⊗ in bedrooms

This imposing house is where, in 1815, Lord Byron, married Annabella Milbanke, the daughter of Seaham Hall's first owner. The hotel offers five types of suites, all with cutting edge technology and an undeniable sense of style. The bathrooms are particularly lavish. The White Room restaurant offers fine dining with superb fresh produce and daily changing menus. Reached by a magical underground walkway, the award-winning Spa offers more than 55 different treatments.

**Recommended in the area**

City of Newcastle & Gateshead; Durham Cathedral; Beamish Open Air Museum

# ESSEX

Weald Country Park

# Maison Talbooth

★★★　◎◎ CHH

**Address:** Stratford Road, DEDHAM  CO7 6HN
**Tel:** 01206 322367
**Fax:** 01206 322752
**Email:** maison@milsomhotels.co.uk
**Website:** www.milsomhotels.com
**Map ref:** 4, TM03
**Directions:** A12 towards Ipswich, 1st turning signed
Dedham, follow road until left bend, take right turn.
Hotel 1m on right

**Rooms:** 12, S £125–£250 D £190–£400 **Facilities:** ↖ Hot tubs, Tennis court, Day Spa - 3 treatment
rooms, STV Wi-Fi in bedrooms **Parking:** 20 **Notes:** ⊗ in bedrooms

Tranquility is the essence of this Victorian country house hotel. Public areas include a comfortable,
spacious drawing room where tea and snacks are available. The bedrooms are truly luxurious, and
decorated with an expert eye for colour. Breakfasts and light meals are available while lunch and dinner
are a stroll, or short courtesy car ride, away at the riverside Le Talbooth Restaurant.

**Recommended in the area**

Flatford Mill; Colchester Castle; Beth Chatto Gardens

# The Pier at Harwich

★★★　83% ◎◎ HL

**Address:** The Quay, HARWICH  CO12 3HH
**Tel:** 01255 241212
**Fax:** 01255 551922
**Email:** pier@milsomhotels.com
**Website:** www.milsomhotels.co.uk
**Map ref:** 4, TM23
**Directions:** from A12, take A120 to Quay. Hotel
opposite lifeboat station
**Rooms:** 14, S £72.50–£122.50 D £105–£185
**Facilities:** STV **Parking:** 10 **Notes:** ⊗ in bedrooms

On the quay in the heart of old Harwich, The Pier is owned by the Milsom family, who also own Maison
Talbooth (see above). Newly refurbished public rooms include a smart lounge bar, claiming to make
the best coffee in town, and plush residents' lounge. The contemporary-style bedrooms are tastefully
decorated and thoughtfully equipped, while many overlook the ever-changing activities of this busy port.
The first-floor Harbourside restaurant has a well-deserved reputation for seafood.

**Recommended in the area**

Flatford Mill; Suffolk Heritage Coast; Mistley Towers

# GLOUCESTERSHIRE

River Windrush, Bourton-on-the Water

Gloucester Cathedral

# Buckland Manor

★★★ ◉◉ HL

Address: BUCKLAND WR12 7LY
Tel: 01386 852626
Fax: 01386 853557
Email: info@bucklandmanor.co.uk
Website: www.bucklandmanor.co.uk
Map ref: 3, SP03
Directions: Off B4632 Broadway to Winchcombe Rd
Rooms: 13, S £255–£450 D £265–£460
Facilities: Tennis STV Internet connection in
bedrooms Parking: 30

Ancient, golden stone greets visitors to this delightful, 13th- century, Cotswold manor house. Inside, light streams in through the stone mullioned windows and huge stone fireplaces glow with log fires in the cooler months. Bedrooms and en suite bathrooms are roomy and cosy, with fine fabrics and period furnishings. The à la carte dinner menu might include roast saddle of Cotswold venison with beetroot gratin, baby onions and a juniper berry sauce. There is also an interesting set-price lunch menu.

Recommended in the area

The Cotswold Way; Snowshill Manor (NT); Sudeley Castle

# Charingworth Manor Hotel

★★★   85% ⊛⊛ CHH

Address: Charingworth Manor, CHARINGWORTH,
Chipping Camden GL55 6NS
Tel:      01386 593555
Fax:      01386 593353
Email:    gm.charingworthmanor@classiclodges.
co.uk
Website:  www.classiclodges.co.uk
Map ref:  3, SP13
Directions: Close to the A429 between Chipping
Camden and Shipston-on-Stour
Rooms: 26 Facilities: ⊗ Tennis Gym STV Parking: 50 Notes: ⊗ in bedrooms

It would be hard to find a more perfect Cotswolds manor house than this – indeed, T.S. Eliot was so struck by it that he wrote an ode. Dating from the early 14th century, the honey-coloured stone house is full of ancient charm, with medieval decoration still visible on the massive, original beams, exposed stone walls, mullioned windows and grand fireplaces. The character of the house,has been enhanced by a heated indoor pool, sauna, steam room and solarium, which add to the already considerable appeal. There are also a modern gym and tennis courts The bedrooms are individually styled, and some offer private terraces and lounges, antique furnishings and tapestries. The John Greville Restaurant provides a real setting in which to enjoy the culinary highlights, with innovative dishes such as baked fillet of Atlantic salmon with a herb crust, garlic and chive mash, black pudding and cider cream, or slowly braised shank of English lamb with roasted parsnip purée and honey and mustard red wine jus. On a fine summer evening, there is nothing nicer than walking off an indulgent meal in the beautiful gardens, with breathtaking views that take in five counties.

Recommended in the area

Hidcote Manor; Stratford-upon-Avon; The Cotswold Way

Pittville Park, Cheltenham

# Charlton Kings Hotel

★★★  77%  SHL

**Address:** London Road, Charlton Kings,
CHELTENHAM  GL52 6UU

**Tel:** 01242 231061

**Fax:** 01242 241900

**Email:** enquiries@charltonkingshotel.co.uk

**Website:** www.charltonkingshotel.co.uk

**Map ref:** 2, SO92

**Directions:** Entering Cheltenham from Oxford on A40, 1st on left

**Rooms:** 13, S £65–£85 D £85–£125 **Facilities:** STV Wi-Fi in bedrooms **Parking:** 26

Quality, comfort and friendliness are the hallmarks of this lovely hotel, standing in an acre of garden with sweeping lawns. All bedrooms have en suite facilities and most have views of the surrounding Cotswold hills. Talented chefs present a varied, weekly changing menu using the finest fresh produce. The Atrium Restaurant offers privacy for an intimate dinner, as well as sufficient space for a family reunion. The bar and conservatory are open all day for snacks and lunches.

**Recommended in the area**

Sudeley Castle; Cheltenham Racecourse; Cotswold villages

# The Greenway

★★★   83% ◉◉ HL

Address: Shurdington, CHELTENHAM  GL51 4UG
Tel:       01242 862352
Fax:      01242 862780
Email:    info@thegreenway.co.uk
Website: www.thegreenway.co.uk
Map ref:  2, SO92
Directions: 2.5m SW on A46 Rooms: 21
Facilities:  Wi-Fi available Parking: 50

This beautiful Elizabethan manor house, is set in nationally renowned gardens. The hotel takes its name from the pre-Roman path that runs alongside. For many years it was the late Queen Mother's favourite base during Cheltenham Gold Cup race week. The elegant hall and public rooms are decorated in tasteful shades of yellow and green, and furnished in the style of an elegant family home, with fresh flowers and antique furniture. The bedrooms and suites in both the main house and the old coach house are light and spacious, with wonderful views of either the Cotswolds or the gardens. Each is tastefully decorated, with bathrooms providing luxury towels, bathrobes and a selection of Molton Brown products; some have double showers. The attractive dining room, overlooking the sunken garden and lily pond, is where Luke Richards, the head chef, serves dishes such as pan-fried Scottish halibut, and Anjou squab pigeon, based firmly on the freshest produce from local suppliers. For something a little lighter, the Terrace menu would be the answer. Old and New World wines come from a carefully selected cellar. In addition to the enjoying the luxury of the hotel you can treat yourself to a massage in your room, or if you a feeling a little more active a gentle game of croquet, followed by afternoon tea in the garden.

Recommended in the area

Cheltenham Literature; Jazz and Music Festivals; Broadway Tower Country Park; Leckhampton Hill

# Tudor Farmhouse Hotel & Restaurant

★★★   72% ◉◉ HL

**Address:** High Street, CLEARWELL, Nr Coleford
GL16 8JS

**Tel:** 01594 833046

**Email:** info@tudorfarmhousehotel.co.uk

**Website:** www.tudorfarmhousehotel.co.uk

**Map ref:** 2, SO50

**Directions:** Off A4136 onto B4228, through Coleford,
turn right into Clearwell, hotel on right

**Rooms:** 22, S £60–£80 D £85–£160 **Facilities:** STV Wi-Fi in bedrooms **Parking:** 30

The Tudor Farmhouse is located within a picturesque village in the heart of the Forest of Dean. Its 14 acres of grounds have been designated an area of Special Scientific Interest, due to the rare and varied flora found on the banks and rocky outcrops. Although called Tudor Farmhouse, its origins go back to the 13th century although, whatever their age, the oak beams, exposed stonework, inglenook fireplaces and wooden spiral staircase are a delight to see. Well-appointed double, twin and family rooms are located either within the main house or in converted buildings in the grounds. All are en suite, and some have four-poster beds and Jacuzzi corner baths. The award-winning candlelit restaurant offers an excellent selection of dishes, using ingredients sourced from local suppliers, such as venison from Lydney Park, and home-grown vegetables. There is a special menu for children. In good weather, guests can eat outside in the garden. Private parties can also be catered for and business guests can hold meetings for up to 20 delegates in one of the function rooms. The area is renowned for its iron mining heritage such as the Clearwell Caves, within walking distance of the hotel.

**Recommended in the area**

Tintern Abbey; Symond's Yat; Chepstow Castle and Races

# Washbourne Court Hotel

★★★ 79% ◉◉ HL

Address: LOWER SLAUGHTER GL54 2HS
Tel: 01451 822143
Fax: 01451 821045
Email: info@washbournecourt.co.uk
Website: www.vonessenhotels.co.uk
Map ref: 3, SP12
Directions: Off A429 at signpost 'The Slaughters',
between Stow-on-the-Wold and Bourton-on-the-
Water. Hotel in centre of village
Rooms: 30 Parking: 40

Nestled in the heart of the Cotswolds and standing in immaculate grounds besides the River Eye Washbourne Court Hotel is a stylish, luxury, country house hotel which dates back to the 17th century. Sophisticated yet informal it is an understated blend of the traditional and funky with a historic exterior and a luxuriously refreshed interior that retains beamed ceilings, stone-mullioned windows, flagstone floors and magnificent open fire places, and complements them with the stunning mirror panelled Eton's Restaurant, stylish bedrooms and the unique 'uber' cool Scholar's Lounge. All bedrooms have private bathrooms some with free standing roll top baths and separate walk in power showers and all are beautifully furnished to the highest of standards. Rooms named Villers, Mustians and Angelo's were once boys' dormitories when Washbourne Court was a crammer school for Eton. In the grounds stand cottage suites which have private lounges attached. Eton's Restaurant is a gastronomic experience creating the ultimate escape and a vibrant place to indulge, enjoy and relax. During the summer, guests enjoy dining on the Riverside Terrace with the pretty river drifting by just yards away. All meeting rooms appointed to a high specification, have natural daylight and are located on the ground floor.

Recommended in the area

Batsford Arboretum; Bourton-on-the-Water; Cotswold Falconry Centre

# Manor House Hotel

★★★   81% ◉◉ HL

Address: High Street, MORETON-IN-MARSH
GL56 0LJ
Tel:        01608 650501
Fax:       01608 651481
Email:     info@manorhousehotel.info
Website: www.cotswold-inns-hotels.co.uk/manor
Map ref:  3, SP23
Directions: Off A429 at south end of town. Take East
St off  High St, hotel car park 3rd on right
Rooms: 36, S  D £135–£175 Facilities:  Wi-Fi in bedrooms Parking: 24

The Manor House Hotel is a 16th-century retreat with a tranquil garden shaded by a 300-year-old mulberry tree. The bedrooms have modern amenities and are furnished in traditional country-house style and some rooms have four-poster beds, open fireplaces and window seats. The Mulberry Restaurant has a vibrant modern styling serving meals made with fresh local produce. It offers both fine dining and a bistro-style menu. Business facilities can accommodate up to 120 people.

Recommended in the area

Royal Shakespeare Company; Stratford-upon-Avon; Batsford Arboretum; Hidcote Manor Gardens

# Calcot Manor

★★★★ ◉◉ HL

Address: Calcot, TETBURY  GL8 8YJ
Tel:        01666 890391
Fax:       01666 890394
Email:     reception@calcotmanor.co.uk
Website: www.calcotmanor.co.uk
Map ref:  2, ST89
Directions: 3m West of Tetbury at junct A4135/A46
Rooms: 35, S £180–£205 D £205–£380
Facilities: ⊛ ⋌ Sauna Jacuzzi Solarium  Gym STV
Wi-Fi in bedrooms Parking: 150 Notes: ⊗ in bedrooms

Fourteenth-century Cistercian monks built the ancient barns and stables amid which stands this lovely English manor house. With no two rooms or suites alike, each is beautifully decorated and equipped with contemporary comforts. Sumptuous sitting rooms, with crackling log fires in winter, overlook the immaculate gardens. There are two dining options: the elegant Conservatory Restaurant or the Gumstool Inn. The luxurious Calcot Spa has outstanding facilities and features a 16-metre pool.

Recommended in the area

Slimbridge Wildfowl Trust; Westonbirt Arboretum; Tetbury

Albert Memorial and stone Statues of Gladstone and Oliver Heywood, Manchester

Bramhall

# ABode Hotel Manchester

Address: 107 Piccadilly,
MANCHESTER M1 2DB
Tel:     0161 247 7744
Fax:     0161 247 7747
Email:   reservationsmanchester@abodehotels.co.uk
Website: www.abodehotels.co.uk
Map ref: 6, SJ89
Directions: M62/M602 follow signs for city centre/
Piccadilly
Rooms: 61, S £130–£265 D £130–£265

ABode's newly acquired hotel is an exciting addition to the city. Situated only minutes from Piccadilly station, this handsome, terracotta-coloured building was once the headquarters of Manchester's textile industry. Rooms feature ABode's trademark hand-built beds, personal DVD player, LCD TV and bathrooms featuring monsoon showers. ABode is also home to Michael Caines' restaurants and bars serving Michael's innovative and award-winning modern British cuisine. Below ground are rooms for meetings and private dining.

**Recommended in the area**

Lowry Art Gallery; Trafford Centre; Urbis Exhibition Centre; Manchester Art Gallery

# Midland Hotel

★★★★ 83% ◉◉ HL

Address: Peter Street, MANCHESTER  M60 2DS
Tel:       0161 236 3333
Fax:      0161 932 4100
Email:    midlandsales@qhotels.co.uk
Website: www.qhotels.co.uk
Map ref:  6, SJ89
Directions: M602 junct 3,  follow Manchester Central
Convention complex  signs.
Hotel opposite the complex
Rooms: 312, S £85–£250 D £85–£250
Facilities: ⊙ Sauna Jacuzzi Solarium  Gym STV Wi-Fi in bedrooms Notes: ⊗ in bedrooms

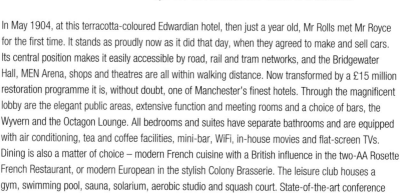

In May 1904, at this terracotta-coloured Edwardian hotel, then just a year old, Mr Rolls met Mr Royce for the first time. It stands as proudly now as it did that day, when they agreed to make and sell cars. Its central position makes it easily accessible by road, rail and tram networks, and the Bridgewater Hall, MEN Arena, shops and theatres are all within walking distance. Now transformed by a £15 million restoration programme it is, without doubt, one of Manchester's finest hotels. Through the magnificent lobby are the elegant public areas, extensive function and meeting rooms and a choice of bars, the Wyvern and the Octagon Lounge. All bedrooms and suites have separate bathrooms and are equipped with air conditioning, tea and coffee facilities, mini-bar, WiFi, in-house movies and flat-screen TVs. Dining is also a matter of choice – modern French cuisine with a British influence in the two-AA Rosette French Restaurant, or modern European in the stylish Colony Brasserie. The leisure club houses a gym, swimming pool, sauna, solarium, aerobic studio and squash court. State-of-the-art conference facilities, including an LCD data projector, can cater for up to 800 delegates.

Recommended in the area

Salford Quays; Lowry Galleries; Old Trafford Football Stadium

# HAMPSHIRE

New Forest

# Esseborne Manor

★★★ 74% ◉ HL

**Address:** Hurstbourne Tarrant, ANDOVER SP11 0ER
**Tel:** 01264 736444
**Fax:** 01264 736725
**Email:** info@esseborne-manor.co.uk
**Website:** www.esseborne-manor.co.uk
**Map ref:** 3, SU34
**Directions:** Halfway between Andover & Newbury on A343, just 1m N of Hurstbourne Tarrant
**Rooms:** 20, S £98–£130 D £125–£250
**Facilities:** Tennis STV Wi-Fi in bedrooms **Parking:** 50

A long drive leads to this privately-owned Victorian country house hotel, set in 3 acres of gardens high on the hill above the lovely Bourne Valley. The surrounding high downland makes this a perfect spot for country walks, with lots of delightful village pubs for refreshment along the way. All the bedrooms, overlooking the gardens and farmlands beyond, are individually decorated, and some have Jacuzzis and four poster beds. Feature rooms include Lymington, with a luxurious Victorian bath overlooking the croquet lawn; Ferndown, with a canopy bed and a private patio; and the Honeymoon Suite, with a separate lounge and rococo-style king-size bed. The Dining Room, with its fabric-lined walls, provides a warm and elegant setting for the chef's fine English cuisine, using local produce and herbs from the hotels own gardens. A choice of fixed-price menus is offered, including a Menu du Vin that includes a specially selected glass of wine with each course. There's also an extensive wine list should you prefer to select your own. A recent dinner menu included such main courses as slow-roast pheasant, steak and Guinness pie with pot-au-feu vegetables, and fillet of cod with crushed new potato and tomato fondue.

**Recommended in the Area**

Highclere Castle; Winchester; Broadlands

Fort Nelson, Portsmouth

# Audleys Wood

★★★★  76%  CHH

**Address:** Alton Road, BASINGSTOKE  RG25 2JT
**Tel:**  01256 817555
**Email:**  info@audleyswood.com
**Website:** www.audleyswood.com
**Map ref:** 3, SU65
**Directions:** M3 junct 6, follow Signs for Alton, after
leaving Basingstoke. Hotel is on right
**Rooms:** 72, S £95–£275 D £95–£295
**Facilities:** Wi-Fi in bedrooms **Parking:** 100

Standing in seven acres of lush woodlands and gardens, with stunning countryside walks all around, this luxurious country house hotel is ideally located for visiting the historic towns and pretty villages that dot the downland countryside of north Hampshire. The house includes superb oak panelling, and the bedrooms include large double rooms and 'special occasion' suites, all with seriously comfortable beds, fluffy towels and fine toiletries. Dining here features modern fusion dishes with classical influences and an international wine list.

**Recommended in the area**

The Vyne (NT); Watercress Line; Stratfield Saye and Wellington Country Park

# Macdonald Botley Park, Golf & Country Club

★★★★   76% ◉ CHH

| | |
|---|---|
| Address: | Winchester Road, Boorley Green, BOTLEY SO32 2UA |
| Tel: | 01489 780 888 |
| Fax: | 01489 789 242 |
| Email: | botleypark@macdonald-hotels.co.uk |
| Website: | www.macdonald-hotels.co.uk/botleypark |
| Map ref: | 3, SU51 |

Directions: A334 towards Botley, left at 1st rdbt past M&S, continue over next 4 mini-rdbts, at 3rd rdbt follow hotel signs

Rooms: 130, S £81–£228 D £93–£240 Facilities: ⊗ Sauna Jacuzzi Solarium Tennis Gym STV Wi-Fi available Parking: 250 Notes: ⊗ in bedrooms

Just outside Southampton and close to Portsmouth, this is a great place for exploring Britain's maritime history or hopping over to the Isle of Wight. Or you could spend the whole time within the 71 hectares of this country-club hotel and take full advantage of its superb golf course, tennis and squash courts, indoor pool and exercise classes. More leisurely activities include spa and beauty treatments and gentle strolls in the grounds. Active or restful, you can end with an aperitif in the Gallery Bar before heading into the restaurant for an elegant meal. There's a fixed-price dinner menu plus a more elaborate à la carte, from which you might choose a starter such as char-grilled wood pigeon or seared diver scallops, followed by poached canon of Highland lamb or grilled John Dory with imaginative trimmings and delicious desserts. All the rooms are en suite, spacious and relaxing with excellent facilities. The Macdonald company are AA Hotel Group of the Year 2007–8.

Recommended in the area

Portsmouth Historic Dockyard and Spinnaker Tower; National Motor Museum at Bieulieu; Marwell Zoo

# Balmer Lawn

★★★ 82% ◉ HL

Address: Lyndhurst Road,
BROCKENHURST SO42 7ZB
Tel: 01590 623116
Fax: 01590 623864
Email: info@balmerlawnhotel.com
Website: www.balmerlawnhotel.com
Map ref: 1, SU30
Directions: A337 towards Lymington, hotel on left
behind village cricket green
Rooms: 55, S £95–£105 D £140–£175 Facilities: ⊛ ⚲ Sauna Jacuzzi Tennis Gym Wi-Fi available
Parking: 100

This imposing, four-storey hotel was built about 1800 as a New Forest hunting lodge. And so it remained until the First World War, when it became a field hospital, then, during the Second, an Army staff college. Namedroppers on the staff may mention King George V, Russian royalty, Churchill and Eisenhower as past guests. Individually designed en suite rooms meet the needs of all, from families to business travellers, providing hospitality tray, direct dial phone, TV, hairdryer and trouser press. Family rooms offer a games console (business guests may consider this unfair!). Many rooms offer views of the forest. With an AA Rosette for fine dining, the comfortable Beresford's Restaurant offers high standards of food, wine and service. At weekends there is live entertainment, with jazz on summer Sundays. Leisure facilities include indoor and outdoor heated pools, spa bath, sauna, air-conditioned gym, squash court, all-weather tennis court and table tennis. Conference rooms are well-equipped, many with broadband access. The hotel is a good base for walking, cycling, riding and mountain-biking through the beautiful open heathland of the New Forest National Park.

Recommended in the area

Beaulieu Palace; Abbey and Motor Museum; Bucklers Hard; Hurst Castle

# Careys Manor & SenSpa

★★★★ 76% ◉◉ HL

Address: BROCKENHURST SO42 7RH
Tel: 01590 623551
Fax: 01590 622799
Email: stay@careysmanor.com
Website: www.careysmanor.com
Map ref: 3, SU30
Directions: M27 junct 3, then M271, then A35 to
Lyndhurst. Then A337 towards Brockenhurst. Hotel
on left after 30mph sign

Rooms: 80 Facilities: ⊗ Gym Spa Freeview Cycle, Golf and Spa breaks available
Parking: 180 Notes: ⊗ in bedrooms

Careys Manor and SenSpa is an award-winning hotel located deep in the heart of the beautiful New Forest National Park. With three restaurants, there is plenty to choose from – whether you prefer fine dining in the two AA-Rosetted Manor Restaurant, in the relaxed atmosphere of Blaireaus French Bistro or want to enjoy authentic Thai cuisine in the Zen Garden Restaurant. All use only the finest ingredients sourced in line with an ethical food policy of using local, free-range and organic produce where possible. SenSpa, the £6 millon Thai spa, offers state-of-the-art facilities including a large hydrotherapy pool, herbal sauna, crystal steam room, ice room, experience showers and much more besides.
A range of indulgent natural treatments include a variety of massage such as traditional Thai and Swedish massage, Ayurvedic head massage, Oriental foot massage and Thai herbal poultice and a range of unique pure spa treatments. Many of SenSpa's therapists are from Thailand and bring with them experience and knowledge to help create an authentic Thai Spa. In effect, English tradition combined with contemporary oriental sophistication, making it the ideal place to enjoy a relaxing break.

Recommended in the area

Beaulieu Palace and Motor Museum; Hurst Castle; Exbury Gardens

# Whitley Ridge Hotel

★★★ 83% ◎◎◎ HL

Address: Beaulieu Road,
BROCKENHURST SO42 7QL
Tel: 01590 622354
Fax: 01590 622856
Email: info@whitleyridge.co.uk
Website: www.whitleyridge.com
Map ref: 3, SU30
Directions: At Brockenhurst onto B3055 Beaulieu
Road. 1m on left up private road
Rooms: 18, S £85–£125 D £199–£280
Facilities: Tennis Wi-Fi in bedrooms
Parking: 35

This 18th-century Georgian house, extended in Victorian times, lies in the New Forest. Whitley Ridge Hotel is set in 14 acres of secluded grounds on the edge of the village of Brockenhurst. An elegant country house, it offers traditional hospitality with a contemporary twist. The hotel's bedrooms are individually styled and furnished and most offer views across gardens and open forest. Among the top-grade rooms there is one with a four-poster bed and a steam cabin, and there are a number of suites. The Michelin starred and three AA-Rossetted Le Poussin restaurant serves an exquisite fusion of contemporary British and French cuisine inspired and created by Master Chef, Alex Aitken. Using local produce where possible, the seasonally changing menu offers extravagant dishes to be enjoyed along with an extensive wine list. With a range of invitingly elegant and comfortable en suite bedrooms and also two beautifully furnished cottages suitable for larger parties, Whitley Ridge is ready to welcome you and make your stay an occasion to savour.

Recommended in the area

National Motor Museum, Beaulieu; Exbury Gardens; Lymington

# Rhinefield House

★★★★ ◎◎ HL

**Address:** Rhinefield Rd, BROCKENHURST SO42 7QB
**Tel:** 01590 622922
**Fax:** 01590 622800
**Email:** rhinefieldhouse@handpicked.co.uk
**Website:** www.handpicked.co.uk
**Map ref:** 3, SU30
**Directions:** A35 towards Christchurch. 3m from Lyndhurst turn left to Rhinefield, 1.5m to hotel
**Rooms:** 50, S £87–£250 D £92–£255
**Facilities:** ⊠ ⳇ Sauna Jacuzzi Solarium Tennis Gym STV Wi-Fi in bedrooms
**Parking:** 100 **Notes:** ⊗ in bedrooms

Deep in the heart of the New Forest, this splendid hotel is approached on a long sweeping driveway lined with rhododendrons, copper beeches and majestic Canadian redwood trees. The house itself is a breathtaking sight, a mixture of Tudor and Gothic styles that actually dates in its present form from the late 19th century, though features from older buildings on the site are incorporated. Among the most imposing rooms is the Armada Restaurant, with a magnificent fireplace, fine oak panelling and huge mullioned windows. The lounge, by contast, is in more contemporary style. Bedrooms and suites are elegantly modern, with restful colour schemes and top quality fabrics and linens. Cuisine in the restaurant offers an interesting melange of international influences, such as a starter of Poole scallops and warm smoked salmon with artichoke stew and sweet curry emulsion, followed, perhaps, by Gressingham duckling, confit boulanger, caramelised kumquat, creamed rocket and bitter coffee lentils, then coconut lime meringue with ten-hour poached pineapple and exotic fruit sorbet. Leisure amenities include a swimming pool, health club, tennis, croquet and a jogging trail.

**Recommended in the area**

New Forest National Park; National Motor Museum; Lymington

Queens Bower, Brockenhurst, New Forest National Park

# Westover Hall Hotel

◎◎

**Address:** Park Lane, MILFORD ON SEA SO41 0PT
**Tel:** 01590 643044
**Fax:** 01590 644490
**Email:** info@westoverhallhotel.com
**Website:** www.westoverhallhotel.com
**Map ref:** 3, SZ29
**Directions:** M3 & M27 W onto A337 to Lymington,
follow signs to Milford-on-Sea onto B3058, hotel
outside village centre towards cliff
**Rooms:** 12, S £130–£220 D £190–£340 **Facilities:** Wi-Fi available **Parking:** 50

A beautiful, Grade II-listed Victorian country house hotel, 150 metres from the beach, with views of the
Isle of Wight and The Needles. The magnificent stained-glass windows, oak panelling and decorated
ceilings invoke much admiration. Stylish bedrooms have private bathroom, tasteful furnishings, luxury
Italian bed linen, phone, radio and TV. Six of them look across Christchurch Bay. The restaurant is open
daily for lunch and dinner, with the kitchen making full use of fresh and abundant New Forest produce.
**Recommended in the area**
Hurst Castle; Hengistbury Head; Beaulieu Palace & Motor Museum

# Chewton Glen Hotel

★★★★★ ◉◉◉ HL

**Address:** Christchurch Road,
NEW MILTON BH25 5QS
**Tel:** 01425 275341
**Fax:** 01425 272310
**Email:** reservations@chewtonglen.com
**Website:** www.chewtonglen.com
**Map ref:** 3, SZ29
**Directions:** A35 from Lyndhurst for 10m, left at
staggered junct. Follow tourist sign for hotel through
Walkford, take 2nd left

**Rooms:** 58, S £295–£1250 D £295–£1250 **Facilities:** 🐕 ⚲ Golf Sauna Tennis Gym STV Wi-Fi in bedrooms **Parking:** 100 **Notes:** ⊗ in bedrooms

The sea is just 10 minutes' walk from this superb 18th-century country-house hotel. Bedrooms are individually styled with luxurious fabrics and furnishings. All bedrooms enjoy the benefits of air-conditioning, satellite television, radio, DVD and CD players, and direct-dial telephone. There are also a number of suites, some duplex, and all with secluded private gardens. Guests can enjoy the health and beauty treatments, both traditional and modern, of the elegant high-tech spa, where everything from a massage to a facial or a body polish is offered. The restaurant offers a wide variety of cuisines, using as much fresh local produce as possible and vegetarian and low-calorie dishes can be provided. The nearby New Forest offers wild mushrooms, vegetables and game; seafood may come from Christchurch and Lymington nearby. The wine list is drawn from a cellar of over 600 bins. Short residential packages are available including: Gourmet Dining Breaks; Spa Breaks and Golf Breaks. Children over five are welcome at the hotel.

**Recommended in the area**

New Forest National Park; National Motor Museum, Beaulieu; Buckler's Hard historic village

Jane Austen's House, Chawton

# Tylney Hall Hotel

★★★★ ◉◉ HL

**Address:** ROTHERWICK, Hook RG27 9AZ
**Tel:** 01256 764881
**Email:** sales@tylneyhall.com
**Website:** www.tylneyhall.com
**Map ref:** 3, SU75
**Directions:** M3 junct 5, A287 to Basingstoke, over junct with A30, over railway bridge, towards Newnham. Right at Newnham Grn. Hotel 1m on left
**Rooms:** 112, S £155–£450 D £205–£500
**Facilities:** ⊕ ⊀ Sauna Solarium Tennis Gym STV Wi-Fi available **Parking:** 120 **Notes:** ⊗ in bdrms

A Grade II-listed, grand Victorian house in 66 acres of beautiful parkland this hotel offers a high level of comfort, as a quick peek into the Library Bar, Wedgwood Drawing Room, Italian Lounge or panelled Oak Room Restaurant will confirm. The hotel prides itself on a modern cooking style, yet one retaining classical hallmarks.Open to non-residents, it offers a full carte menu, with roasts from a carving trolley. The bedrooms are traditionally furnished with telephone, trouser press, hair dryer and toiletries.

**Recommended in the area**

Stratfield Saye; Legoland; Jane Austen's House

Hereford

# Feathers Hotel

★★★   80% ◉ HL

**Address:** High Street, LEDBURY  HR8 1DS
**Tel:** 01531 635266
**Fax:** 01531 638955
**Email:** mary@feathers-ledbury.co.uk
**Website:** www.feathers-ledbury.co.uk
**Map ref:** 2, SO73
**Directions:** S from Worcester on A449, E from Hereford on A438, N from Gloucester on A417
**Rooms:** 19, S £79.50–£125 D £115–£195 (Cottage

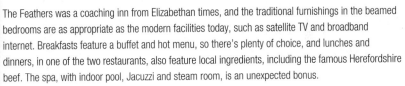

and apartment also available) **Facilities:** ⊙ Sauna Jacuzzi Solarium Gym Wi-Fi in rooms **Parking:** 30

The Feathers was a coaching inn from Elizabethan times, and the traditional furnishings in the beamed bedrooms are as appropriate as the modern facilities today, such as satellite TV and broadband internet. Breakfasts feature a buffet and hot menu, so there's plenty of choice, and lunches and dinners, in one of the two restaurants, also feature local ingredients, including the famous Herefordshire beef. The spa, with indoor pool, Jacuzzi and steam room, is an unexpected bonus.
**Recommended in the area**
The Malvern Hills; Eastnor Castle; Hereford, Worcester and Gloucester cathedrals

# Best Western Pengethley Manor

★★★   80% HL

**Address:** Pengethley Park, ROSS-ON-WYE  HR9 6LL
**Tel:** 01989 730211
**Email:** reservations@pengethleymanor.co.uk
**Website:** www.pengethleymanor.co.uk
**Map ref:** 2, SO52
**Directions:** 4m N on A49 Hereford road, from Ross-on-Wye
**Rooms:** 25, S £79–£115 D £120–£160
**Facilities:** ⊀ Wi-Fi available **Parking:** 70

Set in 15 acres of lovely grounds overlooking National Trust parkland, this elegant Georgian manor house offers relaxing tranquillity and easy access to the local spa towns, picturesque villages and unspoiled countryside. The individually-styled bedrooms include ground-floor rooms and particularly spacious rooms up in the roof that feature grand old timbers. The menus in the restaurant make the best use of local produce and the wine list includes white wines from the hotel's own vineyard within the grounds. Amenities include an outdoor swimming pool, and the hotel is licensed for civil weddings.
**Recommended in the area**
Symond's Yat and the Forest of Dean; Goodrich Castle; Tintern Abbey

The garden at Hatfield House

# Sopwell House

★★★★   76% ◉ HL

**Address:** Cottonmill Lane, Sopwell, ST ALBANS
AL1 2HQ
**Tel:** 01727 864477
**Fax:** 01727 844741
**Email:** enquiries@sopwellhouse.co.uk
**Website:** www.sopwellhouse.co.uk
**Map ref:** 3, TL10
**Directions:** M25 junct 22, follow A1081 St Albans.
At traffic lights, turn left into Mile House Lane, over
mini-rdbt into Cottonmill Lane
**Rooms:** 129, S £99–£129 D £121–£189 **Facilities:** ⊗  Sauna Jacuzzi Solarium  Gym STV
**Parking:** 350 **Notes:** ⊗ in bedrooms

This imposing Georgian house was once the country home of Lord Mountbatten. In his time, stable lads and horses probably still lived in Sopwell Mews; today their accommodation has been turned into self-contained apartments, complete with kitchenette and lounge. Bedrooms in the main building vary in style and include satellite TV, tea and coffee tray, direct-dial phones and internet. There are several places to relax: for drinks make for the Cocktail Bar and Lounge; for light meals, sandwiches, traditional afternoon tea or a nightcap, it has to be the Terrace Lounge Bar; for an informal meal in a buzzy atmosphere, there's the Brasserie; and for good contemporary British cuisine, served under the direction of award-winning chef Leigh Diggins, seek out the hotel's latest addition, The Restaurant at Sopwell House. Leigh is committed to using the best locally sourced ingredients he can lay his hands on to create a widely appealing seasonal menu. The huge world wine collection is housed in an impressive wine wall. In summer, enjoy dining al fresco on the terrace, overlooking the gardens.

**Recommended in the area**

St Albans Clock Tower; Verulamium Museum; The Organ Museum

# St Michael's Manor

★★★★ 74% ◉◉ HL

Address: Fishpool Street, ST ALBANS  AL3 4RY
Tel:      01727 864444
Fax:      01727 848909
Email:    reservations@stmichaelsmanor.com
Website:  www.stmichaelsmanor.com
Map ref:  3, TL10
Directions: From St Albans Abbey follow Fishpool
Street toward St Michael's village. Hotel 0.5m on left
Rooms: 30, S £145–£260 D £180–£335
Facilities: STV Wi-Fi in bedrooms Parking: 70 Notes: ⊗ in bedrooms

This magnificent country house hotel stands in five acres of country gardens overlooking a lake, yet is still within walking distance of modern St Albans and its Roman predecessor. The house, which is over 500 years old,was a private house until the early 1960s, when the Newling Ward family recognised its potential and bought it – and they're still the owner/managers today. Many of the individually designed rooms overlook the lake and garden and, as well as providing the generally accepted extras, thoughtfully include board games, biscuits, sweets, books and magazines too, not to mention 24-hour room service. From the restaurant there are excellent views across the gardens and lake which, together with the award-winning modern British cuisine, is responsible for drawing in food lovers from a wide area. Two examples from the carte illustrate the style: Lapsang tea-smoked salmon, and rump of lamb with sweetbreads. Dining can also be enjoyed on the garden terrace, by the lake, in the bar, or in one of the private dining rooms. St Michael's is a romantic house and thus in great demand for weddings, but businesses, with possibly a different sort of merger in mind, could make good use of its conference facilities and meeting rooms.

Recommended in the area

Roman Verulamium; St Albans Cathedral & Abbey; Hatfield House

# ISLE OF WIGHT

Compton Bay, Freshwater

The Needles, Isle of Wight

# The Royal Hotel

★★★★ 75% ◉◉ HL

**Address:** Belgrave Road, VENTNOR,
Isle of Wight PO38 1JJ
**Tel:** 01983 852186
**Fax:** 01983 855395
**Email:** enquiries@royalhoteliow.co.uk
**Website:** www.royalhoteliow.co.uk
**Map ref:** 2, SZ57
**Directions:** A3055 into Ventnor follow one-way
system, after lights l into Belgrave Road. Hotel on r
**Rooms:** 55, S £85–£125 D £140–£220 **Facilities:** ⚲ Wi-Fi available **Parking:** 56

The largest of the Isle of Wight's premier-class hotels is set in large and colourful gardens, with views of the island's south coast. All rooms are en suite and individually furnished, with tea- and coffee-making facilities, television and direct-dial telephone. Guests can take their morning coffee in the conservatory. The bar is cosy, and the lounges are sumptuously furnished. Packages of three to seven nights are available throughout the year, together with Christmas and New Year packages.

**Recommended in the area**

Ventnor Botanic Garden; Appuldurcombe House; Osborne House.

# George Hotel

★★★ ◎◎ HL

Address: Quay Street, YARMOUTH,
Isle of Wight , PO41 0PE
Tel: 01983 760331
Fax: 01983 760425
Email: res@thegeorge.co.uk
Website: www.thegeorge.co.uk
Map ref: 3, SZ38
Directions: Between the castle and the pier
Rooms: 17, S £110–£180 D £150–£250
Facilities: STV Wi-Fi in bedrooms

This delightful 17th-century hotel stands at the water's edge, overlooking the bustling harbour, right next door to the castle. Built in 1668 by Sir Robert Holmes, a former governor of the island, it has inevitably been altered and extended, but the principal features remain, including the fine four-abreast staircase. Incidentally, Sir Robert interpreted governorship to mean that he was entitled to keep two thirds of the value of any non-English ship and her cargo he captured in local waters – a perk that amounted to piracy. Public areas include a cosy bar and an inviting lounge. Individually styled bedrooms are provided with full room service, bathrobes, hairdryer, direct dial phone and satellite TV, while some have spacious balconies with table, chairs, umbrella and harbour views. Guests may take advantage of an holistic therapy and beauty service. In the brasserie, Jose Graziosi's seasonal menus of contemporary, European-influenced dishes make extensive use of as much organic and local produce as possible, particularly fish and seafood. Guests reluctant to return to their own cooking may buy from The George at Home range – just heat and eat. The hotel is ideal for small business meetings and its own motor yacht is available for hire by guests.

**Recommended in the area**

Yarmouth Castle; Osborne House; Ventnor Botanic Garden

# KENT

Kent countryside

# Eastwell Manor

★★★★  ◉◉ HL

**Address:** Eastwell Park, Boughton Lees,
ASHFORD TN25 4HR
**Tel:** 01233 213000
**Email:** enquiries@eastwellmanor.co.uk
**Website:** www.eastwellmanor.co.uk
**Map ref:** 4, TR04
**Directions:** On A251 from Ashford, 200yds on left
when entering Boughton Aluph
**Rooms:** 62, S £110–£415 D £140–£445
**Facilities:** ⊕ ⬟ Sauna Jacuzzi Solarium Tennis Gym STV Wi-Fi **Parking:** 200

Eastwell Manor, with a history going back to the Norman Conquest, lies in 62 acres of grounds, including a formal Italian garden, attractive lawns and parkland. In the 16th century Richard Plantagenet lived here, and Queen Victoria and King Edward VII were frequent visitors. Its age is apparent in the lounges, restaurant and bar, with their original fireplaces, carved panelling and fine antiques. Twenty-three individually designed bedrooms, all with private bathrooms, are named after previous owners and other worthies. The 19 luxury Mews Cottages in the grounds have been converted from Victorian stables. They have one, two or three bedrooms and all are en suite with kitchen, sitting room and dining facilities and are also available on a self catering basis. The informal, all-day Brasserie in The Pavilion looks out across the Kent countryside, while the more formal dining destination is the Manor Restaurant with a French and modern English menu. The Pavilion Spa houses a 20-metre pool in a Roman baths-like setting, hydrotherapy pool, sauna, Jacuzzi, steam room and technogym. The beauty and therapy area, Dreams, pampers both men and women. There is also a 20-metre outdoor swimming pool and an all weather tennis court. The 9 hole Golf Course is opening in June 2008.

**Recommended in the area**

Canterbury Cathedral; Sissinghurst Castle; Leeds Castle

Oast house near Chiddingstone

# Thistle Brands Hatch

★★★★  83% ◉◉ HL

**Address:** BRANDS HATCH, Dartford DA3 8PE
**Tel:** 0870 333 9128
**Fax:** 0870 333 9228
**Email:** BrandsHatch@Thistle.co.uk
**Website:** www.thistlehotels.com/brandshatch
**Map ref:** 4, TQ56
**Directions:** Follow signs for Brands Hatch, hotel on left of racing circuit entrance
**Rooms:** 121 **Facilities:** ⓢ Sauna Jacuzzi Solarium Gym STV **Parking:** 180

Obviously a premier choice for motor racing fans since it stands right at the entrance to the famous Brands Hatch circuit, this hotel is also ideally located for visiting all the delights of the 'Garden of England'. This is a modern building, offering standard, deluxe and executive rooms, 18 meeting rooms, and leisure facilities that include an indoor swimming pool, health treatments and fitness equipment. A highlight of a stay here is a meal in Genevieves Restaurant and The Bugatti sports bar also serves food.
**Recommended in the area**
Lullingstone Castle; Knole (NT); North Downs Way

# Rowhill Grange Hotel & Utopia Spa

★★★★ 82% ◉◉ HL

Address: DARTFORD, Dartford DA2 7QH
Tel: 01322 615136
Fax: 01322 615137
Email: admin@rowhillgrange.co.uk
Website: www.rowhillgrange.co.uk
Map ref: 4, TQ57
Directions: M25 junct 3 take B2173 to Swanley, then B258 to Hextable
Rooms: 38, S £175–£260 D £200–£370 Facilities: ⓢ Sauna Jacuzzi Gym STV Wi-Fi in bedrooms
Parking: 150 Notes: ⊗ in bedrooms

A partly thatched hotel in nine acres of grounds encompassing a lake with Australian black swans, Victorian walled garden, private woodlands and sweeping lawns. From one exceptional setting to another – the hotel itself was built in 1868 as a 'summer house' for a seemingly very fortunate 18-year-old girl. Original period features, solid-wood furniture, top-end designer fabrics and attractive artwork all contribute to Rowhill's stylish character. The bedrooms and suites feel homely, in no small measure due to their comfortable beds, upholstered armchairs, elegant side tables and cushioned window seats. Many of the en suite bathrooms are lined with Italian marble. Diners in Truffles Restaurant, the informal Brasserie, or out on the terrace, may choose from an extensive international menu. In the Utopia spa, one of the world's top 50 according to a national newspaper, qualified therapists offer beauty treatments, massage and aromatherapy. The indoor swimming pool is surrounded by a convincing Tuscan trompe l'oeil.

Recommended in the area

Leeds Castle; Brands Hatch; Bluewater Shopping Centre

133

# Chilston Park Hotel

★★★★  ◉◉ HL

**Address:** Sandway, LENHAM, Maidstone ME17 2BE
**Tel:** 01622 859803
**Email:** chilstonpark@handpicked.co.uk
**Website:** www.handpicked.co.uk
**Map ref:** 4, TQ85
**Directions:** From A20 turn off to Lenham Village, turn right onto High St, pass station on right, 1st left, over crossroads, hotel 0.25 mile on left
**Rooms:** 53, S £85–£280 D £110–£340 **Facilities:** Tennis STV Wi-Fi in bedrooms **Parking:** 100

Set in rolling Kent countryside, this beautifully proportioned Grade I listed mansion dates from the 17th century. Inside, the gracious rooms are furnished with exquisite antiques, fine paintings adorn the walls, and log fires cast a warm glow on cooler days, setting the scene for a relaxing stay amid a welcoming atmosphere. The bedrooms are highly distinctive, named rather than numbered to reflect the theme of the décor and furnishings: Tudor, Regency, Camelot, Raj, and so on. Several have four-poster beds, and all have plasma screen TVs with Sky channels and DVDs, hospitality trays and Broadband access (wired; wireless is available in public areas and meeting rooms). The finest rooms are in the Old House, while some of the Classic and Executive rooms are in the New House and Courtyard, and many have lovely parkland views. There are several locations for enjoying the fine food, including private dining rooms, a terrace, room service or out in the grounds with a luxury picnic hamper. Culpeper's Restaurant is where the chef works his magic using traditional local produce and rare ingredients. For a small charge, guests can use the facilities at The Greens Health Club in nearby Charing Village.

**Recommended in the area**

Leeds Castle; Canterbury; Howletts and Port Lymphe Wild Animal Parks

# The Spa Hotel

★★★★　79% ⚜ HL

**Address:** Mount Ephraim, ROYAL TUNBRIDGE WELLS　TN4 8XJ
**Tel:**　01892 520331
**Email:**　info@spahotel.co.uk
**Website:** www.spahotel.co.uk
**Map ref:** 4, TQ53
**Directions:** Off A21 to A26, follow signs to A264 East Grinstead, hotel on right
**Rooms:** 69, S £80–£113 D £97–£170 **Facilities:** 🕸 Sauna Tennis Gym STV Wi-Fi in bedrooms **Parking:** 150

Royal Tunbridge Wells is one of Britain's most famous spa towns, and this elegant country mansion on its outskirts dates back to the town's 18th-century heyday. Set in 14 acres of gardens and parkland, the mellow stone mansion now offers individually-styled bedrooms on three floors, most with lovely views and some with four-poster beds and spa bathrooms. There are also some suites, with king-size beds and separate lounges. Weddings and conferences are among the services offered. The Chandelier Restaurant has one AA Rosette, and offers modern English cuisine together with a well-chosen wine list. A recent dinner menu included starters such as home-smoked cornfed chicken and leek terrine, and marinated fresh tuna tartare with soy, sesame oil and seeds. Main courses included pan-seared calves liver with smoked cure bacon mash, fine beans and rosemary jus, and wild sea trout and seared scallops with wilted spinach, orange emulsion and fennel pollen. The afternoon teas and Sunday lunches are also popular. Leisure facilities include an outdoor tennis court, a jogging trail, and a spa and leisure club within a modern, purpose-built extension. It includes an indoor swimming pool, steam room and sauna, two gymnasiums and a range of health and beauty treatments.

**Recommended in the area**

Shopping in The Pantiles in Royal Tunbridge Wells; Penshurst Place; Bayham Abbey

# LANCASHIRE

Whalley Abbey

# Barton Grange Hotel

★★★★ 76% ◉ HL

**Address:** Garstang Road, BARTON, Preston PR3 5AA

**Tel:** 01772 862551

**Fax:** 01772 861267

**Email:** stay@bartongrangehotel.com

**Website:** www.bartongrangehotel.co.uk

**Map ref:** 6, SD53

**Directions:** M6 junct 32, follow signs to Garstang (A6) for 2.5 miles. Hotel on right

**Rooms:** 51, S £60–£90 D £70–£125 **Facilities:** ⓣ Swimming Pool Sauna Jacuzzi Gym STV Wi-Fi in bedrooms **Parking:** 250 **Notes:** ⊗ in bedrooms

The former mansion of a cotton-mill owner, built in 1900, it has been lovingly developed by the Topping family into a fine 51-bedroom hotel. The third generation are now at the helm, and recent refurbishment has given a smart, contemporary look while retaining the traditional charm of the old manor house. Bedrooms vary in size, but all are beautifully decorated and have stylish bathrooms. There are two restaurants, and the family also run a garden centre nearby.

**Recommended in the area**

Garden Centre; National Football Museum at Preston; Beacon Fell Country Park; Blackpool

# Garstang Country Hotel & Golf Club

★★★ 75% HL

**Address:** Garstang Road, Bowgreave, GARSTANG PR3 1YE

**Tel:** 01995 600100

**Fax:** 01995 600950

**Email:** reception@ghgc.co.uk

**Website:** www.garstanghotelandgolf.co.uk

**Map ref:** 3, SD44

**Directions:** M6 junct 32 take 1st right after Rogers Esso garage on A6 onto B6430. Continue for 1m and hotel on left

**Rooms:** 32, S £60–£95 D £85–£100 **Facilities:** STV **Parking:** 172 **Notes:** ⊗ in bedrooms

This modern, family-owned hotel has the golfer very much in mind. It has its own 18-hole, par 68 course, designed by former PGA Cup captain, Richard Bradbeer, and a floodlit driving range. Guests can watch the play from the en suite bedrooms and then dine in the Kingfisher Restaurant.

**Recommended in the area**

National Football Museum; Blackpool Pleasure Beach; Hoghton Tower

# Northcote Manor

★★★★ 75% ❀❀❀ SHL

**Address:** Northcote Road, LANGHO,
Blackburn BB6 8BE
**Tel:** 01254 240555
**Fax:** 01254 246568
**Email:** sales@northcotemanor.com
**Website:** www.northcotemanor.com
**Map ref:** 6, SD73
**Directions:** M6 junct 31, 9m to Northcote. Follow
Clitheroe (A59) signs, Hotel on left before rdbt
**Rooms:** 14, S £150–£195 D £180–£225 **Facilities:** STV Wi-Fi in bedrooms **Parking:** 50 **Notes:** ⊗ in
bedrooms

Built in the 1880s, Northcote Manor still has the ambience of a Victorian family home and the focus is
on eating well, as, no doubt, it was when it belonged to a textile baron. Its former ownership explains its
proximity to Lancashire's industrial heartland to the south, but stretching northwards across the River
Ribble is Longridge Fell and the Forest of Bowland. The excellent road network also makes it easy to
reach the Yorkshire Dales and Blackpool. Proprietors Nigel Haworth and Craig Bancroft describe their
venture as a restaurant with rooms, and the food is certainly a very good reason to come here. Nigel is
the chef, a staunch supporter of the county's many artisan food producers and, with their ingredients
and organic fruit, vegetables and herbs from the manor's own gardens, creates memorable culinary
delights. The bedrooms have individual, contemporary décor that is stunning in its originality and the
quality of the fabrics and wall coverings. Each room has a high-tech sound system with iPod connector,
TVs with 200 satellite stations, DVD and CD players and complimentary wireless internet connection.
Cosy bathrobes are provided, along with Molton Brown hair and skin-care products.

**Recommended in the area**

Clitheroe; Ribble Valley; Gawthorpe Hall (NT)

# Best Western Leyland Hotel

★★★★ 77% HL

**Address:** Leyland Way, LEYLAND,
Preston PR25 4JX
**Tel:** 01772 422922
**Fax:** 01772 622282
**Email:** leylandhotel@feathers.uk.com
**Website:** www.feathers.uk.com
**Map ref:** 6, SD52
**Directions:** M6 junct 28 turn left at end of slip road, hotel 100mtrs on left
**Rooms:** 93, S £79–£94 D £89–£119 **Facilities:** ⊗ Sauna Jacuzzi Solarium Gym STV
**Parking:** 150

This purpose-built hotel is just off junction 28 of the M6, so strategically well placed for those heading to Scotland or the south. All of the bedrooms have been refurbished by the hotel's owners, the Feathers Group, to provide full en suite facilities, satellite tv, direct dial phone, tea- and coffee-making kit and broadband internet. There are several dining options - à la carte, brasserie-style, casual bar snacks or room service. Sounding a bit like a brand of fruit juice, although obviously named after the motorway junction, the J28 Meetings, Lounge and Café Bar offers refreshment for residents, as well as for corporate clients who might well want to run through their Powerpoint presentation of the latest sales figures with a café latte and freshly baked muffin. The more formal Four Seasons restaurant offers a variety of freshly prepared meals, such as aubergine and ratatouille tian and classic beef bourguignonne. The hotel has recently undergone a major refurbishment of its leisure club to provide an indoor swimming pool, spa bath, steam room and sauna and exercise room. Modern Italian sculptures dot the newly created gardens, which are just perfect for wedding photography.

**Recommended in the area**

Blackpool Pleasure Beach; Camelot Theme Park; Martin Mere; Shopping in Southport

Steamtown Museum, Carnforth

# West Tower Country House Hotel

★★★  82%  HL

**Address:** Mill Lane, Aughton, ORMSKIRK  L39 7HJ
**Tel:** 01695 423328
**Fax:** 01695 420704
**Email:** info@westtower.com
**Website:** www.westtower.co.uk
**Map ref:** 6, SD40
**Rooms:** 12, S £45–£80 D £90–£120
**Parking:** 100 **Notes:** ⊗ in bedrooms

Within the 3-hectare estate of a fine mansion once owned by shipping magnate Lord Alfred Holt (the tower was a lookout for staff to view his ships approaching port), this small hotel is well placed for visiting the coast around Southport as well as conducting business in Merseyside. The bedrooms are modern and beautifully decorated in contemporary style, with stylish en suite bathrooms. There are also two suites with Jacuzzi baths. The restaurant offers a tempting choice of beautifully presented dishes, created from the best fresh ingredients. The cellar of West Tower contains the sophisticated Café West, with an old stone floor and sumptuous leather furniture.

**Recommended in the area**

Martin Mere Wildfowl & Wetlands Trust; Liverpool; Rufford Old Hall (NT)

# LEICESTERSHIRE

Great Central Railway at Loughborough

Leicester

# Best Western Belmont House Hotel

★★★ 85% HL

**Address:** De Montfort Street, LEICESTER LE1 7GR
**Tel:** 0116 254 4773
**Fax:** 0116 247 0804
**Email:** info@belmonthotel.co.uk
**Website:** www.belmonthotel.co.uk
**Map ref:** 3, SK50
**Directions:** From A6 southbound, take 1st right after rail station. Hotel 200yds on left
**Rooms:** 77, S £115–£140 D £125–£145
**Facilities:** Freeview Wi-Fi in bedrooms **Parking:** 75

This well-established, elegant town house hotel in the city's leafy New Walk conservation area is within an easy stroll of the shops via an ancient walkway laid out in 1785. The extensive public rooms are smartly appointed and include the informal Bowie's Brasserie, with French-style, zinc-topped bar, Jamie's Bar & Lounge, a popular place for light bites and a drink, and Cherry's Restaurant for quality, modern, European cuisine. Individually designed, well-equipped bedrooms offer Wi-Fi and Freeview.

**Recommended in the area**

Rockingham Castle; National Space Centre; Foxton Locks

# Stapleford Park

★★★★  ◉◉ HL

**Address:** Stapleford, MELTON MOWBRAY
LE14 2EF
**Tel:** 01572 787000
**Fax:** 01572 787001
**Email:** reservations@stapleford.co.uk
**Website:** www.staplefordpark.com
**Map ref:** 3, SK71
**Directions:** 1m SW of B676, 4m E of Melton
Mowbray and 9m W of Colsterworth
**Rooms:** 55 **Facilities:** ⊕ Sauna Jacuzzi Tennis Gym STV **Parking:** 120

A magnificent 17th-century house in 500 acres of parkland, lake and woods, originally created by 'Capability' Brown. One of England's finest stately homes, Stapleford Park offers a stunning blend of architecture, history and landscape. Although no longer in regular use, the Church of St Mary Magdalene graces the gardens. But there is far more to it than its magical environment. The splendid reception rooms, for example, mirror the traditional character of the house, while the 55 individually designed and furnished bedrooms reflect the styles of their creators, among them Crabtree & Evelyn, David Hicks, Pirelli, Sanderson and Zoffany, ensuring that every guest has a unique experience.
Just choose your favourite. The Grinling Gibbons dining room offers inspired traditional English and European dishes, while the more relaxed and informal Pavilion restaurant can be found at the golf club house. The challenging golf course itself was designed by Donald Steel, but if golf doesn't appeal, try the falconry school, clay pigeon shooting, fishing, archery, tennis or giant chess. Stapleford Park offers the whole estate of wellness from the pool, steam room, sauna and Jacuzzi in the main house to the seven unique treatment rooms and gym in the Victorian stable block.
**Recommended in the area**
Rutland Water; Burghley House; Rockingham Castle

# LINCOLNSHIRE

Lincoln Cathedral

# Best Western Bentley Hotel & Leisure Club

★★★  85%  HL

**Address:** Newark Road, South Hykeham,
LINCOLN LN6 9NH
**Tel:** 01522 878000
**Fax:** 01522 878001
**Email:** infothebentleyhotel@btconnect.com
**Website:** www.thebentleyhotel.uk.com
**Map ref:** 8, SK97
**Directions:** From A1 take A46 E towards Lincoln for 10m. Over 1st rdbt on Lincoln Bypass to hotel 50yds on left
**Rooms:** 80, S £88–£97 D £102–£135 **Facilities:** ⊗ Sauna Jacuzzi Gym STV Wi-Fi in bedrooms
**Parking:** 170 **Notes:** ⊗ in bedrooms

In a lovely rural location, this fine modern hotel is only 6 miles south of the centre of Lincoln, making it ideal for visits to that historic city as well as the largely undiscovered but beautiful countryside around. The hotel has a very pleasing contemporary style and a range of bedrooms that includes some four-poster rooms and a spacious suite with a separate lounge area. All of the rooms have en suite bathrooms and include satellite TV, trouser presses, hairdryers, tea- and coffee-making facilities and wireless internet connection. The restaurant offers a good choice, from one-dish dining to table d'hôte and a full à la carte menu, and is particularly renowned for its carvery lunches. Snacks and lighter meals are available in the Saracens Bar. This is Lincoln's only hotel with a leisure and health centre. It includes a superb indoor swimming pool, steam room, sauna and whirlpool, plus a gymnasium with qualified staff and a beauty salon offering various treatments and therapies – best to book in advance.

**Recommended in the area**

Lincoln; Doddington Hall and Gardens; Newark Aircraft Museum

# LONDON

Houses of Parliament and Westminster Bridge

Regents Park, London

# The Landmark London

★★★★★ ◉◉ HL

**Address:** 222 Marylebone Road,
LONDON NW1 6JQ
**Tel:** 020 7631 8000
**Fax:** 020 7631 8080
**Email:** reservations@thelandmark.co.uk
**Website:** www.landmarklondon.co.uk
**Map ref:** 4, TQ38
**Directions:** Adjacent to Marylebone Station and
near Paddington Station

**Rooms:** 299, S £230–£370 D £255–£395 **Facilities:** ⊗ Sauna Jacuzzi  Gym STV Wi-Fi available
**Notes:** ⊗ in bedrooms

The Landmark was built in 1899 opposite Marylebone Station. Classic Victorian opulence combine with contemporary Thai influences (it has a sister hotel in Bangkok), most evidently in the eight-storey atrium, where the Winter Garden Restaurant is an impressive place to dine underneath towering palm trees. The bedrooms are particularly well equipped for comfort, convenience  and entertainment.

**Recommended in the area**

Madame Tussauds Waxwork Museum; Regent's Park; Lords Cricket Ground

# Melia White House

★★★★  83% HL

**Address:** Albany Street, Regents Park,
LONDON  NW1 3UP
**Tel:** 020 7391 3000
**Fax:** 020 7388 0091
**Email:** melia.white.house@solmelia.com
**Website:** www.melia-whitehouse.com
**Map ref:** 4, TQ38
**Directions:** opposite Gt Portland St tube station
**Rooms:** 581, S £135–£160 D £160–£185
**Facilities:** Sauna Gym STV Wi-Fi available **Parking:** 7 **Notes:** ⊗ in bedrooms

Managed by the Spanish Sol Melia company, this impressive art deco property is located just to the south of Regents Park, and just a few blocks north of Oxford Street. Spacious public areas offer a high degree of comfort and include an elegant cocktail bar. Stylish en suite bedrooms come in a variety of sizes, although they all offer high levels of air-conditioned comfort and are well equipped with hair dryer, magnifying mirror, satellite TV, direct-dial phone, high-speed internet connection via laptop or TV, radio, tea and coffee tray, safe and trouser press. Room service is available 24 hours a day. Diners looking for somewhere fashionable to eat will approve of L'Albufera, an elegant, award-winning Spanish restaurant; for greater informality, The Place Brasserie offers buffet breakfast, lunch and dinner, with an emphasis on Mediterranean dishes. Relax in comfortable Longfords Bar, while listening to one of the jazz singers and pianists who perform there from Tuesday to Sunday. Among the hotel's other amenities are an air-conditioned gym, with the latest cardiovascular equipment, and a modern therapy room chock-full of treatments that 'alleviate and rejuvenate'. For those looking to stay longer in the capital, there are studios and apartments to choose from.

**Recommended in the area**

Madame Tussaud's; London Eye; London Zoo

# Crown Moran Hotel

★★★★  75%  HL

Address: 142–152 Cricklewood Broadway,
        Cricklewood, LONDON  NW2 3ED

Tel:      020 8452 4175

Fax:      020 8452 0952

Email:    crownres@moranhotels.com

Website:  www.crownmoranhotel.co.uk

Map ref:  4, TQ38

Directions: M1 junct 1 follow signs onto North
Circular (W) A406. Junct with A5 (Staples Corner).
At rdbt take 1st exit onto A5 to Cricklewood Rooms: 116, S £105–£170 D £105–£190

Facilities: ℞ Sauna Jacuzzi Gym STV Wi-Fi 5 event spaces including the Bentley Room for 300 people

This striking, Irish-owned hotel is cleverly (no need to drive into central London) located in Cricklewood.
Although ultra modern in design, it retains the human touch that some design-led hotels lack and offers
a warm Irish welcome, good service and plenty of smiles. Amenities include function and conference
facilities, leisure club, choice of stylish lounges, bars and contemporary restaurant. The spacious,
air-conditioned bedrooms are appointed to a high standard and include several trendy suites. The King
Sitric Bar & Grill (named after an 11th-century Norse king of Dublin) specializes in 28-day-aged Irish
beef steaks from the charcoal grill, simply served seasonal dishes and house specialties. The good-
value fixed price menu changes frequently while, next door through an impressive glass atrium,
is the popular Crown Pub, where a bar food and snacks menu is served. Four of the hotel's five bars
are located within The Crown, which retains its original fireplaces and stained glass. The leisure centre
is only for hotel residents, which means there are no queues to use gym equipment and the pool is
never crowded. Personal trainers, sports masseurs and beauty therapists can be booked in advance.

Recommended in the area

Wembley Stadium and Arena

# London

Tate Modern

# Hendon Hall Hotel

★★★★ 77% ◉◉ HL

**Address:** Ashley Lane, Hendon, LONDON NW4 1HF
**Tel:** 020 8203 3341
**Fax:** 020 8457 2502
**Email:** info@hendonhall.com
**Website:** www.hendonhall.com
**Map ref:** 4, TQ38
**Directions:** M1 junct 2 follow A406. Right at lights onto Parson St, right onto Ashley Ln. Hotel on right
**Rooms:** 57, S £105–£195 D £115–£210
**Facilities:** STV Wi-Fi in bedrooms **Parking:** 70

Close to the southern end of the M1 and with excellent transport links to central London, this late 17th century mansion is a real gem. Once the home of the famous 18th-century actor, David Garrick, it is full of character and run by a caring and imaginative team. From the entrance hall a series of elegant, rooms includes the Fringe Restaurant, serving modern English cuisine, and a cocktail bar. An elegant staircase leads up to the bedrooms, where there is a welcome tipple awaiting

**Recommended in the area**

The RAF Museum; Wembley Stadium and Alexandra Palace events; Kenwood House (EH)

**150**

# London Bridge Hotel

★★★★ 79% HL

**Address:** 8–18 London Bridge Street,
LONDON SE1 9SG
**Tel:** 020 7855 2200
**Fax:** 020 7855 2233
**Email:** sales@londonbridgehotel.com
**Website:** www.londonbridgehotel.com
**Map ref:** 4, TQ38
**Directions:** From London Bridge Station bus/taxi
yard, into London Bridge St. Hotel 50yds on left

**Rooms:** 138, S £219 D £219 **Facilities:** Sauna Solarium Gym STV Wi-Fi available **Notes:** ⊗ in bedrooms

In the heart of vibrant Southwark, an area rich in architecture, museums, theatres and shopping opportunities, this is a tremendously chic, privately owned hotel with a stately entrance and a stunning interior that blends classical features with an ultra-modern interior. A calming blend of cream and earth tones combines with textures contrasting between smooth leather, polished wood, suede and coarse-weave fabrics. There's a touch of colour in the Londinium restaurant, named in recognition of the Roman artefacts unearthed during the building development, where red suede upholstery is set against polished walnut floors. Modern British cuisine is served in these elegant surroundings, with Malaysian food offered in the stylish Georgetown restaurant and more simple dishes available in the Borough Bar. The bedrooms are supremely relaxing and comfortable; fibre-optic reading lights, flat-screen TVs and high-speed internet among the in-room facilities. Deluxe rooms have a king-size bed, plus a sofabed and walk-in closet, while the executive rooms and suites are designed with business guests in mind. The City, London's financial heart, is, after all, just a short walk away, across London Bridge.

**Recommended in the area**

Borough Market; The Tate Modern; Shakespeare's Globe

# London Marriott Hotel County Hall

★★★★★　88% ◉ HL

**Address:** Westminster Bridge Road, County Hall,
LONDON SE1 7PB
**Tel:** 020 7928 5200
**Email:** mhrs.lonch.salesadmin@marriotthotels.com
**Website:** www.marriottcountyhall.com
**Map ref:** 4, TQ38
**Directions:** on Thames South Bank, between
Westminster Bridge & London Eye
**Rooms:** 200, from £180 **Facilities:** Club & Spa with
Ⓧ Sauna Jacuzzi Solarium Gym Steam Room Pilates Dance studio STV Wi-Fi in bedrooms **Parking:** 20

Occupying the elegant former seat of the Greater London Council, this fine hotel has breathtaking views across the Thames to the Houses of Parliament. The conversion of the building to a hotel has retained many original features, including the huge bronze doors and polished marble floors. Air-conditioned, spacious bedrooms are set up for work as well as relaxation and many have river views. The fine-dining County Hall Restaurant offers modern European cuisine in a grand setting.

**Recommended in the area**

British Airways London Eye; London Aquarium; Houses of Parliament and Big Ben

# Cavendish London

★★★★　78% ◉ HL

**Address:** 81 Jermyn Street, LONDON SW1Y 6JF
**Tel:** 020 7930 2111
**Fax:** 020 7839 2125
**Email:** info@thecavendishlondon.com
**Website:** www.thecavendishlondon.com
**Map ref:** 4, TQ38
**Directions:** From Piccadilly, 1st right into Duke St
**Rooms:** 230 **Facilities:** STV Wi-Fi in bedrooms
**Notes:** Ⓧ in bedrooms

In the heart of the prestigious St James's area, the Cavendish is just a few minutes' walk from Green Park, Piccadilly and Mayfair. In Edwardian times it was run by Rosa Lewis, immortalised on TV as the 'Duchess of Duke Street'; her famously high standards live on. The cutting-edge design treatment throughout makes a strong impact in both the public areas and the well-equipped bedrooms, studios and suites. Recently awarded an AA Rosette, the restaurant's seasonal British menu marries old favourites with more contemporary dishes. An excellent wine list accompanies it.

**Recommended in the area**

Fortnum & Mason; Trafalgar Square; Hyde Park

# The Halkin Hotel

★★★★★  ◉◉◉ TH

Address: Halkin Street, Belgravia,
LONDON SW1X 7DJ
Tel:      020 7333 1000
Fax:      020 7333 1100
Email:    res@halkin.como.bz
Website:  www.halkin.como.bz
Map ref:  4, TQ38
Directions: Hotel between Belgrave Sq & Grosvenor Place. Via Chapel St into Headfort Place and left into Halkin St
Rooms: 41, S £315 D £375 Facilities: STV Wi-Fi in bedrooms Notes: ⊗ in bedrooms

Behind the Georgian-style facade is one of London's smartest hotels. Discreetly situated in a quiet street, The Halkin is surrounded by elegant buildings, smart shops, and is just a short stroll from Hyde Park Corner, Knightsbridge and Buckingham Palace. Inside, the style is contemporary Italian, much of the impact being derived from the use of luxury textiles in cool shades of taupe and cream. The bedrooms and suites are equipped to the highest standard with smart, all-marble bathrooms – among the largest in London – and many extras, including three dual-line phones with voice mail and modem connection, high-speed internet, fax, interactive cable television with CD and DVD services, air conditioning and personal bar. Each floor has been designed thematically – earth, wind, fire, water and the universe. Public areas include a lounge, an airy bar for light meals, drinks and cocktails, and then there's Nahm, David Thompson's award-winning Thai restaurant. Service from Armani-clad staff is attentive and friendly. Guests may use the COMO Shambhala Health Club at The Halkin's sister hotel, The Metropolitan.

Recommended in the area

Science Museum; Harrods; Green Park

# Mandarin Oriental Hyde Park

★★★★★  ◎◎◎◎◎ HL

Address: 66 Knightsbridge, LONDON SW1X 7LA
Tel: 020 7235 2000
Fax: 020 7235 2001
Email: molon-reservations@mohg.com
Website: www.mandarinoriental.com/london
Map ref: 4, TQ38
Directions: Harrods on right, hotel 0.5m on left opp
Harvey Nichols
Rooms: 198 D £488–£5552 Facilities: The Spa at
Mandarin Oriental, Gym STV Notes: ⊗ in bedrooms

Facing fashionable Knightsbridge and overlooking the Royal acres of Hyde Park to the rear, this grand late-Victorian hotel was once a gentlemen's club. Today the frock-coated, top-hatted doormen greet highfliers, celebrities and the young and fashionable, for whom this is a popular destination. How many times, one wonders, have these liveried sentries watched the Household Cavalry clatter by on their way from Knightsbridge Barracks to Buckingham Palace? In keeping with the rest of the hotel, the bedrooms, many with park views, are unquestionably opulent, with antique furniture, plush carpets, marble bathrooms and the finest Irish linen and goose-down pillows. Guests have a choice of dining options, from the brasserie-style, all-day Park Restaurant, to the chic, award-winning Foliage Restaurant, where modern European cuisine is served against a backdrop of Hyde Park. The 'über trendy' Mandarin Bar serves light snacks and cocktails and features live jazz nightly. The stylish Spa is consistently voted one of the best in the country, and guests may find themselves easily seduced into unwinding in the steam room, vitality pool, sanarium or the calming Zen colour therapy relaxation room. All of central London is within easy reach by tube, bus or most rewarding of all, on foot.

**Recommended in the area**

Victoria & Albert Museum; Royal Albert Hall; Harrods

# Sofitel St James London

★★★★★ 85% ◉◉ HL

**Address:** 6 Waterloo Place,
LONDON SW1Y 4AN
**Tel:** 020 7747 2222
**Fax:** 020 7747 2210
**Email:** H3144@accor.com
**Website:** www.sofitelstjames.com
**Map ref:** 4, TQ38
**Directions:** On corner of Pall Mall & Waterloo Place
**Rooms:** 186, S £358.37–£616.88 D £358.37–
£881.25 **Facilities:** Gym STV Wi-Fi available

Surely the corner of Pall Mall and Waterloo Place in exclusive St James's must be one of London's finest addresses. It was certainly prestigious enough for Cox & Kings bank to make it the site for what was their headquarters building, now protected by Grade II listing. The hotel's trademarks are its rich fabrics in shades of chocolate, almond and olive, lacquered mahogany furniture, thick carpets and sophisticated lighting. The modern bedrooms and suites are equipped to a high standard, with luxurious beds, high-tech TV, laptop-sized safe, hairdryer, ironing board and tea- and coffee-making facilities. Albert Roux's eponymous restaurant occupies the former banking hall and offers first class French brasserie cuisine. Just off the lobby, the St James bar – famous for its range of Champagnes – recreates the atmosphere of a gentlemen's club, with dark blue carpets, mahogany parquet floors, black leather chairs, pin-stripe walls and an inviting fireplace. For continental breakfast or afternoon tea make for the Rose Lounge – pink and cream to be precise – featuring deep wool rugs, a Fifties chandelier, fresh roses, the sound of a harp and books on French and English culture, London and roses. Conference and banqueting facilities comprise eight state-of-the-art suites.

**Recommended in the area**

St. James's Park; Buckingham Palace; Trafalgar Square

# The Draycott Hotel

★★★★★ 82% TH

Address: 26 Cadogan Gardens, LONDON SW3 2RP
Tel: 020 7730 6466
Fax: 020 7730 0236
Email: reservations@draycotthotel.com
Website: www.draycotthotel.com
Map ref: 4, TQ38
Directions: From Sloane Sq station towards Peter Jones, keep l.
At Kings Rd take 1st r into Cadogan Gdns, 2nd r, hotel on left
Rooms: 35, S £148–£160 D £207–£263 Facilities: STV Wi-Fi

Combining Edwardian grandeur with the feel of a private
residence, albeit a luxurious one, the hotel is a skilful conversion
of three elegant town houses. It is part of the Cadogan estate, built by the eponymous peer around
Sloane Square, the hub of this ever-fashionable district. The bedrooms all have high ceilings, fireplaces
and carefully selected antiques. Each is named after a theatrical personality and decorated around a
print, poster or other memento associated with that character. More practical considerations include
a well-proportioned en suite bathroom, air conditioning, satellite TV and CD music system, and Sea
Island sheets covering the specially made large beds with some rooms looking out over the peaceful
garden below. Start the day in the Breakfast Room, adorned with masks of famous artistes, such as
Dame Kiri Te Kanawa, and framed programmes of plays performed at the nearby Royal Court Theatre.
Although there is no formal restaurant, a 24-hour room service menu offers a selection of seasonal
meals and snacks. There is also a private dining room that combines the decadence of The Draycott
Hotel with the cosiness of a private home. The fully-airconditioned Donald Wolfit Suite is a conference
room with a beautiful oak-panelled interior that, via patio doors, opens up into a private garden square.
Recommended in the area
Harrods; Hyde Park; Kensington Gardens Serpentine Gallery; Natural History Museum; V&A Museum

# The Bentley Kempinski Hotel

★★★★★   87% ◎◎ HL

**Address:** 27–33 Harrington Gardens,
LONDON SW7 4JX
**Tel:** 020 7244 5555
**Fax:** 020 7244 5566
**Email:** info@thebentley-hotel.com
**Website:** www.thebentley-hotel.com
**Map ref:** 4, TQ38
**Directions:** S of A4 into Knightsbridge at junct with
Gloucester Rd, r, 2nd r turn, hotel on l after mini-rdbt
**Rooms:** 64 **Facilities:** Sauna Jacuzzi Gym STV Wi-Fi available

This exclusive hotel in the residential heart of Kensington is wonderfully close to the smart shops of Knightsbridge and Chelsea's Kings Road. What were built in 1880 as four grand private residences have now been tastefully and sympathetically restored behind their original facades. Lavishly styled public areas, air-conditioned luxury bedrooms and suites, and a superb spa all benefit from generous attention to detail. Exquisite designs, materials and colours create a very South Ken ambience in the spacious guestrooms. Their marble-clad bathrooms offer Jacuzzis and walk-in showers, while technology is discreetly fed into each in the form of touch-screen phones, high-speed internet and a fully interactive audio-visual system with infra-red keyboards. The handsomely appointed Imperial Suite comes complete with a dining room for up to twelve guests and a grand piano. Take traditional breakfast or lunch in the naturally lit Peridot restaurant, relax with a post-shopping martini in Malachite cocktail lounge, then stir yourself into heading to the 1880 award-winning restaurant for dinner, where avant garde, five-course grazing and carte menus are accompanied by carefully selected world wines. Le Kalon Spa is home to the only authentic hammam, or Turkish bath, in a London hotel.

**Recommended in the area**

Victoria & Albert Museum; Royal Albert Hall; Hyde Park

# The Dorchester

★★★★★  ◉◉◉ HL

Address:   Park Lane, LONDON W1A 2HJ
Tel:          020 7629 8888
Fax:         020 7629 8080
Email:      info@thedorchester.com
Website:  www.thedorchester.com
Map ref:  4, TQ38
Directions: Halfway along Park Ln between Hyde
Park Corner & Marble Arch
Rooms: 250, S £265–£385 D £405–£465
Facilities: Sauna Jacuzzi Solarium Gym STV Wi-Fi in bedrooms Notes: ⊗ in bedrooms

From the day it opened in 1931, this legendary hotel has witnessed the comings and goings of many a limousine. Pass by at any time and there'll be a Rolls-Royce, Bentley or Porsche disgorging a world statesman, film star or industry magnate. Standing on the edge of Mayfair, it is minutes away from the exclusive shops of Bond Street and Knightsbridge. The spacious bedrooms and suites, beautifully decorated in English country house style, all overlook Hyde Park or the hotel's landscaped terraces. Their capacious, Italian-marble bathrooms are believed to have the deepest baths in London.  The Dorchester is celebrated for its food, but first head for the bar where the Martini, Manhattan and White Lady cocktails were created. The Grill Room specialises in British cooking, whilst China Tang offers highly rated Cantonese cuisine. Afternoon tea to live piano music in The Promenade is an institution among Londoners of a certain social persuasion. The Spa is a calm and peaceful retreat with steam rooms, spa baths, a fully equipped gymnasium and an extensive range of beauty and therapeutic treatments. At the front is a huge plane tree - one of the 'Great Trees of London' – it is stunning at Christmas time.

Recommended in the area

Buckingham Palace; Royal Academy of Arts; Piccadilly Circus

# The Metropolitan

★★★★★   86% ◉◉◉ HL

Address: Old Park Lane,
         LONDON W1K 1LB
Tel:     020 7447 1000
Fax:     020 7447 1100
Email:   res.lon@metropolitan.como.bz
Website: www.metropolitan.como.bz
Map ref: 4, TQ38
Directions: On corner of Old Park Ln and Hertford St, within 200mtrs from Hyde Park Corner
Rooms: 150, S £375 D £425
Facilities: Sauna Gym STV Wi-Fi throughout

In one of London's best locations – overlooking Hyde Park and close to some of the most upmarket shopping areas – this hotel is cool and classy, with a contemporary air of understated luxury. It is also home to Nobu, a fine Japanese Peruvian restaurant, opened by celebrated Japanese chef Nobu Matsuhisa in partnership with Robert de Niro, among others. Drawing on classic sushi, it adds innovative new Japanese cuisine. The Met Bar, for hotel guests and members only, is a sophisticated venue for drinks, snacks, and live music. The sleek urban style of the bedrooms features light wood, suede upholstery and subtle décor, and natural light floods in through big windows overlooking the park or the rooftops of Mayfair. All the bedrooms have the finest Egyptian cotton linen, goosedown duvets and a host of high-tech entertainment, business and communications devices, including CD juke box and movie library, and complimentary Wi-Fi and high-speed internet. The health club has a gym, but focuses on the Urban Escape element of its name, with experienced professionals offering shiatsu, reiki, reflexology, Thai massage and other treatments to ward off city stress.

Recommended in the area

Buckingham Palace; Royal Academy of Arts; Hyde Park

# Millennium Hotel London Mayfair

★★★★   79% ◉ HL

Address:  Grosvenor Square, LONDON W1K 2HP
Tel:      020 7629 9400
Fax:      020 7629 7736
Email:    sales.mayfair@mill-cop.com
Website:  www.millenniumhotels.com
Map ref:  4, TQ38
Directions: S side of Grosvenor Square
Rooms: 348, S £185–£255 D £205–£275 Facilities: Gym STV
Wi-fi available Notes: ⊗ in bedrooms

Built as a magnificent townhouse in the 18th century, this
hotel, in the heart of London's most exclusive and fashionable
shopping district, still exudes an ambience of cultured luxury. The air-conditioned bedrooms, never
less than 36 square metres in size, all have king-size beds, seating areas and, of course, en suite
bathrooms. Most have fine views over Grosvenor Square. Facilities include internet access (there's
also Wi-Fi in all public areas), mini bar and tea- and coffee-making supplies, and a rollaway bed can
be provided in some of the rooms for a child. The principal restaurant at the hotel is the retro-chic
Brian Turner Mayfair, where the celebrity chef creates first-rate, traditional British cuisine in his own
inimitable style, using a hand-picked selection of UK specialist and organic suppliers. The Shogun
Restaurant has a wide menu of authentic Japanese dishes, including hand-rolled sushi. Bars include
the trendy, contemporary Turner Bar and the ultra-stylish new Pine Bar. Business guests have the use
of a 24-hour Business Centre with computer stations and office equipment, plus mobile phone and
pager rentals. The hotel also has a wedding licence, and ten function rooms provide facilities for events
with up to 700 guests.

Recommended in the area

West End shopping; West End theatres; Hyde Park

# The Washington Mayfair Hotel

★★★★ 77% HL

**Address:** 5–7 Curzon Street, Mayfair,
LONDON W1J 5HE
**Tel:** 020 7499 7000
**Fax:** 020 7495 6172
**Email:** sales@washington-mayfair.co.uk
**Website:** www.washington-mayfair.co.uk
**Map ref:** 4, TQ38
**Directions:** From Green Park station take Piccadilly exit & turn right. 4th street on right into Curzon Street
**Rooms:** 171, S £165–£295 D £165–£295 **Facilities:** Gym STV Wi-Fi in bedrooms

This is an art deco gem in the heart of chic Mayfair, a distinguished hotel that has been sympathetically renovated to preserve its elegant 1913 ambience and style. It's perfectly located for the high-end shopping of Bond Street and Regent Street, with Knightsbridge just a short taxi ride away. Friendly, helpful service includes 24-hour porterage and room service, a weekday valet service, shoe-shine and laundry, and turn-down service. Together with the range of business services, mobile phone hire, and full concierge service, this makes for a caring atmosphere. The chic and spacious contemporary bedrooms have computer coded security systems, two telephone lines, personal phone number and voicemail, internet connection and large desks. Of the suites, the Master Suites are the most spacious, with dining as well as sitting areas, but Executive Studio Suites have the biggest bathrooms. The open-plan bar and lounge, a clubby space with piano, are where guests congregate for afternoon tea or pre-dinner drinks, while Madison's Restaurant offers formal dining on creative international cuisine. Pre-theatre meals are also available. Up on the fifth floor guests can work off any overindulgences in the well equipped gym, with various exercise machines.

**Recommended in the area**

Buckingham Palace; Royal Academy of Art; Hyde Park

# Milestone Hotel & Apartments

★★★★★ ◎◎ HL

Address: 1 Kensington Court, LONDON W8 5DL
Tel: 020 7917 1000
Fax: 020 7917 1010
Email: bookms@rchmail.com
Website: www.milestonehotel.com
Map ref: 4, TQ38
Directions: From Warwick Rd right into Kensington High St. Hotel 400yds past Kensington underground
Rooms: 57, S £235–£295 D £265–£325
Facilities: ⊕ Sauna Jacuzzi Gym STV Wi-Fi in bedrooms

The Milestone's combination of country-house ambience and chic city elegance is something of a mirror to its surroundings, with Hyde Park and Kensington Gardens across the road and some of London's most fashionable shopping just around the corner. The dedication to personal attention and service includes a welcome with champagne, sherry or tea, a turn-down service and limousine shopping trips, and that is just the beginning. Take a luxury suite and you will also get 24-hour butler service and canapés each evening. The bedrooms each have an individual style, featuring exquisite fabrics, soft furnishings and antique and hand-painted furniture. The stunning Safari Suite, for instance, has a vast tented ceiling and exotic earth-tone décor. The public areas are equally sumptuous, including elegant, wood-panelled lounges, a clubby bar and a choice of restaurants: the intimate Cheneston's serving the finest international cuisine; the informal Conservatory; and the cosy Park Lounge, perfect for afternoon tea. The health suite is for residents only and includes a resistance pool, fully equipped gym and resident beauty therapist. The Milestone belongs to the Red Carnation group, AA Small Hotel Group of the Year 2007–8.

Recommended in the area

Kensington Palace; Royal Albert Hall; South Kensington Museums

# Royal Garden Hotel

★★★★★ HL

**Address:** 2–24 Kensington High Street,
LONDON W8 4PT
**Tel:** 020 7937 8000
**Fax:** 020 7361 1991
**Email:** sales@royalgardenhotel.co.uk
**Website:** www.royalgardenhotel.co.uk
**Map ref:** 4, TQ38
**Directions:** Next to Kensington Palace
**Rooms:** 396, S £149–£209 D £179–£239
**Facilities:** Sauna Gym STV **Notes:** ⊗ in bedrooms

The views from the upper floors of the Royal Garden Hotel extend over Hyde Park and Kensington Gardens to the financial district of the city and London's riverside landmarks. The hotel has 396 beautifully-appointed bedrooms. all of modern design, high-speed Wi-Fi connection, interactive television and radio, DVD and CD player, mini-bar, air-conditioning and safe. Room grades range from Standard and Superior through to Deluxe and Executive. Deluxe rooms are for double occupancy and all enjoy views over the gardens and the park, they are light and spacious with work and lounge areas. There are 37 suites, the four highest-grade being on the hotel's highest floors with unequalled views. Min Jiang is due to open in spring 2008, a brand new contemporary Asian style restaurant replacing the famous Tenth Restaurant with stunning views of the Capital's exquisite skyline. Throughout the day guests can also dine in the Park Terrace Restaurant, with its seasonal menu derived from the highest quality ingredients. A choice of two bars is available at the hotel with either Bertie's Bar, recently

refurbished and amongst Kensington's most fashionable venues or the relaxing atmosphere of the Park Terrace Bar. The hotel offers various promotions throughout the year with festive occasions including not only Christmas and New Year but also Thanksgiving. The hotel offers 11 conference and banqueting rooms able to accommodate events with up to 550 delegates, the fully equipped business centre is open 24 hours a day. The Soma Centre is the hotel's health club and spa, offering a wide range of beauty and fitness treatments, a steam room, a sauna, and coaching in yoga, martial arts, aerobics and Pilates.

**Recommended in the area**

Harrods; Hyde Park; Kensington Gardens
Serpentine Gallery; Natural History
Museum; V&A Museum

Covent Garden

# Jurys Great Russell Street

★★★★ 77% ◎ HL

| Address: | 16–22 Great Russell Street, |
| | LONDON WC1B 3NN |
| Tel: | 020 7347 1000 |
| Fax: | 020 7347 1001 |
| Email: | restaurant_grs@jurysdoyle.com |
| Website: | www.jurysdoyle.com |
| Map ref: | 4, TQ38 |

Directions: A40 onto A400, Gower St then south to Bedford Sq. Turn right, then 1st left to end of road

Rooms: 170, S £79–£240 D £79–£240 Facilities: STV Wi-Fi available Notes: ⊗ in bedrooms

Designed by Sir Edwin Lutyens for the YWCA, Jurys Doyle Group bought and converted the building in 1998. Original features have been retained throughout the major interior spaces, particularly in the grand reception lobby and lounge. A choice of accommodation includes classic and executive rooms and junior suites. Lutyens Restaurant is recommended for impressive European cuisine. Pre-theatre menu available.

Recommended in the area

British Museum; Oxford Street; Covent Garden; Theatreland; Dominion Theatre

# Renaissance Chancery Court

★★★★★  86% ◉◉◉ HL

**Address:** 252 High Holborn, LONDON WC1V 7EN
**Tel:** 020 7829 9888
**Fax:** 020 7829 9889
**Email:** sales.chancerycourt@renaissancehotels.com
**Website:** www.renaissancechancerycourt.co.uk
**Map ref:** 4, TQ38
**Directions:** A4 along Piccadilly onto Shaftesbury Av. Into High Holborn, hotel on right
**Rooms:** 356 **Facilities:** Sauna Gym STV Wi-Fi available
**Notes:** ⊗ in bedrooms

Sublime old-world class links arms here with contemporary standards of five-star luxury situated amidst the dramatic architecture of Holborn and close to the pretty streets and squares of historic Bloomsbury. Just a stone's throw from the shops and restaurants of Covent Garden and trendy Clerkenwell, the hotel is ideally located for both business and leisure guests. Enter the beautiful classical courtyard and this grand building makes an immediate impression with its stunning public areas, decorated in rich mahogany, rare marble and fine crystal. The bedrooms are some of the largest in London and feature luxurious marble bathrooms with luxury amenities, high speed internet access and Marriott's new Revive bedding. Walking into the Pearl restaurant means being momentarily mesmerised by breathtaking chandeliers and shimmering cascades of real pearls. This sophisticated room is the domain of world-renowned head chef, Jun Tanaka, who brings to the tables a menu of international cuisine. The CC Bar, embellished with restored period features, feels like an exclusive members' club, while the marble-columned Lounge must be one of the finest open spaces to be found in a hotel. Indulge in a relaxation and therapy programme in the Spa at Chancery Court.

**Recommended in the area**

London Eye; Somerset House; British Museum

# MERSEYSIDE

Liverpool's Roman Catholic Cathedral of Christ the King

HMS Plymouth and submarine HMS Onyx, Birkenhead

# RiverHill Hotel

★★★   79%  HL

**Address:** Talbot Road, Prenton,
BIRKENHEAD CH43 2HJ
**Tel:** 0151 653 3773
**Fax:** 0151 653 7162
**Email:** reception@theriverhill.co.uk
**Website:** www.theriverhill.co.uk
**Map ref:** 5, SJ38
**Directions:** 1m from M53 junct 3, along A552. Turn left onto B5151 at lights hotel 0.5m on right)
**Rooms:** 15, S £69.75 D £79.75–£89.75 **Facilities:** STV Wi-Fi available **Parking:** 32 **Notes:** ⊗ in bedrooms

The RiverHill stands in its own beautiful grounds in Oxton, a quiet residential neighbourhood near Birkenhead. It is run by Nick and Michelle Burn, who also run the Grove House Hotel in nearby Wallasey. The attractively furnished en suite bedrooms, all have TV, phone, hot drinks facilities, trouser press and hair dryer. The RiverHill has two bridal suites, each with four-poster bed. An excellent choice of carte and fixed price menus and good quality wines can be found in the Bay Tree Restaurant.
**Recommended in the area**
Speke Hall (NT); Bidston Observatory; Ness Botanic Gardens

**167**

# Hillbark

★★★★   88% ⑨⑩ CHH

Address:   Royden Park, FRANKBY,
           Wirral CH48 1NP
Tel:       0151 625 2400
Fax:       0151 625 4040
Email:     enquiries@hillbarkhotel.co.uk
Website:   www.hillbarkhotel.co.uk
Map ref:   5, SJ28
Rooms: 19, S £175–£475 D £175–£475
Facilities: Jacuzzi STV Parking: 140
Notes: ⊗ in bedrooms

In the heart of the beautiful Wirral peninsula, just 15 minutes, yet seemingly a million miles away from vibrant Liverpool and historic Chester, this magnificent Grade II listed hotel provides the finest luxury coupled with discreet yet friendly service. It is set in 250 acres of beautiful parkland overlooking the scenic Dee estuary and the hills of North Wales beyond. The house has a fascinating history. It was originally built in 1891 in Birkenhead for soap manufacturer Robert William Hudson, a founder of Lever Fabergé, but was sold in 1921 to Cunard shipping magnate Sir Ernest Royden and in 1928 was moved to its present site, brick by brick. The Great Hall has a 1527 Jacobean fireplace from Sir Walter Raleigh's house in Ireland, a set of William Morris stained-glass windows and a pair of 13th-century church screen doors; the library came from a Gloucestershire stately home; and the opulent Yellow Room restaurant contains a magnificent 1795 Robert Adam fire surround. Here, and in the stylish Hillbark Grill, imaginative and delicious haute cuisine is complemented by a splendid 500-bin cellar. Rolls-Royces and Bentleys are available to collect guests from airports and stations, and leisure activities include golf and windsurfing.

Recommended in the area

Williamson Art Gallery and Museum; Ness Botanic Garden; Port Sunlight

Knowsley Safari Park.

# Grove House Hotel

★★★　78%　HL

**Address:** Grove Road, WALLASEY  CH45 3HF
**Tel:** 0151 639 3947
**Fax:** 0151 639 0028
**Email:** reception@thegrovehouse.co.uk
**Website:** www.thegrovehouse.co.uk
**Map ref:** 5, SJ29
**Directions:** M53 junct 1, A554 (Wallasey New Brighton), right after church onto Harrison Drive, left after Windsors Garage onto Grove Rd
**Rooms:** 14, S £75 D £95–£135 **Facilities:** STV Wi-Fi available **Parking:** 28 **Notes:** ⊗ in bedrooms

Pretty lawns and gardens are the setting for this friendly hotel, situated in a quiet residential area of Wallasey. Nick and Michelle Burn have owned it since 1998; they also own the nearby RiverHill Hotel. The attractively furnished ground floor, family and four-poster en suite bedrooms have TV, phone, hot drinks facilities, trouser press and hair dryer. Relax with an aperitif in the cocktail bar before dinner; a liqueur in the cocktail lounge afterwards. The Oak Tree Restaurant offers a wide choice of dishes.
**Recommended in the area**
Speke Hall (NT); Bidston Observatory; Ness Botanic Gardens

# NORFOLK

Burnham Overy Staithe

Sandringham House

# Hoste Arms Hotel

★★★   86% ⧳⧳ HL

**Address:** The Green, BURNHAM MARKET, King's
Lynn PE31 8HD
**Tel:**        01328 738777
**Fax:**       01328 730103
**Email:**    reception@hostearms.co.uk
**Website:**  www.hostearms.co.uk
**Map ref:**  4, TF84
**Directions:** signed on B1155, 5m W of Wells-next-the-
Sea

**Rooms:** 35, S £90–£165 D £122–£437 **Facilities:** STV Wi-Fi available **Parking:** 45

Behind the traditional 17th-century façade overlooking the village green there are surprises in store.
Once Nelson's local and still the social hub of the village, it is also a sumptuous hotel with stunning
style and décor. The well-travelled hosts have injected ideas gleaned from around the world and
the result is quite breathtaking. The food, using the finest local produce, displays similarly global
inspirations. Truly a one-of-a-kind place.

**Recommended in the area**

Holkham Hall; Titchwell RSPB Reserve; Sandringham

# Elderton Lodge Hotel & Langtry Restaurant

★★★　87% ❀ HL

Address: Gunton Park, CROMER  NR11 8TZ
Tel:　　01263 833547
Fax:　　01263 834673
Email:　enquiries@eldertonlodge.co.uk
Website: www.eldertonlodge.co.uk
Map ref: 4, TG24
Directions: At North Walsham take A149 towards
Cromer, hotel 3m on left, just before Thorpe Market
Rooms: 11, S £65 D £100–£120 Parking: 50

Positioned in beautiful wooded grounds, and overlooking 800 acres of deer park, this 200-year-old former shooting lodge to Gunton Hall is lovingly run as a country house hotel. Rachel and Pat, both natives of Norfolk, have worked hard refurbishing the property and training staff. Enjoy pre-dinner drinks or after-dinner coffee in the comfortable lounge. En suite bedrooms are individually decorated and furnished, with careful attention to detail. Every room has TV, DVD player (free DVDs from Reception), phone, alarm clock, tea-making facilities and hair dryer. The candlelit Langtry Restaurant, named after Lillie, the celebrated Victorian beauty and mistress of the Prince of Wales, is open daily to residents and non-residents, with seasonal and regularly changing fixed price menus. The emphasis is on fresh, locally sourced produce, particularly fish and seafood, and game from neighbouring estates, including Gunton itself. Adjoining the Langtry is the Conservatory, used also for breakfast and lunch. The hotel building and grounds provide a wonderful backdrop for wedding photographs (licensed for civil ceremonies). There is also a top-of-the-range marquee with wooden dance floor and chandeliers.

**Recommended in the area**

Norfolk Broads; Norwich City Centre and Cathedral; Blickling Hall

Norwich Cathedral

# Congham Hall Country House Hotel

★★★ ◎◎ HL

**Address:** Lynn Road, GRIMSTON,
King's Lynn PE32 1AH
**Tel:** 01485 600250
**Fax:** 01485 601191
**Email:** info@conghamhallhotel.co.uk
**Website:** www.conghamhallhotel.co.uk
**Map ref:** 4, TF72

**Directions:** At A149/A148 junct, take A148 towards Fakenham. Right to Grimston, hotel 2.5m on left
**Rooms:** 14, S £90–£95 D £110–£345 **Facilities:** Tennis **Parking:** 50 **Notes:** ⊗ in bedrooms

This Georgian manor house, set in parklands and gardens, has a homely feel, with log fires and antique furniture. The bedrooms, individually decorated in traditional English style, all overlook the gardens or parkland. In the intimate Orangery restaurant, with its french windows giving on to the terrace, the cuisine features seasonal local produce including specialities such as Cromer crab.
**Recommended in the area**
Sandringham House and Estate; Holkham Hall; Norfolk Lavender and wildflowers

# Caley Hall Hotel

★★★  80%  HL

Address: Old Hunstanton Road,
HUNSTANTON  PE36 6HH
Tel:        01485 533486
Fax:       01485 533348
Email:     mail@caleyhallhotel.co.uk
Website:  www.caleyhallhotel.co.uk
Map ref:  4, TF64
Directions: 1m from Hunstanton, on A149
Rooms: 40, S £49–£99 D £70–£150
Facilities: STV Wi-Fi in bedrooms Parking: 80

Located where the north Norfolk coast curves southwest into The Wash, this is a good base for long walks along wide beaches and exploring unspoilt countryside dotted with sleepy villages. Caley Hall is a lovely 17th-century brick-and-flint house which, from the front, presents a fairly modest farmhouse appearance, but former barns, stables and extensions tucked away at the back have been beautifully converted to provide additional accommodation. Most of the rooms, all with en suite bathrooms, are at ground level, grouped around several sheltered patio areas, and have satellite TV, DVD and CD players, a refrigerator and tea- and coffee-making facilities. There's individual heating in each room, so guests can get the temperature just how they like it. The deluxe rooms are more spacious – one has a four-poster bed – and there's a suite with a whirlpool bath, plus some rooms for mobility-impaired guests. The restaurant is housed in the old stables, but the décor is chic rather than rustic, with high-back leather chairs and modern light-wood tables. Breakfast, lunch and dinner are served, with an evening menu that might include grilled seabass, braised local beef, a traditional roast and vegetarian options. There's also a bright, spacious bar, open all day, with lots of cosy soft leather sofas.

Recommended in the area

Sandringham; Titchwell RSPB Reserve; Holkham Hall

# Titchwell Manor Hotel

★★★ 82% ◉◉ HL

Address: TITCHWELL,
Brancaster PE31 8BB
Tel: 01485 210221
Fax: 01485 210104
Email: margaret@titchwellmanor.com
Website: www.titchwellmanor.com
Map ref: 4, TF74
Directions: On A149 coast road between Brancaster and Thornham
Rooms: 26, S £45–£150 D £90–£200 Parking: 50

Golfers come here for the two championship courses nearby; nature lovers come for the rich bird-life of the marshes that are directly overlooked by the hotel; foodies come for the cuisine of head chef Eric Snaith, and others come just for the relaxing ambience and stylish accommodation. The main building is a brick-and-flint Victorian farmhouse dating from 1890, and further accommodation is in a converted barn, a traditional cottage and around a scented, herb-filled courtyard. All of the rooms boast chic contemporary furnishings and up-to-the-minute bathroom suites, and the majority are very spacious, with queen- or king-size beds. Some rooms have sea views; some can accommodate families; some are particularly suitable for guests with mobility problems; and some are dog-friendly, with bowls and biscuits (there's also a kennel and run available by the car park). The dinner menu in the restaurant offers a selection of innovative, beautifully presented dishes, with starters such as an 'almost sashimi' of tuna with lime puree, pumpkin seed and muscovado sugar salt; main courses might include rack of Norfolk lamb with roast saffron potatoes, salsify, chorizo, fresh peas and muscovado jelly. The bar offers simpler, but no less accomplished choices and the kids' menu is a cut above the usual.

Recommended in the area

RSPB Titchwell Marsh Reserve; Peddars Way and Norfolk Coast Path; Norfolk Lavender

Church of St Mary and All Saints near the River Nene

# Rushton Hall

★★★★ 83% ☺☺ CHH

**Address:** Rushton Hall, Rushton,
KETTERING NN14 1RR
**Tel:** 01536 713001
**Fax:** 01536 713010
**Email:** enquiries@rushtonhall.com
**Website:** www.rushtonhall.com
**Map ref:** 3, SP87
**Directions:** A14 junct 7. A43 to Corby then A6003
to Rushton turn after bridge

**Rooms:** 44, S £140–£300 D £140–£300 **Facilities:** Sauna Jacuzzi Solarium Tennis Gym Wi-Fi
available **Parking:** 140 **Notes:** ⊗ in bedrooms

Rushton Hall is a magnificent Grade I listed Elizabethan country house, surrounded by beautiful, tranquil countryside where a wide range of activities, country pursuits and attractions are available. The east Midlands road network makes it easy to get to, which makes it a popular conference and wedding venue. The grandeur of the building is balanced by an ambience of comfort and relaxation, where guests can relax by one of the big open fireplaces and enjoy the attentive hospitality. Bedrooms are richly decorated in individual style, from elegant superior rooms to wood-panelled rooms with magnificent four-poster beds. All have internet access and flat-screen TVs, and some of the en suite bathrooms have a large bath and separate shower. The restaurant occupies the grand oak panelled dining room and as much attention is paid to the sourcing of ingredients as to the creation of one of the best menus in the country. There is also a brasserie, and afternoon tea is served in the Great Hall, or out in the courtyard when the weather is good. Guests have the use of a gym, outdoor tennis courts and a billiard table, and a new spa and indoor swimming pool is scheduled to open early in 2008.

**Recommended in the area**

Triangular Lodge; Boughton House; Wicksteed Park

River Aln, Alnmouth

# White Swan Hotel

★★★ 80% HL

Address: Bondgate Within,
ALNWICK NE66 1TD
Tel: 01665 602109
Fax: 01665 510400
Email: info.whiteswan@classiclodges.co.uk
Website: www.classiclodges.co.uk
Map ref: 10, NU11
Directions: From A1 follow town centre signs. Hotel in town centre near Bondgate Tower
Rooms: 56, S £60–£90 D £90–£180
Parking: 25

Right in the heart of the historic town, this charming 300-year-old coaching inn has recently benefited from a major refurbishment. Not only has it paid off by bringing the whole hotel up to date, but it has done so by treading carefully around the many authentic period features. All the bedrooms have been fully modernised to produce a range of classic standard, classic superior and classic suite rooms, all with LCD TVs and DVD players. The public areas have been transformed and now include the new Hardy's Bistro, where you can get anything from a café latte to a classic club sandwich or a traditional steak and ale pie. The refurbishment also included the restoration of the Olympic Suite dining room, famous for its original oak panelling, mirrors and stained glass windows salvaged from the SS Olympic. Unlike her sister ship, the Titanic, she didn't sink but was pensioned off and the hotel bought the fittings at auction after she had been scrapped in a Scottish shipyard in 1937. The head chef's Olympic menus subtly blend continental flavours and local fare to suit all tastes. A brand new conference/meeting room and residents' lounge adds to the facilities.

Recommended in the area

Alnwick Castle and Gardens; Holy Island; Metro Centre

# Langley Castle Hotel

★★★★   82%  HL

Address: Langley on Tyne, HEXHAM  NE47 5LU
Tel:      01434 688888
Fax:      01434 684019
Email:    manager@langleycastle.com
Website:  www.langleycastle.com
Map ref:  7, NY96
Directions: From A69 S on A686 for 2m. Castle on right
Rooms: 19, S £99.50–£189.50 D £129–£249
Facilities: STV Parking: 70 Notes: ⊗ in bedrooms

This really is a castle. It was built in 1350 and is now a rare example of an English medieval fortified castle hotel. A local historian, Cadwallader Bates, bought it as a near ruin in 1882 and spent the rest of his life restoring it; after he died his widow, Josephine, continued the task, rebuilding the original chapel on the castle roof in memory of her husband. She died in 1933 and is buried alongside him in the 10-acre woodland estate. The building preserves what are probably Europe's finest examples of 14th-century garderobes, the name our ancestors gave to their toilets. All the bedrooms have private facilities, four-poster beds and window seats set into the 7-foot thick walls, while additional luxury features may include a sauna or spa bath. Castle View and the Lodge, restored listed buildings situated in the grounds, contain a further 10 rooms and suites decorated and furnished to the same high standard as rooms in the Castle. In the candlelit Josephine Restaurant a fixed-rate menu of continental, regional and local dishes specialises in fresh fish and local game and the wine list extends to vintage Château Lafite. Afterwards guests can retire to the magnificent Drawing Room for a coffee or liqueur in front of a crackling log fire. Not surprisingly, the hotel makes a fine setting for a wedding reception.

Recommended in the area

Hadrian's Wall; Bamburgh Castle; Hexham Abbey

Newstead Abbey Kitchen Gardens

Sherwood Forest's ancient woodland

# Langar Hall

★★★  81% ◉◉ HL

**Address:** LANGAR  NG13 9HG
**Tel:**      01949 860559
**Fax:**      01949 861045
**Email:**    info@langarhall.co.uk
**Website:** www.langarhall.com
**Map ref:** 8, SK73
**Directions:** Via Bingham from A52 or Cropwell
Bishop from A46, both signed. Hotel behind church
**Rooms:** 12, S £75–£110 D £150–£210
**Facilities:** Wi-Fi in bedrooms **Parking:** 20 **Notes:** ⊗ in bedrooms

Langar Hall was built in 1837 on the site of a great historic house, the home of Admiral Lord Howe. It stands in the Vale of Belvoir overlooking lovely gardens, complete with a croquet lawn and medieval fishponds. The family home of Imogen Skirving, Langar offers the hospitality of an informal country house. Most of the comfortable bedrooms have countryside views. The restaurant, an elegant pillared hall, is well regarded for fresh seasonal food. Langar is a popular venue for civil marriages.

**Recommended in the area**

Belvoir Castle; Trent Bridge Cricket Ground; Newark International Antiques and Collectors Fair

# The Grange Hotel

★★★  82% ◉ HL

**Address:** 73 London Road, NEWARK-ON-TRENT
NG24 1RZ
**Tel:** 01636 703399
**Email:** info@grangenewark.co.uk
**Website:** www.grangenewark.co.uk
**Map ref:** 8, SK75'
**Directions:** From A1 follow signs to Balderton, hotel is opposite Polish War Graves
**Rooms:** 19, S £75–£100 D £100–£150
**Facilities:** Wi-Fi in bedrooms **Parking:** 17 **Notes:** ⊗ in bedrooms

A family-run, Victorian-era hotel in a conservation area, just a short walk from the town centre. Skilfully renovated, Newark Civic Trust gave it an award for the way original features, such as a beautiful tiled floor in one of the entrance areas, have been retained. Public rooms include a bar called Potters, with framed illustrations of old crockery, and a residents' lounge. Beyond Potters is a stone-flagged patio shaded by tall yews and the immaculate landscaped garden, winner of a Newark in Bloom award. The bedrooms, some with four-posters, all feature newly-designed bathrooms with bath and shower, co-ordinated soft furnishings, desk space with phone and computer access point, TV, radio alarm, beverage-making and ironing facilities, hair dryer, trouser press and, last but not least, a rubber duck for the very young (or perhaps the harassed business executive). High-ceilinged Cutlers restaurant, named after the antique cutlery on display, offers a frequently changing, à la carte menu, with main courses such as pan-fried fillet of pork; baked herb-crusted sea bass; and broccoli, cheese and potato bake. That it attracts non-residents as well as hotel guests says much about the restaurant's appeal. Weddings and business functions are expertly catered for.

**Recommended in the area**

Newark Castle and Gardens; Newark International Antiques Fair; Newark Air Museum

# Restaurant Sat Bains with Rooms

★★★  ◉◉◉◉ HL

**Address:** Trentside, Lenton Lane,
NOTTINGHAM NG7 2SA
**Tel:** 0115 986 6566
**Fax:** 0115 986 0343
**Email:** info@restaurantsatbains.net
**Website:** www.restaurantsatbains.com
**Map ref:** 8, SK53
**Directions:** M1 junct 24 take A453 Nottingham S.
Over River Trent in central lane to rdbt. Left then left
again towards river. Hotel on left after bend
**Rooms:** 8, S £90–£120 D £110–£140 **Facilities:** STV **Parking:** 22 **Notes:** ⊗ in bedrooms

Chic boutique hotel, or restaurant with rooms? Take your pick. Named after the chef-patron, who runs it with his wife Amanda, this sympathetic conversion of farm buildings by the River Trent is close to the city's industrial area, yet manages to remain tucked away in idyllic seclusion. The individually designed bedrooms create a warmth and magic using quality soft furnishings and antique and period furniture; suites and four-poster rooms are also available. Cosy public rooms comprise the reception/lounge bar and two small linked dining rooms, whose outstanding cuisine earned the title of AA Restaurant of the Year for 2006–7. A delighted Sat Bains described this as "A great surprise and fantastic news for Nottingham". Behind this accolade is what he acknowledges as an obsession with quality and traceability of produce, declaring that everything from the lobster to the mackerel is worthy of the chef's time. A popular choice is the tasting menu, prepared for the whole table and designed to balance tastes, textures and temperatures. There's even a bespoke tasting menu tailored to individual preferences, although this requires 48 hours notice.

**Recommended in the area**

Trent Bridge Cricket Ground; Nottingham Castle; Nottingham Concert Arena

# OXFORDSHIRE

Magdalen College, Oxford University

# The Bay Tree Hotel

★★★   79% ◉ HL

Address: Sheep Street, BURFORD  OX18 4LW
Tel:        01993 822791
Fax:        01993 823008
Email:      info@baytreehotel.info
Website:  www.cotswold-inns-hotels.co.uk/bay_tree
Map ref:  3, SP21
Directions: From Burford High St turn into Sheep St,
next to the old market square. Hotel is on right
Rooms: 21, S £119–£129 D £145–£175
Facilities: Wi-Fi available Parking: 50

Much of this delightful old inn's character comes from the flagstone floors, tapestries, high-raftered hall, galleried stairs and tastefully furnished oak-panelled bedrooms, some with four-poster or half-tester beds. Public areas consist of the country-style Woolsack Bar, a sophisticated airy restaurant with original leaded windows, a selection of meeting rooms and an attractive walled garden. An alternative to the restaurant's candle-lit atmosphere is the Woolsack's extensive menu of lighter meals.

Recommended in the area

Burford Wildlife Park; Blenheim Palace; Oxford

# The Lamb Inn

★★★   81% ◉◉ HL

Address: Sheep Street, BURFORD  OX18 4LR
Tel:        01993 823155
Fax:        01993 822228
Email:      info@lambinn-burford.co.uk
Website:  www.cotswold-inns-hotels.co.uk/lamb
Map ref:  3, SP21
Directions: Turn off A40 into Burford, downhill, take
1st left into Sheep St, hotel last on right
Rooms: 17, S  D £145–£165 Facilities: Wi-Fi in bedrooms

To quote the owners, "The phrase 'charming old inn' is used much too freely, but the Lamb has a genuine right to it". Indeed it has, with stone-flagged floors, log fires and many other time-worn features. The cosy lounges, warmed by those self-same fires, and with deep armchairs, are tranquillity itself. The en suite bedrooms contain fine furniture, much of it antique, in addition to all the usual amenities, including homemade cookies. All overlook leafy side streets, or the hotel courtyard. The light, airy restaurant serves traditional English cuisine with a modern twist.

Recommended in the area

Cotswold Wildlife Park; Blenheim Palace; City of Oxford

# The Mill House Hotel & Restaurant

★★★   81% ◉◉ HL

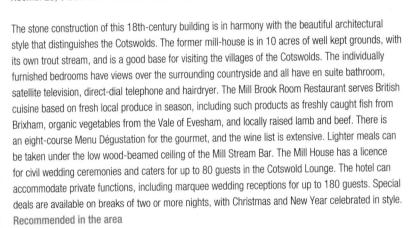

**Address:** KINGHAM  OX7 6UH
**Tel:**       01608 658188
**Fax:**      01608 658492
**Email:**    stay@millhousehotel.co.uk
**Website:** www.millhousehotel.co.uk
**Map ref:** 3, SP22
**Directions:** Off A44 onto B4450. Hotel indicated by tourist sign
**Rooms:** 23, S £90–£100 D £130–£150 **Facilities:** STV Wi-Fi available **Parking:** 60

The stone construction of this 18th-century building is in harmony with the beautiful architectural style that distinguishes the Cotswolds. The former mill-house is in 10 acres of well kept grounds, with its own trout stream, and is a good base for visiting the villages of the Cotswolds. The individually furnished bedrooms have views over the surrounding countryside and all have en suite bathroom, satellite television, direct-dial telephone and hairdryer. The Mill Brook Room Restaurant serves British cuisine based on fresh local produce in season, including such products as freshly caught fish from Brixham, organic vegetables from the Vale of Evesham, and locally raised lamb and beef. There is an eight-course Menu Dégustation for the gourmet, and the wine list is extensive. Lighter meals can be taken under the low wood-beamed ceiling of the Mill Stream Bar. The Mill House has a licence for civil wedding ceremonies and caters for up to 80 guests in the Cotswold Lounge. The hotel can accommodate private functions, including marquee wedding receptions for up to 180 guests. Special deals are available on breaks of two or more nights, with Christmas and New Year celebrated in style.

**Recommended in the area**

Blenheim Palace; Stratford-upon-Avon; Warwick Castle.

# Westwood Country Hotel

★★★ 74% HL

**Address:** Hinksey Hill Top, Boars Hill,
OXFORD OX1 5BG
**Tel:** 01865 735408
**Fax:** 01865 736536
**Email:** reservations@westwoodhotel.co.uk
**Website:** www.westwoodhotel.co.uk
**Map ref:** 3, SP50
**Directions:** Off Oxford ring road at Hinksey Hill junct
towards Boars Hill & Wootton. At hilltop Hotel on right
**Rooms:** 20, S £65–£75 D £110–£125
**Facilities:** Wi-Fi in bedrooms and throughout hotel **Parking:** 50 **Notes:** ⊗ in bedrooms

Proprietor Anthony Healy has realised his dream to create a peaceful retreat, free from the hustle and bustle of everyday living. Just two miles from the centre of the 'City of Dreaming Spires', and surrounded by 400 acres of ancient woodland and gardens, the Westwood was built by an Edwardian gentleman in 1910. Public areas include a contemporary bar, cosy lounge and restaurant overlooking the pretty garden. Many of the bedrooms have been recently refurbished, each individually styled to provide maximum comfort, with the help of an en suite bath and/or shower, fluffy cotton towels, TV, phone, and beverage tray. Different room shapes and sizes suit all needs; two have four-posters and many enjoy views over the gardens and woods. The general manager and head chef both come from AA-Rosette backgrounds and are building a formidable reputation for fine-dining here. Taken from a typical menu are slow-roasted salmon with carrots julienne, new potatoes and herb cream; roasted duck breast on spinach and basil mash; and penne pasta with Mediterranean vegetables. In the restaurant, or out on the terrace, order a fine wine from the world's most renowned vineyards.

**Recommended in the area**

Ashmolean Museum; Bodleian Library; Blenheim Palace; Bicester Village Retail Outlet

# The Springs Hotel & Golf Club

★★★ 78% ◉ HL

**Address:** Wallingford Road, North Stoke,
WALLINGFORD OX10 6BE
**Tel:** 01491 836687
**Fax:** 01491 836877
**Email:** info@thespringshotel.com
**Website:** www.thespringshotel.com
**Map ref:** 3, SU68
**Directions:** Off A4074 (Oxford–Reading road) onto
B4009 (Goring). Hotel approx 1m on right

**Rooms:** 32, S £95–£120 D £110–£135 **Facilities:** ⤳ SaunaSTV Wi-Fi in bedrooms **Parking:** 150

The Springs, built in 1874, is a fine example of a Victorian country house, one of the first to be built in Mock-Tudor style. Standing in rolling parkland, possibly on the site of a Roman forum, it overlooks the Thames Valley and a lake fed by a million gallons of spring water daily. After several changes of ownership, it was bought in 1973 by Ian Gillan of rock group Deep Purple, who set about restoring its oak-panelled rooms and carved fireplaces and turning it into a luxury hotel. Its present owners acquired it in 2001, embarking on a continuing programme of further improvements, including luxury suites, heated outdoor pool, an excellent 18-hole golf course, croquet lawn and putting green. Public rooms include the beamed, richly carpeted lounge, and the Lord Nelson dining room, which has a wonderful decorative ceiling copied from a now-destroyed original in James I's Scottish hunting lodge. Among the variously sized en suite bedrooms are two bridal suites with four-poster beds. The bedrooms are all supremely comfortable and very well equipped. The lattice-windowed Lakeside Restaurant offers an award-winning, daily changing menu of dishes such as saltmarsh lamb, 28 day hung beef,and pumpkin and oyster mushroom risotto.

**Recommended in the area**

Ridgeway Path; Child Beale; Stonor Park

# RUTLAND

Rutland Water

# Hambleton Hall

★★★★ ◉◉◉◉ CHH

Address: Hambleton, OAKHAM  LE15 8TH
Tel:       01572 756991
Fax:       01572 724721
Email:     hotel@hambletonhall.com
Website: www.hambletonhall.com
Map ref: 3, SK80
Directions: 3m E off A606
Rooms: 17, S £170–£200 D £200–£600
Facilities: ⊀ Tennis STV Wi-Fi available Parking: 40

This family-run hotel is a magnificent Victorian house, standing
in its own beautiful gardens and enjoying fine views over Rutland
Water, the largest man-made lake in Western Europe. Its rooms are highly individual in character,
furnished with fine fabrics and sumptuous furniture, many having hand-stencilled walls. The Master
rooms are the largest, and many of them have wonderful views overlooking the lake. The smaller
Standard rooms overlook the hotel's lawn and handsome cedar trees. The most luxurious rooms are
in the two-bedroom Croquet Pavilion, a folly 50 yards from the main building. In the hotel's public
areas there are open fireplaces in the cosy bar and sumptuous drawing-room. The restaurant serves
outstanding cuisine, using local produce as far as possible. The food incorporates fresh and seasonal
ingredients, and menus change frequently. Three private dining-rooms are available. Each month there
is a Wine Dinner. Adventurous residents can participate in rock-climbing, windsurfing or canoeing in
the local area. The hotel is a popular venue for business meetings, held in the ground floor of the main
house. Full business support is available, including secretarial, fax, OHP, email and other services. The
hotel is popular for prestigious private functions of all kinds, including wedding parties.

**Recommended in the area**

Burghley House; Rutland Water; Grimsthorpe Castle; Kelmarsh Hall Gardens

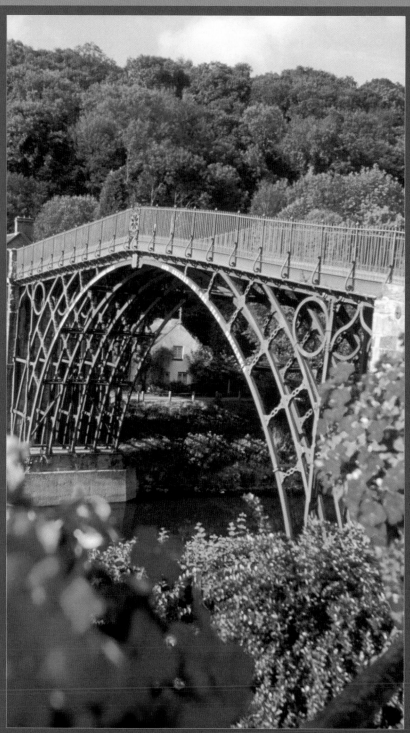

Ironbridge

# Best Western Wynnstay Hotel

★★★  87% ◉◉ HL

**Address:** Church Street, OSWESTRY  SY11 2SZ
**Tel:**  01691 655261
**Fax:**  01691 670606
**Email:**  info@wynnstayhotel.com
**Website:** www.wynnstayhotel.com
**Map ref:** 5, SJ22
**Directions:** B4083 to town, fork left at Honda Garage, right at lights. Hotel opposite church
**Rooms:** 34, S £60–£85 D £77–£160 **Facilities:** ⊗
Sauna Jacuzzi Solarium Gym STV Wi-Fi in bedrooms Conference and Banqueting **Parking:** 80

Once a coaching inn and posting house on the London–Holyhead and Liverpool–Cardiff routes, this largely Georgian property is entered from the street through an imposing four-columned portico. Elegant public areas include the former Coach House, now a health, leisure and beauty centre with gym, Finnish sauna, aromatic steam room, 10-person jet spa, pool, spray tan booth, sun shower and 3 purpose built beauty therapy rooms offering an extensive range of spa treatments. The rooms are complete with private facilities including welcome tray, digital TVs , modem points, Wi-Fi internet connection, trouser press and hairdryer. There are family rooms and eight executive rooms which have various individual features, including four poster and king size beds, whirlpool baths and sitting room. The Four Seasons Restaurant which prides itself on its use of fresh and local ingedients, offers an eclectic mix of dishes created and developed by the head chef, ranging from the traditional roast to a balance of lighter more creative dishes of an international appeal. The Pavilion Lounge Bar also offers excellent bar meals both at lunch and dinner, seven days a week. A new addition, Wilson's Wine Bar, is the ideal location for pre dinner drinks or to spend an enjoyable evening with friends

**Recommended in the area**

Chirk Castle; Shrewsbury; Chester

# Prince Rupert Hotel

★★★ 82% HL

**Address:** Butcher Row, SHREWSBURY SY1 1UQ
**Tel:** 01743 499955
**Fax:** 01743 357306
**Email:** reservations@prince-rupert-hotel.co.uk
**Website:** www.prince-rupert-hotel.co.uk
**Map ref:** 2, SJ41
**Directions:** Follow town centre signs, over English Bridge & Wyle Cop Hill. Right into Fish St, 200yds
**Rooms:** 70, S £75 D £105 **Facilities:** Sauna Jacuzzi Gym Wi-Fi in bedrooms **Parking:** 70 **Notes:** ⊗ in bedrooms

Situated in the heart of medieval Shrewsbury, this privately owned hotel is the former home of Prince Rupert, grandson of James I. Surrounded by cobblestone streets and Tudor buildings, it stands cheek-by-jowl with the town's main attractions. Many bedrooms, including the 12th-century Mansion House Suites (some with four-poster canopy bed) and 15th-century Tudor Suites, retain exposed beams and other original features. All are en suite and tastefully furnished with pocket-sprung beds, fluffy towels, velvet-textured blankets, hair dryer and welcome tray. The rooms at the front have views of the historic and famous St. Alkmunds Square, while many at the rear overlook the Mansion House courtyard garden. Wi-Fi extends to all, as well as to public areas and conference suites. For dining, head for the newly refurbished Royalist Restaurant, featuring an à la carte menu which focuses on fresh seasonal produce; the oak-panelled Chambers Brasserie serves typical British food, and the oak beamed La Trattoria – just three minutes' walk away – is, of course, Italian. Camellias Tea Rooms offers relaxation to the sound of a grand piano. The health suite includes a fully equipped Nautilus weights room, Jacuzzi, sauna and steam shower. Guests may also try to snooker each other on a full-size table.

**Recommended in the area**

Shrewsbury Abbey and Castle; Ironbridge Gorge; Stokesay Castle

Shrewsbury

# Old Vicarage Hotel

★★★ ◉◉◉ HL

**Address:** Worfield, WORFIELD  WV15 5JZ
**Tel:** 01746 716497
**Fax:** 01746 716552
**Email:** admin@the-old-vicarage.demon.co.uk
**Website:** www.oldvicarageworfield.com
**Map ref:** 2, SO79
**Directions:** Off A454 between Bridgnorth &
Wolverhampton, 5m S of Telford's southern
business area
**Rooms:** 14, S £85–£115 D £99.50–£180 **Facilities:** Wi-Fi available **Parking:** 30

This small, privately owned hotel, formerly an Edwardian vicarage, offers individually styled rooms with antique furniture; one has a four-poster bed and those in the Coach House annexe have their own private gardens. In the Orangery Restaurant, with its fine country views, diners can enjoy a modern British treatment of seasonal local produce, with a fine wine list and cheeseboard. Conference capacity is up to 20, and the hotel and gardens provide unforgettable surroundings for wedding receptions.

**Recommended in the area**

Ironbridge Gorge (World Heritage Site); Severn Valley Railway; David Austin Roses

# SOMERSET

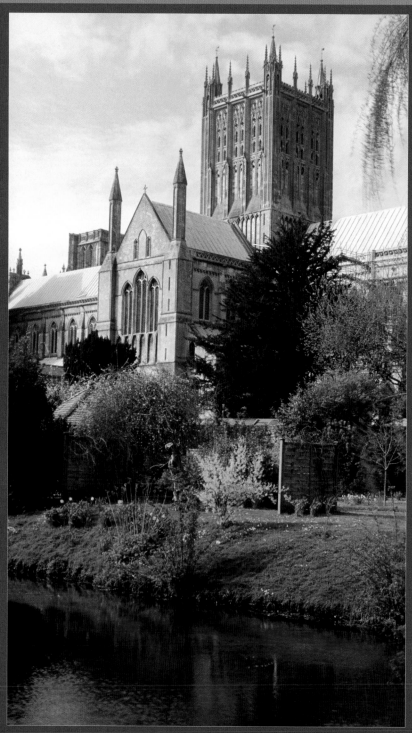

Wells Cathedral

# The Bath Priory Hotel Restaurant & Spa

★★★★ ◉◉◉ HL

| | |
|---|---|
| Address: | Weston Road, |
| | BATH BA1 2XT |
| Tel: | 01225 331922 |
| Fax: | 01225 448276 |
| Email: | mail@thebathpriory.co.uk |
| Website: | www.thebathpriory.co.uk |
| Map ref: | 2, ST76 |

Directions: Adjacent to Victoria Park

Rooms: 27, S  D £200–£360 Facilities: ☯ ↻ Sauna Jacuzzi Solarium Gym STV Wi-Fi in bedrooms Parking: 40 Notes: ⊗ in bedrooms

Every bit the country house hotel, this Gothic-style, former private residence stands discreetly behind high walls in a quiet tree-lined road close to the historic city centre. Since 1994, Andrew and Christina Brownsword have tastefully and lovingly refurbished it, acquiring along the way an extensive collection of paintings and fine art for the sumptuous public rooms. The en suite bedrooms are luxurious and well proportioned, with most rooms enjoying views over the south-facing four acres of landscaped gardens. Each room is named after a flower: Carnation, for example, has a dressing room and a four-poster, while Heather and Lilac have beautiful marble bathrooms and small balconies above the gardens. Head Chef Chris Horridge's cuisine is prepared from carefully sourced ingredients and is complemented by an impressive wine list. His passion shines through in the dishes he creates, with more than a nod to former mentor, Raymond Blanc. Despite Bath's many attractions the hotel's award-winning gardens and luxurious health and leisure Garden Spa, could prove quite a diversion.

Recommended in the area

Thermae Bath Spa; Roman Baths; Bath Abbey

The Circus, Bath

# Best Western The Cliffe Hotel

★★★   85% ◉ HL

Address:   Cliffe Drive, Crowe Hill, Limpley Stoke,
           BATH  BA2 7FY
Tel:       01225 723226
Email:     cliffe@bestwestern.co.uk
Website:   www.bw-cliffehotel.co.uk
Map ref:   2, ST76
Directions: A36 S from Bath onto B3108 at lights
left towards Bradford-on-Avon,  0.5m. Right before
bridge through village, hotel on right

Rooms: 11, S £107-£162 D £130-£180 Facilities: ⤲ STV Wi-Fi in bedrooms Parking: 20

The peace and tranquillity here is not surprising, given its setting in over three acres of woodland, with spectacular views over the Avon Valley. Individually styled bedrooms include two with four-posters and one with whirlpool bath, and after a delicious meal in the AA Rosette-awarded restaurant, you can relax in the comfortable lounge. A small meeting room is available. A heated outdoor pool is open from June to September, weather permitting, and canal day boats and bikes can be hired locally.

Recommended in the area

World Heritage City of Bath; Lacock Abbey and Village (NT); Westwood Manor (NT)

# Dukes Hotel

★★★  82%  SHL

Address: Great Pulteney Street, BATH  BA2 4DN
Tel:       01225 787960
Fax:       01225 787961
Email:     info@dukesbath.co.uk
Website:   www.dukesbath.co.uk
Map ref:   2, ST76
Directions: M4 junct 18 onto A46. At Bath turn left
towards A36, right at next lights and right again onto
Great Pulteney St
Rooms: 17, S £100–£125 D £135–£225

An expertly restored, bow-fronted, Grade I-listed Georgian town house where the rooms are decorated with period furniture, fine fabrics, prints and portraits. Surviving original plasterwork includes delicate features such as Adams-style urns and floral swags. In winter a blazing log fire in the lounge gives a warm welcome, while in summer the peaceful courtyard terrace, with a sparkling fountain, is perfect for a relaxing meal or drink. The en suite bedrooms and six suites (two with four-posters) have been restored to their original spacious dimensions. Many have enormous sash windows and splendid views over Great Pulteney Street, the Bath skyline or the surrounding countryside. Each differs in size and design, some Georgian themed, others more contemporary. All have bath and/or power shower, large fluffy towels and bathrobes, digital TV and hairdryers. The refurbished Cavendish Restaurant and Bar offers chef Fran Shell's modern British seasonal cooking, for which he sources locally grown and reared organic and free range produce. A fixed-price lunch menu offers two or three courses and the dinner menu is à la carte. There are two smaller, more intimate, dining rooms which can be reserved for private receptions.

Recommended in the area

Thermae Bath Spa; Roman Baths; Royal Crescent and Circus

# The Queensberry Hotel

★★★ ◉◉ HL

Address: Russell Street, BATH  BA1 2QF
Tel:      01225 447928
Fax:      01225 446065
Email:    reservations@thequeensberry.co.uk
Website: www.thequeensberry.co.uk
Map ref: 2, ST76
Directions: 100mtrs from the Assembly Rooms
Rooms: 29, S £120–£420 D £120–£420
Facilities: Wi-Fi available Parking: 6
Notes: ⊗ in bedrooms

Four Georgian townhouses form this charming hotel, which is located in a quiet residential street close to the centre of this beautiful city, and run by husband and wife team Laurence and Helen Beere. It is the only contemporary boutique hotel in Bath, and has a choice of sumptuously furnished drawing rooms, an inviting bar and secluded terraced gardens. The spacious bedrooms are individually designed, harmoniously combining up-to-date comfort with original features. Expect marble bathrooms, deep armchairs, flat screen television, DAB radio, CD player and luxurious White Company toiletries. The stylish Olive Tree restaurant specialises in contemporary British cuisine with Mediterranean influences, and the kitchen has a firm commitment to locally produced ingredients and local suppliers. Main courses might include courgette and aubergine charlotte, with onion ravioli and olive and caper dressing, as a vegetarian option, alongside pan-fried sea bass with creamed wild mushrooms, lettuce, pancetta and croutons; or roast loin of venison with a beetroot and apple pasty and port wine sauce. Start and finish with the likes of galantine of wood pigeon, duck and rainbow chard, with spiced gooseberry chutney; and dark chocolate panacotta with griottine cherries and nougatine.
Recommended in the area

Thermae Bath Spa; Beckford's Tower; Claverton Pumping Station

# The Royal Crescent Hotel

★★★★★ 84% HL

**Address:** 16 Royal Crescent, BATH BA1 2LS
**Tel:** 01225 823333
**Fax:** 01225 339401
**Email:** info@royalcrescent.co.uk
**Website:** www.vonessenhotels.co.uk
**Map ref:** 2, ST76
**Directions:** From A4, right at lights. 2nd left onto Bennett St. Continue into The Circus, 2nd exit onto Brock St

**Rooms:** 45, D £245–£865 **Facilities:** ⊛ Sauna Gym STV Wi-Fi available **Parking:** 10

John Wood the Younger's masterpiece of fine Georgian architecture provides the setting for this elegant hotel in the centre of the world-famous Royal Crescent. Spacious, individually designed bedrooms, some of which are named after personalities connected with Bath, such as Jane Austen and Sir Thomas Gainsborough. Each has a luxuriously appointed en suite bathroom, and is furnished with antiques and graced with freshly cut flowers. Most rooms enjoy lovely views over the surrounding gardens and lawns. The award-winning Dower House Restaurant's three distinctively designed areas begin with a naturally lit dining area overlooking a garden so secluded that secret might be a better word. From a central zone, with a stunning central banquette and working fire, mahogany doors lead to the lobby, with works by contemporary artists. Beyond lies the rear dining space with a huge art installation of natural seaweed in crystal. In summer months the sunny terrace and manicured lawns are the perfect setting. The signature dish of quail tart with creamed leeks and Puy lentils features on a world-influenced contemporary British menu. For real style, why not enjoy a Champagne cruise along the Kennet and Avon waterway in Lady Sophina, the hotel's fine 1923 former River Thames launch.

**Recommended in the area**

Thermae Bath Spa; The Cotswolds; Longleat

# Ash House Country Hotel

★★★ 77% ⬢ CHH

Address: 41 Main Street, Ash, MARTOCK
          TA12 6PB
Tel:       01935 822036
Email:     reception@ashhousecountryhotel.co.uk
Website: www.ashhousecountryhotel.co.uk
Map ref: 2, ST41
Directions: Off A303 at Tintinhull Forts junct and left at top of slip road. 0.5m into Ash, on right opposite Ash recreation ground
Rooms: 9, S £60–£75 D £95–£120 Facilities: STV Parking: 35 Notes: ⊗ in bedrooms

This listed Georgian country house, set in an acre and a half of beautiful mature gardens, has been carefully restored to provide individually furnished bedrooms which, while offering modern comforts, retain the grace and elegance of earlier times. Modern British cuisine is served in the light and airy Conservatory Restaurant overlooking the floodlit garden, or in the main dining room – particularly snug when its log fire blazes. Although small, Ash House is licensed to hold civil weddings.
Recommended in the area
Montacute House; East Lambrook Manor Gardens; Fleet Air Arm Museum

# Charlton House

★★★★ ⬢⬢ CHH

Address: Charlton Road, SHEPTON MALLET,
          Nr Bath BA4 4PR
Tel:       01749 342008
Fax:       01749 346362
Email:     enquiry@charltonhouse.com
Website: www.charltonhouse.com
Map ref: 2, ST64
Directions: On A361 towards Frome, 1m from town centre
Rooms: 26, S £140–£290 D £180–£465 Facilities: Sauna Gym STV Wi-Fi available Parking: 70

Charlton House is just about as far away from the stuffy, formal country house of old as you can get. So say owners Roger Saul, founder of the luxury Mulberry brand, and his wife, Monty. Fine fabrics and furnishings are a feature throughout, and the bedrooms, each equipped with the latest technology, are full of character. The highly regarded restaurant is backed by the Sauls' enthusiastically stocked wine cellar. Monty's spa offers treatments and therapies, while The Orangery is perfect for special events.
Recommended in the area
Cheddar Gorge; Stourhead; Wells Cathedral

Cheddar Gorge

# Bindon Country House Hotel & Restaurant

★★★ ◎◎ CHH

**Address:** Langford Budville, WELLINGTON TA21 0RU

**Tel:** 01823 400070

**Email:** stay@bindon.com

**Website:** www.bindon.com

**Map ref:** 2, ST12

**Directions:** From Wellington B3187 to Langford Budville, through village, r towards Wiveliscombe, r at junct, pass Bindon Farm, r after 450yds

**Rooms:** 12, S £95–£145 D £115–£215 **Facilities:** ↘ Tennis  Wi-Fi in bedrooms **Parking:** 30

This lovely rural retreat occupies a delightful 17th-century house, and each of the bedrooms and suites have an individual style and charm, with beautiful co-ordinating fabrics and fine furniture. The bathrooms each have a large bath with overhead shower and Molton Brown products. Dining is a real treat here, with modern British cuisine that is unpretentious yet artistically presented and full of flavour.

**Recommended in the area**

Blackdown Hills; Taunton; Sheppy's Cider Farm Centre

**203**

# Lanes

★★★   79% ◉ HL

**Address:** West Coker, YEOVIL  BA22 9AJ
**Tel:**       01935 862555
**Fax:**       01935 864260
**Email:**     stay@laneshotel.net
**Website:**  www.laneshotel.net.
**Map ref:**  2, ST51
**Directions:** 2m W of Yeovil on A30 in centre of West Coker
**Rooms:** 27, S £88 D £110 **Facilities:** Sauna Jacuzzi Gym Wi-Fi available **Parking:** 40 **Notes:** ⊗ in bedrooms

At the heart of an attractive village of mellow hamstone cottages, within a conservation area, this fine former rectory is set in its own walled and landscaped gardens. The whole building has been recently refurbished with modern additions, but it retains its country-house elegance and style. The bedrooms are decorated in restful tones, and have contemporary furnishings of a high standard. Each room's facilities include an en suite bathroom, mini-bar, digital television, DVD player, and broadband internet connection, and accommodation on offer includes a penthouse suite and an apartment. The hotel's brasserie-style restaurant is a modern addition to the building – bright, spacious and airy, with large windows and high ceilings, and with original paintings on the walls. The menu makes much use of local produce in season, and changes regularly. Guests and local people mingle in the Piano Bar, with its open fire and deep leather armchairs, where an extensive list of wines, spirits and beers is on offer. The hotel has its own leisure suite, available exclusively for residents, with a spa pool, sauna and gym. West Coker is well placed for excursions, with the historic towns of Yeovil and Sherborne close by, and within easy reach of the many attractions of Somerset, while the Dorset coast is only 20 miles away.

**Recommended in the area**

Lyme Regis; Yeovilton Fleet Air Arm Museum; Montacute House and Gardens.

# STAFFORDSHIRE

Cannock Chase

War Memorial and Stoke Minster, Stoke-on-Trent

# Three Queens Hotel

★★★   81% ◉ HL

Address:   One Bridge Street,
            BURTON UPON TRENT DE14 1SY
Tel:        01283 523800
Fax:        01283 523823
Email:      hotel@threequeenshotel.co.uk
Website:   www.threequeenshotel.co.uk
Map ref:   3, SK22
Directions: Located on A511 in Burton Upon Trent at
the junct of Bridge St & High St. **Rooms:** 38,
S £55–£99 D £65–£120 **Facilities:** STV Wi-Fi in bedrooms **Parking:** 40 **Notes:** ⊗ in bedrooms

Parts of this historic hotel date back to the 16th century. Bedrooms and suites have many facilities, including en suite bathrooms, satellite TV, internet access, hot drinks supplies, and service extends to bringing morning tea/coffee to rooms, and washing midweek guests' cars. The Grill Room offers excellent AA-Rosetted food with a wide-ranging à la carte menu. Air-conditioned meeting and conference facilities are available and delegate packages can be arranged.

Recommended in the area

Alton Towers; Staffordshire and Derbyshire Moorlands National Forest; Museum of Brewing

# Swinfen Hall Hotel

★★★★ ◎◎ HL

Address: Swinfen, LICHFIELD WS14 9RE
Tel: 01543 481494
Fax: 01543 480341
Email: info@swinfenhallhotel.co.uk
Website: www.swinfenhallhotel.co.uk
Map ref: 3, SK10
Directions: Set back from A38, 2.5m outside Lichfield, towards Birmingham
Rooms: 17, S £125 D £145–£275 Facilities: Tennis STV Wi-Fi in bedrooms Parking: 80 Notes: ⊗ in bedrooms

Standing grandly at the end of a long driveway, this lavishly decorated Georgian mansion is surrounded by 100 acres of deer park, formal gardens, meadows and woodland. Painstakingly restored by the present owners, the public rooms are particularly stylish, with intricately carved ceilings and impressive oil portraits. First floor guest rooms retain their tall sash windows and other period features, while those on the second floor (the former servants' quarters) are smaller and more contemporary. All provide goose-down duvets, Egyptian cotton sheets, large white fluffy towels and free Wi-Fi, satellite TV, DVD and well-stocked hospitality tray. Plans are currently in hand to convert a derelict wing and outbuildings into additional bedrooms and leisure facilities. The oak-panelled Four Seasons Restaurant has a reputation for fine dining, while lighter meals may be eaten in the bar or on the cocktail terrace. Local produce is used wherever possible, including fruit, vegetables and herbs from the Victorian walled garden, while home-reared organic venison is making its first appearance on the menu. The menus are complemented by frequently changing wines bought directly from vineyards, through specialist merchants and at auction. And if you need them for walking there's a good stock of Wellington boots!

Recommended in the area

Lichfield Cathedral; Shugborough Hall; The Potteries

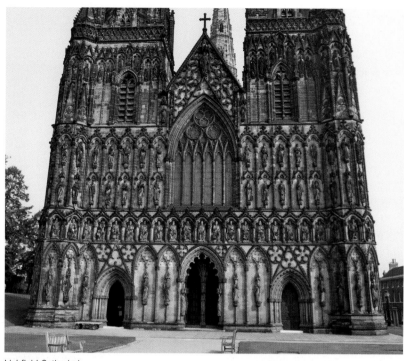

Lichfield Cathedral

# Best Western Stoke-on-Trent Moat House

★★★★  76%  HL

Address:  Etruria Hall, Festival Way, Etruria,
STOKE-ON-TRENT ST1 5BQ
Tel:  0870 225 4601
Email:  reservations.stoke@qmh-hotels.com
Website:  www.bestwestern.co.uk
Map ref:  7, SJ84
Directions: M6/A500. Turn off at A53 Festival Park
Rooms: 147, S £64–£129 D £64–£129 Facilities: ☒ Sauna Jacuzzi Solarium  Gym STV Wi-Fi in
bedrooms Parking: 350 Notes: ☒ in bedrooms

Not only is this hotel perfectly placed for visiting the Potteries, it is actually built within the grounds of
Etruria Hall, the former home of Josiah Wedgwood, which is now a conference centre. The hotel has
a range of leisure facilities and a varied menu is on offer in the Viva Bar and Brasserie. The bedrooms,
which include family rooms and spacious suites, are decorated in contemporary style.
Recommended in the area
Etruria Industrial Museum; Wedgwood Visitor Centre; Gladstone Pottery Museum

# SUFFOLK

Dunwich beach

# Wentworth Hotel

★★★   86% ◉◉ HL

Address: Wentworth Road, ALDEBURGH  IP15 5BD
Tel:      01728 452312
Fax:      01728 454343
Email:   stay@wentworth-aldeburgh.co.uk
Website: www.wentworth-aldeburgh.com
Map ref: 4, TM45
Directions: off A12 onto A1094, 6m to Aldeburgh,
with church on left and left at bottom of hill
Rooms: 35, S £65–£99 D £136–£234
Facilities: Wi-Fi available Parking: 30

This triple-gabled hotel has been managed by the Pritt family since 1920, and this continuous thread is responsible for the fact that the Wentworth is everything a seaside hotel should be. The attractive and well-maintained public rooms include three lounges furnished with comfortable chairs and sofas, which are sunny spots in summer and cosy places to relax by an open fire in winter. Outside are two sea-facing gardens in which to soak up the sun with a morning coffee, light lunch or cream tea. Many of the regularly refurbished en suite bedrooms have good views of the North Sea, for which the hotel thoughtfully provides binoculars. Seven rooms in Darfield House, just opposite the main building, are particularly spacious and well appointed. For those who find stairs difficult (there's no lift) there are five ground floor rooms. Room sizes and outlook do vary, and these differences are reflected in the tariff. . You can start the day here with a locally smoked kipper, as part of your 'full-house' cooked breakfast. At lunchtime, the terrace bar menu offers a wide choice, from a fresh crab sandwich to traditional cod and chips, and the elegant candlelit restaurant has a daily changing dinner menu based on fresh local produce.

Recommended in the area

Minsmere (RSPB) Reserve; Snape Maltings (Aldeburgh Festival); Suffolk Heritage Coast

# The Bildeston Crown

★★★   85% ◉◉◉ HL

Address: 104 High Street, BILDESTON,
         Ipswich IP7 7EB
Tel:     01449 740510
Fax:     01449 741843
Email:   hayley@thebildestoncrown.co.uk
Website: www.thebildestoncrown.co.uk
Map ref: 4, TL94
Directions: B1070 to Hadleigh. At t-junct turn left
onto A1141, then right onto B1115. Hotel 0.5m
Rooms: 10, S £60–£90 D £110–£170 Facilities: STV Wi-Fi in bedrooms Parking: 30

This small and intimate hotel is a coaching inn with its roots in the 15th century. Its public areas
retain much of its period character, but it has been refurbished to the highest modern standards.
The individually styled en suite bedrooms have outstanding facilities. The restaurant, furnished with
dark woods and leather furniture, offers both traditional and modern cuisine based on produce locally
sourced in Suffolk and neighbouring counties. There is also a private dining-room.
Recommended in the area
Kentwell Hall; Lavenham village; Christchurch Park, Ipswich

# Best Western Priory Hotel

★★★   81% ◉◉ HL

Address: Mildenhall Road,
         BURY ST EDMUNDS IP32 6EH
Tel:     01284 766181
Fax:     01284 767604
Email:   reservations@prioryhotel.co.uk
Website: www.prioryhotel.co.uk
Map ref: 4, TL86
Directions: From A14 take Bury St Edmunds W slip
road. Follow signs to Brandon. At mini-rdbt turn right
Rooms: 39 Facilities: STV Wi-Fi in bedrooms (connection charge) Parking: 60

In a delightful town surrounded by pretty countryside, this is a charming hotel with spacious, individually
designed bedrooms. All include an en-suite bathroom, 10-channel TV and high speed Wi-Fi. The food
is exceptional with British and European influences. One main course item from a recent menu was
a duo of grilled pork fillet and slow-cooked belly with black truffle mash, wilted spinach, red onion
marmalade and Madeira jus. The gardens are attractively landscaped and car parking is free.
Recommended in the area
St Edmundsbury Cathedral and Abbey Gardens; Greene King Visitors Centre; Ickworth House

# Hintlesham Hall Hotel

★★★★ ◉◉◉ HL

Address: George St, HINTLESHAM, Ipswich IP8 3NS
Tel: 01473 652334
Fax: 01473 652463
Email: reservations@hintleshamhall.com
Website: www.hintleshamhall.com
Map ref: 4, TM04
Directions: 4m W of Ipswich on A1071 to Hadleigh
Rooms: 33, S £120–£165 D £150–£450
Facilities: ⤚ Tennis Gym Parking: 80

Hospitality and service are absolute priorities at this imposing 16th-century, Grade I-listed country house hotel in 175 acres of landscaped gardens and grounds. The building is distinguished by its Georgian additions, most notably the façade, as well as by earlier Stuart interior embellishments. Works of art and antiques abound throughout, particularly in the spacious public rooms and restaurants. Individually decorated bedrooms and suites come in varying shapes, sizes and styles, but consistently applied are their high degree of comfort, tasteful furnishings and thoughtful extras. Wander around the grounds before heading for the grand Salon, largest of the three dining rooms, and Head Chef Alan Ford's well-balanced carte, from which examples include grilled fillet of haddock served in a mussel and clam chowder, and tournedos of beef with braised oxtail and horseradish. Many of the dishes encompass fresh herbs from the famous garden, designed by the late Robert Carrier, who bought the then–derelict Hall in 1972. The award-winning 350-bin wine list includes a generous selection of half-bottles. Health and beauty and other specialist treatments, and a newly equipped gym with helpful instructors, now complement the small but perfectly formed seasonal pool. A championship PGA golf course is adjacent to the Hall.

### Recommended in the area

Constable Country; Aldeburgh; Newmarket Racecourse

River Blyth, Blythburgh

# Swan Hotel

★★★ 80% ◉◉ HL

**Address:** Market Place, SOUTHWOLD  IP18 6EG
**Tel:** 01502 722186
**Email:** swan.hotel@adnams.co.uk
**Website:** www.adnams.co.uk
**Map ref:** 4, TM57
**Directions:** A1095 to Southwold. Hotel in town centre. Parking via archway to left of building
**Rooms:** 42, S £86 D £152 **Parking:** 35

Set on the market place of one of Suffolk's most delightful towns, the Swan dates back to the 14th century, though today it represents a mixture of 18th-century ambience in its public areas and 21st-century comforts in the bedrooms. These range from single rooms to suites, all beautifully and individually furnished. Menus in the restaurant and bar offer interesting, well-constructed dishes, such as the pan-seared calves liver with red onion marmalade, or sautéed fillet of black bream with wilted spinach, roasted garlic and Puy lentil and coriander sauce. Entertainment ranges from literary lunches to wine weekends.

**Recommended in the area**

Suffolk Heritage Coast; RSPB Minsmere Reserve; Suffolk Wildlife Park

# SURREY

River Thames, Hampton Court

# Mercure Burford Bridge Hotel

★★★★  81% ◉◉ HL

**Address:** Burford Bridge, Box Hill,
DORKING RH5 6BX
**Tel:** 01306 884561
**Fax:** 01306 880386
**Email:** h6635@accor.com
**Website:** www.mercure.com
**Map ref:** 3, TQ14
**Directions:** M25 junct 9/A243 towards Dorking,
Hotel within 5m on A24
**Rooms:** 57, S £99 D £109 **Facilities:** ◟ STV Wi-Fi in bedrooms **Parking:** 130 **Notes:** ⊗ in bedrooms

Lord Nelson reputedly canoodled here with Lady Hamilton before heading off for his fatal engagement
with Napoleon at Trafalgar. Whether the lovers knew, or cared, that the original inn was founded in
1254, history doesn't record. The inn obviously marketed itself well because John Keats, Jane Austen,
William Wordsworth, Richard Brinsley Sheridan, Robert Louis Stevenson and Queen Victoria have
all stayed here. Despite all the history, the hotel has an elegant, contemporary feel. It sits below the
famous Box Hill, with the River Mole at the bottom of its extensive gardens. Guests in the beautifully
appointed en suite bedrooms can enjoy satellite TV, iron and board, trouser press, tea- and coffee-
making facilities, mini bar, complimentary mineral water and air-conditioning. The executive rooms
have the extra luxury of an enclosed balcony with stunning views over the gardens as well as bathrobes
and slippers plus a CD and DVD player. The restaurant is open for breakfast, lunch and dinner, with
fixed price, seasonal menus offering English and international cuisine. Local wines feature among
the extensive international selection. The nearest leisure centre is in Dorking and the hotel's outdoor
heated pool is open in summer.

**Recommended in the area**

Polesdon Lacey (NT); RHS Garden Wisley; Denbies Wine Estate

# Runnymede Hotel & Spa

★★★★ 78% HL

Address: Windsor Road, EGHAM TW20 0AG
Tel:     01784 436171
Fax:     01784 436340
Email:   info@runnymedehotel.com
Website: www.runnymedehotel.com
Map ref: 3, TQ07
Directions: M25 junct 13, onto A308 towards Windsor
Rooms: 180, S £222–£330 D £265–£330
Facilities: ⓧ Sauna Jacuzzi Tennis Gym STV Wi-Fi available Parking: 280 Notes: ⊗ in bedrooms

From its peaceful location beside the River Thames, this large modern hotel offers an excellent range of leisure and corporate facilities. Guest rooms are comfortably furnished and offer many delights, from cosy duvets to fast broadband access, while a good few have views of the river. In the Leftbank Restaurant, produce is carefully sourced: organic salmon from the Shetlands, fish and shellfish delivered daily from Brixham, free range eggs from North Devon and Aberdeen Angus beef from Scotland. Local market gardener, Mario, supplies salads, spinach, tomatoes and rocket, and also imports fruit and vegetables from his extended family in Sicily. The result is 'an eclectic fusion' of Mediterranean and British food. An extensive wine list includes some imaginative bins. Informal Charlie Bell's restaurant, named after a 19th-century local lock-keeper, provides everything from a rib-eye steak to a Caesar salad, all prepared in an open kitchen. With its riverside terrace and gardens, The Conservatory is the place for a pot of Earl Grey or a classic cocktail or two. In the health spa swim in the 18-metre pool, relax in the whirlpool bath, saunas or eucalyptus steam room, or work up a sweat in the dance studio, gym or playing tennis.

**Recommended in the area**

Windsor Castle; Legoland; Magna Carta Memorial

# Lythe Hill Hotel & Spa

★★★★   77% ◉◉ HL

**Address:** Petworth Road, HASLEMERE GU27 3BQ
**Tel:**        01428 651251
**Fax:**       01428 644131
**Email:**    lythe@lythehill.co.uk
**Website:** www.lythehill.co.uk
**Map ref:** 3, SU93
**Directions:** Left from High St onto B2131. Hotel 1.25m on right
**Rooms:** 41, S £140–£295 D £140–£295 **Facilities:** 🕲 Sauna
Jacuzzi Tennis Gym Wi-Fi in bedrooms **Parking:** 200

The hotel consists of several buildings, the earliest dating from
the 15th century, set in 30 acres of attractive parkland. The
bedrooms are all individually furnished in keeping with the building. Each bedroom is equipped with
en suite bathrooms, television, and broadband wireless internet access. Some have twin showers and
Jacuzzis. There are five luxury suites in the listed buildings, which retain their original oak beams and
wood panelling. New for 2007 are 31 refurbished bedrooms as well as meeting rooms and public
areas. The Auberge de France restaurant, in the 15th-century building, is an oak-panelled dining-room
and includes a garden room that overlooks the lake and parkland. The cuisine is French-inspired,
but uses the full range of local produce according to season. The wine list has over 200 wines. More
informal dining is offered by the Italian Garden, the Pantry and the Dungeon. The Amarna Spa offers a a
variety of treatment days and breaks and is available to guests together with a complete range of health
and beauty treatments. The hotel can host business conferences, team-building events and private
celebrations. It has a licence for civil wedding ceremonies, using the wedding rooms, the extensive
gardens, and marquees as required.

**Recommended in the area**

Haslemere; Petworth House (NT); Goodwood horse and motor racing; Lurgashall Winery.

# EAST SUSSEX

Fulking Escarpment

# Deans Place

★★★   81% ◉ HL

Address: Seaford Road,
ALFRISTON,
Polegate BN26 5TW
Tel: 01323 870248
Fax: 01323 870918
Email: mail@deansplacehotel.co.uk
Website: www.deansplacehotel.co.uk
Map ref: 4, TQ50
Directions: Off A27, signed Alfriston & Drusillas Zoo
Park. Continue south through village
Rooms: 36, S £74–£120 D £95–£168 Facilities: ⚲ STV Wi-Fi in bedrooms
Parking: 100

Situated in the picturesque village of Alfriston, with its quaint buildings and narrow streets, the privately owned 14th-century Deans Place Hotel is set in four acres of beautifully landscaped gardens and has the rolling South Downs as an outstanding backdrop. This location creates the perfect retreat where experienced and attentive staff provide an atmosphere of comfortable sophistication. Bedrooms have views over the meadow and hills beyond; many overlook the heated swimming pool. Others look out to the garden, croquet lawn and stream. The rosette awarded restaurant offers fine International cuisine, using fresh local produce when available, prepared by the hotel's chef, whose creativity provides a memorable dining experience within a spacious, light atmosphere. The adjacent Friston Bar is the ideal place for meeting friends over a quiet drink in front of a roaring log fire. The large terrace, offers al fresco dining on balmy summer evenings. Deans Place is an ideal base for walkers and there are many routes available in the local area.

**Recommended in the area**

Glyndebourne Opera; Drusillas Zoo; Beachy Head

# The Grand Hotel

★★★★★   85% ◉◉ HL

Address: King Edward's Parade,
         EASTBOURNE BN21 4EQ
Tel:     01323 412345
Email:   reservations@grandeastbourne.com
Website: www.grandeastbourne.com
Map ref: 4, TV69
Directions: On seafront W of Eastbourne, 1m from
railway station
Rooms: 152, S £150–£480 D £180–£510
Facilities: ◉ ↖ Sauna Jacuzzi Solarium Gym STV Parking: 60

Affectionately known as 'The White Palace', the 19th-century Grand stands at Eastbourne's classy
Beachy Head end, across a green from the beach. There are 46 suites, including the Presidential, with
a four-poster and luxurious lounge, and the Penthouse, which like many of the rooms has a panoramic
view of the busy English Channel. The menus created for the Mirabelle and Garden Restaurants have
won many awards. Seventeen conference and meeting rooms cater for all business needs.
Recommended in the area
Drusillas Zoo; Pevensey Castle; Battle Abbey

# Ashdown Park Hotel and Country Club

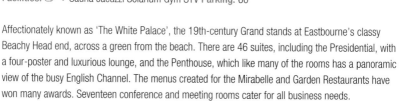

★★★★ ◉◉ HL

Address: Wych Cross, FOREST ROW  RH18 5JR
Tel:     01342 824988
Email:   reservations@ashdownpark.com
Website: www.ashdownpark.com
Map ref: 3, TQ43
Directions: A264 to East Grinstead, then A22 to
Eastbourne, 2m S of Forest Row at Wych Cross traffic
lights. Left to Hartfield, hotel on right 0.75m
Rooms: 106, S £160–£390 D £190–£420 Facilities: ◉ Sauna Jacuzzi Solarium Tennis Gym STV
Wi-Fi available Parking: 200 Notes: ⊗ in bedrooms

In the heart of Ashdown Forest, this magnificent hotel has evolved from an old country mansion. The
bedrooms, all quite different in shape, style and decor, overlook the extensive grounds and each has
modern facilities. The Anderida Restaurant sources ingredients locally or from London markets.
Recommended in the area
Hever Castle; Bluebell Railway; Wakehurst Place

# Newick Park Hotel & Country Estate

★★★ ◉◉ HL

**Address:** NEWICK  BN8 4SB
**Tel:** 01825 723633
**Fax:** 01825 723969
**Email:** bookings@newickpark.co.uk
**Website:** www.newickpark.co.uk
**Map ref:** 3, TQ42
**Directions:** Turn off A272 at Newick Green continue 1m past church and pub. Turn left, hotel 0.25m on the right
**Rooms:** 16, S £125 D £165–£285 **Facilities:** ↖ Tennis STV Wi-Fi available
**Parking:** 50

Newick Park is a beautiful Georgian country house hotel set in over two hundred acres of landscaped gardens and parkland with stunning views across the Sussex countryside towards the South Downs. Being both privately owned and run guests enjoy an outstanding level of service along with complete peace and privacy. The bedrooms are all beautifully furnished with wonderfully comfortable beds and fine antique furniture and the award-winning restaurant excels with fruit and vegetables from the organically run walled garden, and game from the estate. Newick Park is the perfect place for a relaxing, yet luxurious break but for those of you that can't leave the office, complimentary Wi-Fi is available in the reception rooms, along with broadband internet access in all the bedrooms. If you are looking for a more adventurous trip away Quad Biking, Tank Driving and Clay pigeon shooting are also on offer, to name but a few pre-booked activities.

**Recommended in the area**

Glyndebourne Opera; Sheffield Park Gardens; Brighton's Lanes

# The George in Rye

★★★★ 80% HL

**Address:** 98 High Street, RYE  TN31 7JT
**Tel:** 01797 222114
**Fax:** 01797 224065
**Email:** stay@thegeorgeinrye.com
**Website:** www.thegeorgeinrye.com
**Map ref:** 4, TQ92
**Directions:** M20 junct 10, then A2070 to Brenzett then A259 to Rye
**Rooms:** 24, S £95–£125 D £125–£225 **Facilities:** Wi-Fi in bedrooms **Notes:** ⊗ in bedrooms

Occupying a warren of interconnecting buildings dating from the 16th century, The George in Rye recently underwent a major restoration under its new owners, Alex and Katie Clarke. The hotel is now one of the most stunning hideaways on the south coast. All twenty-four rooms and suites are individually designed with antiques, bespoke furniture and work from local artists to create a stylish home-away-from-home for guests. There is thoughtful attention to detail: Vi-spring beds, marble-topped baths, and Frette Italian Bed linen are standard, while Deluxe and Junior Suites are particularly luxurious with some offering feature beds and walk-in showers. In-room Aveda massages are available. In the dining room, a modern Mediterranean menu makes the most of local ingredients, particularly fish from Rye Harbour. Local wines from Kent and Sussex are also celebrated here and in the hotel's own historic pub, The George Tap. The original Regency Ballroom is a beautiful venue for events and weddings, for which The George is licensed. A number of seasonal, special interest breaks are available (including yoga and gastronomic stays). The hotel is in the middle of Rye, one of Britain's best preserved medieval towns; a magical base from which to explore 1066 country.
**Recommended in the area:**
Rye; Camber Sands; Great Dixter House & Gardens; Chapel Down vineyard.

# Dale Hill Hotel & Golf Club

★★★★   82% ◉ HL

Address: TICEHURST, Wadhurst TN5 7DQ
Tel:      01580 200112
Fax:      01580 201249
Email:    info@dalehill.co.uk
Website:  www.dalehill.co.uk
Map ref:  4, TQ63
Directions: M25 junct 5/A21. 5m after Lamberhurst turn R at lights onto B2087 to Flimwell. Hotel 1m on l
Rooms: 35, S £110–£130 D £120–£250
Facilities: ⊕ Sauna Gym STV Parking: 220 Notes: ⊗ in bedrooms

Set in magnificent countryside, with views across the High Weald, this modern hotel is only a short drive from the village. Extensive public rooms include a lounge bar, conservatory brasserie, formal restaurant and the lively Spike Bar, which is where golfers, fresh from playing one of the two 18-hole courses, like to congregate (and commiserate). Dale Hill also has an indoor heated swimming pool and gym. Spacious en suite bedrooms feature radio, TV, direct-dial phones, modem access, hairdryer, tea and coffee facilities, safe and trouser press. Those on the south side of the hotel overlook the golf course, the executive rooms having the extra advantage of balconies. The menu in the elegant AA-Rosette Wealden View Restaurant offers dishes such as braised lamb shank, seared tuna loin and butternut squash and sage ravioli, complemented by an international wine list. For simpler dishes head for The Eighteenth Restaurant, to the Lounge for a traditional Sussex afternoon tea, or to the Club House Bar to catch up on the latest sports scores. The new conference and banqueting suite can accommodate up to 200 delegates. Ian Woosnam, 1991 Masters winner, designed the championship-standard, 6,500-yard golf course; the Old Course attracts the high handicappers.

Recommended in the area

Groombridge Place; Bodiam Castle; Kent & East Sussex Railway

# WEST SUSSEX

Weald and Downland Open Air Museum

# Bailiffscourt Hotel & Spa

★★★ 83% ◉◉ HL

Address: Climbing Street, CLIMPING  BN17 5RW
Tel:      01903 723511
Fax:      01903 718987
Email:    bailiffscourt@hshotels.co.uk
Website: www.hshotels.co.uk
Map ref:  3, SU90
Directions: A259, follow Climping Beach signs. Hotel 0.5m on right
Rooms: 39, S £185–£455 D £205–£510 Facilities: ⌨ ⚲
Sauna Jacuzzi Tennis Gym STV Wi-Fi available Parking: 100

Appearances can be deceptive. From the outside, Bailiffscourt is
a classic, part-thatched, part-tiled manor house, reached down a quiet lane behind unspoilt Climping beach. But actually, it dates from only the 1920s, when Sir Walter Guinness (Lord Moyne) gathered stone and wood from all over England to create the buildings that are Bailiffscourt as a family retreat. Gothic mullioned windows overlook the rose-clad courtyard, whilst narrow passageways lead through a series of intimate lounges and sitting rooms. Many of the public rooms feature open log fires and fine antiques, tapestries and fresh flowers. Bedrooms vary from the atmospheric, with log fires, oak beams and four-poster beds to the spacious and contemporary, located in the grounds. Baylies, the master suite, with its huge vaulted ceiling, open fire and vast bathroom with walk-in shower and twin baths is for that special occasion. Classic European cooking is the mainstay of The Tapestry Restaurant, and during the summer lunch and afternoon tea may be enjoyed in the courtyard. The award-winning spa has heated indoor and outdoor pools, sauna, steam room, hot tub, gym and treatment rooms. Take a walk through the 30-acre grounds to the beach, counting peacocks on the way.

Recommended in the area

Arundel Castle; Chichester; South Downs National Park

# Ockenden Manor

★★★ ◉◉◉ HL

Address: Ockenden Lane, CUCKFIELD  RH17 5LD
Tel:     01444 416111
Fax:     01444 415549
Email:   reservations@ockenden-manor.com
Website: www.hshotels.co.uk
Map ref: 3, TQ32
Directions: A23 towards Brighton. 4.5m left onto
B2115 towards Haywards Heath. Cuckfield 3m.
Ockendon Lane off High St. Hotel at end

Rooms: 22, S £105–£185 D £170–£350 Facilities: STV Wi-Fi available Parking: 43

Tucked away down a little country lane lies this charming Elizabethan manor house. With open views across nine acres of beautifully maintained grounds to the South Downs, the hotel is within easy reach of some of the region's great houses and gardens, as well as raffish Brighton and rather genteel Eastbourne. The public rooms, including an elegant sitting room, retain much of their original character. En suite bedrooms are all individually furnished and provided with satellite TV, direct-dial phone, trouser press, hairdryer and hospitality tray. All are named after members of the two families that have owned the hotel since 1520. Merrick, for example, has its own dining room, while Elizabeth is reached by a private staircase and is apparently home to a 'friendly but sad' ghost. In the wood-panelled Restaurant, with its ornately painted ceiling and stained glass windows, a sample main course might be monkfish noisettes with Parma ham, tomato and basil mayonnaise and new potato salad. A seven-course 'tasting' menu is worth starving in advance for. A small dining room is suitable for semi-private dining, while in summer light meals can be taken on the Conservatory Terrace or in the gardens. Ockenden has a huge wine cellar, sourced from all over the world.

Recommended in the area

Wakehurst Place; Hever Castle; Glyndebourne Opera House

Standen, East Grinstead

# Gravetye Manor Hotel

★★★ ◎◎◎ HL

**Address:** EAST GRINSTEAD  RH19 4LJ
**Tel:** 01342 810567
**Fax:** 01342 810080
**Email:** info@gravetyemanor.co.uk
**Website:** www.gravetyemanor.co.uk
**Map ref:** 3, TQ33
**Directions:** B2028 to Haywards Heath. 1m after
Turners Hill fork left towards Sharpthorne, immediate
1st left into Vowels Lane
**Rooms:** 18, S £110–£175 D £165–£340 **Facilities:** Wi-Fi in bedrooms **Parking:** 35
**Notes:** ⊗ in bedrooms

This Elizabethan mansion, built in 1598, still enjoys its tranquil setting in 35 acres of historic gardens,
surrounded by a thousand acres of forest. Expect great country house hospitality in a timeless
atmosphere – neither trendy, nor stuffy. Relax in oak-panelled day rooms with open fires and fresh
flowers. Daily three-course menus make full use of fruit and vegetables from the kitchen garden.
**Recommended in the area**
Chartwell; Penshurst Place; Standen

# Langshott Manor

★★★ ◍◍ CHH

Address: Langshott Lane,
GATWICK AIRPORT  RH6 9LN
Tel:         01293 786680
Fax:         01293 783905
Email:     admin@langshottmanor.com
Website:  www.langshottmanor.com
Map ref:  3, TQ24
Directions: From A23 take Ladbroke Rd, off
Chequers rdbt to Langshott, after 0.75m hotel
on right
Rooms: 22, S £150–£320 D £170–£320 Facilities: STV Wi-Fi in bedrooms
Parking: 25 Notes: ⊗ in bedrooms

A brick and timber-framed Tudor manor house, with roses around the door, pretty gardens and even a section of moat, Langshott Manor exudes the grandeur of a former age. This, of course, makes it a perfect place to recuperate after a long-haul flight or to spend the night before the honeymoon flight. In fact, you can exclusively hire the entire hotel for a house-party style wedding. Bedrooms are either in the main house or the mews, and all are sumptuous, some with four-poster beds, open fireplaces and perhaps a private deck. There's even a four-poster bath in one of the bathrooms, all of which are individually styled and absolutely stunning. Dining in the Mulberry restaurant is always an occasion, with innovative dishes served in elegant surroundings. Less formal dining is offered in the lounge. Surrounded by beautiful countryside, Langshott Manor is less than 25 miles from London and in very close proximity (8 minutes) to Gatwick Airport. It is an ideal place to relax on your first and last stop in the country.

Recommended in the area

Wakehurst Place Gardens; Chartwell; Denbies Vineyard

# Sofitel London Gatwick

★★★★ 78% HL

Address: North Terminal,
GATWICK AIRPORT RH6 0PH
Tel: 01293 567070
Fax: 01293 567739
Email: h6204-re@accor.com
Website: www.sofitel.com
Map ref: 3, TQ24
Directions: M23 junct 9, follow to 2nd rdbt
Rooms: 500, S £95–£220 D £95–£220
Facilities: Sauna Solarium  Gym STV Wi-fi available Parking: 200 Notes: ⊗ in bedrooms

Who would have thought that staying overnight before or after a flight could be so desirable. The Sofitel also offers handy 'Park and Fly' packages to those on the outbound journey. It is the only hotel directly linked to Gatwick's North Terminal (with a monorail link to South Terminal), and an overnight stay is a holiday in itself. The air-conditioned bedrooms are modern and stylish. Three restaurants include the Oriental, an outpost of chef Ken Hom's group, and there's a café, two bars and 24-hour room service.

Recommended in the area

Brighton; Bluebell Railway; Standen (NT)

# Spread Eagle Hotel and Spa

★★★ 80% ⊛⊛ HL

Address: South Street, MIDHURST  GU29 9NH
Tel: 01730 816911
Fax: 01730 815668
Email: spreadeagle@hshotels.co.uk
Website: www.hshotels.co.uk/spread/spreadeagle-main.htm
Map ref: 3, SU82
Directions: M25 junct 10, A3 to Milford, take A286 to Midhurst. Hotel adjacent to market square
Rooms: 39, S £90–£400 D £99–£400 Facilities: ⊗ Sauna Jacuzzi Gym STV Wi-Fi available
Parking: 75

Offering accommodation since 1430, the hotel was described by Hilaire Belloc as "...that oldest and most revered of all the prime inns of this world". The sloping floors, huge inglenook fireplaces and Tudor bread ovens remain unchanged. The individually styled bedrooms – oak-panelled in the main house – provide up-to-the-minute comforts. The Tapestry Restaurant serves Modern British cuisine.

Recommended in the area

Goodwood Estate; Petworth House; Cowdray Park

# TYNE & WEAR

The Tyne Bridge and the Sage Centre (centre background), Newcastle upon Tyne

# Vermont Hotel

★★★★   79% ◉ HL

Address:   Castle Garth, NEWCASTLE UPON TYNE
           NE1 1RQ
Tel:       0191 233 1010
Fax:       0191 233 1234
Email:     info@vermont-hotel.co.uk
Website:   www.vermont-hotel.com
Map ref:   7, NZ26
Directions: City centre by high level bridge and Castle Keep
Rooms: 101, S £120–£190 D £120–£190
Facilities: Solarium  Gym STV Wi-Fi in bedrooms
Parking: 100

Adjacent to the castle and close to the buzzing Quayside area, this imposing, 12-storey, independently owned hotel enjoys fine views of the Tyne and Millennium Bridges. With an exterior style described as '1930s Manhattan tower', its plush interior is both traditional and contemporary. All bedrooms, including the grand suites, are equipped with three telephones, computer modem fax port, work desk, fully stocked mini-bar, satellite TV, and complimentary tea and coffee facilities. The elegant reception lounge encourages relaxation, while the Bridge Restaurant is open for breakfast, lunch and dinner. Through its windows, the Tyne Bridge looks close enough to reach out and pluck the suspension cables. The Blue Room provides the perfect setting for private dining in luxurious surroundings for up to 80 guests. The informal Redwood Bar is an intimate meeting place serving a large selection of wines and light meals until the early hours. Martha's Bar and Courtyard is popular too, particularly with the 20-somethings. Seven meeting and conference rooms cater as effortlessly for 300 people at a cocktail function as they do for a one-to-one meeting. A Health and Fitness Centre is also available.

**Recommended in the area**

Newcastle Cathedral; Baltic Centre for Contemporary Art; Sage Centre, Gateshead

Royal Shakespeare Theatre, Stratford-upon-Avon

# Ettington Park Hotel

★★★★ ◉◉ HL

Address: ALDERMINSTER, Stratford-upon-Avon
CV37 8BU
Tel: 01789 450123
Fax: 01789 450472
Email: ettingtonpark@handpicked.co.uk
Website: www.handpicked.co.uk
Map ref: 3, SP24
Directions: Off A3400, 5m S of Stratford, just
outside Alderminster

Rooms: 48, S £120–£220 D £220–£390 Facilities: ⊕ Sauna Jacuzzi Tennis STV Wi-Fi available
Parking: 100 Notes: ⊗ in bedrooms

All the delights of the Heart of England are on the doorstep of this grand historic estate, which has been owned by one of the county's oldest families, the Shirleys, for more than 1,000 years. Many alterations were carried out over the centuries, and exploring behind the imposing Gothic exterior is a revelation – even if you don't encounter one of the reputed ghosts (Ettington Park was nominated by the AA as 'The Most Haunted Hotel in Britain'). Be sure to see the stained glass windows in The Chapel. Rooms come in various shapes, sizes and styles, from the stunning 'Feature Suites' to the contemporary, split-level Courtyard Rooms, and some occupy more recent garden wings. The dining experience at Ettington Park combines a formal setting with friendly, well-informed service and a creative menu based largely on seasonal local produce. You might start, for instance, with warm Gressingham duck leg salad with a damson compote, followed by baked fillet of red mullet with a tower of Mediterranean vegetables. There is also a table d'hôte and fixed-price gourmet tasting menu. The approach to feeding children is refreshingly flexible. The hotel has facilities for weddings and conferences.

**Recommended in the area**

Stratford-upon-Avon; Hidcote Manor (NT); The Cotswolds

## Warwickshire

Kenilworth Castle

# Best Western Lea Marston Hotel

★★★★ 75% HL

**Address:** Haunch Lane, LEA MARSTON,
Sutton Coldfield B76 0BY
**Tel:** 01675 470468
**Fax:** 01675 470871
**Email:** info@leamarstonhotel.co.uk
**Website:** www.leamarstonhotel.co.uk
**Map ref:** 3, SP29
**Directions:** M42 junct 9, A4097 to Kingsbury. Hotel
signed 1.5m on right
**Rooms:** 88, S £70–£200 D £90–£220 **Facilities:** ⊗ Sauna Jacuzzi Solarium Tennis Gym
STV Wi-Fi available **Parking:** 220 **Notes:** ⊗ in bedrooms

The Lea Marston is a modern hotel within easy reach of motorway, rail and air links. Lounges are
spacious, airy and comfortable, while all bedrooms and the larger suites come with all the expected
facilites. Enjoy fine dining in the Adderley Restaurant, or the bistro-style menu in Hathaways gastropub.
The hotel offers facilities for conference rooms, weddings and civil ceremonies.
**Recommended in the area**
Drayton Manor Theme Park; Lichfield Cathedral; Staffordshire Regimental Museum; Twycross Zoo

# Menzies Welcombe Hotel Spa & Golf Club

★★★★   85% ◉◉ HL

**Address:** Warwick Road, STRATFORD-UPON-AVON, CV37 0NR
**Tel:** 01789 295252
**Fax:** 01789 266336
**Email:** welcombe@menzieshotels.co.uk
**Website:** www.menzieshotels.co.uk
**Map ref:** 3, SP25
**Directions:** A46 towards Stratford-upon-Avon, at rdbt follow signs for A439. Hotel 3m on right
**Rooms:** 78 **Facilities:** Indoor Pool, Sauna Tennis Gym STV **Parking:** 100 **Notes:** ⊗ in bedrooms

This Jacobean-style house, built in 1866, stands in a 157-acre private estate with extensive formal gardens on the outskirts of Stratford-upon-Avon. The public rooms are good examples, especially the lounge with its wood panelling and ornate marble fireplace, and a bar that resembles nothing so much as a West End gentlemen's club. Bedrooms in the original building are stylish and gracefully proportioned; those in the garden wing are comfortable and thoughtfully equipped. Through the lounge is the two-Rosette, award-winning restaurant, offering a seasonal menu of English and European dishes, made all the more enjoyable by the view over the beautiful Italian gardens, water features and the rolling hills of the Warwickshire countryside beyond. The head chef insists on using only the finest ingredients and seasonal produce for the most satisfying flavours. This luxury resort offers some of the finest leisure facilities in the heart of England, including an 18-hole championship golf course, an all-weather floodlit tennis court, and a luxurious spa with level-deck swimming pool, and thermal experience and treatment rooms. Private function suites are tailor-made for residential meetings.

**Recommended in the area**

Royal Shakespeare Company Theatre; Shakespeare's Birthplace; Warwick Castle

# Ardencote Manor Hotel, Country Club & Spa

★★★★  77% ◉◉ HL

**Address:** Lye Green Road, Claverdon,
WARWICK  CV35 8LT
**Tel:**      01926 843111
**Fax:**     01926 842646
**Email:**   hotel@ardencote.com
**Website:** www.ardencote.com
**Map ref:** 3, SP26
**Directions:** In Claverdon centre follow Shrewley signs off A4189.
Hotel 0.5m on right
**Rooms:** 75, S £105–£110 D £130–£165 **Facilities:** ⊗ Sauna
Jacuzzi Steam Room Tennis Gym STV Wi-Fi available **Parking:** 150 **Notes:** ⊗ in bedrooms

Ardencote Manor Hotel is a privately owned independent venue with high standards of service. It offers tasteful accommodation, fine dining and a wonderful array of leisure amenities including a testing 9 hole golf course and the luxurious Ardencote Spa. Surrounded by landscaped grounds in 82 acres of Warwickshire countryside, the Hotel's proximity to several castles and the attractions of Shakespeare Country makes it an ideal base for a sightseeing break. The award-winning Lodge Restaurant overlooking the lake provides an informal and contemporary interior offering a modern international style of cuisine. The best of fresh local produce is sourced by the Head Chef and his team including Warwickshire's famous Lighthorne Lamb and herbs from the hotel's own Kitchen Garden. Originally built in 1860, the Hotel was extensively and sympathetically extended in 2001 to provide all the modern comforts of a 21st century hotel and hotel spa destination.

**Recommended in the area**

Warwick Castle; Kenilworth Castle; Stratford-Upon-Avon

Gas Street Basin, Birmingham

Council House, Birmingham

# Fairlawns Hotel & Spa

★★★ 85% ◉◉ HL

| | |
|---|---|
| **Address:** | 178 Little Aston Road, |
| | WALSALL WS9 0NU |
| **Tel:** | 01922 455122 |
| **Fax:** | 01922 743148 |
| **Email:** | reception@fairlawns.co.uk |
| **Website:** | www.fairlawns.co.uk |
| **Map ref:** | 3, SP09 |

**Directions:** Off A452 towards Aldridge at x-roads with A454. Hotel 600yds on right

**Rooms:** 59, S £79.5–£165 D £95–£175 **Facilities:** ⓢ Sauna Solarium Tennis Gym STV Wi-Fi in bedrooms **Parking:** 150

The hotel stands in 9 acres of landscaped grounds in a rural location, yet is only 8 miles from central Birmingham. The en suite bedroom interiors range from traditional to modern style. and are very well equipped. The Fairlawns Restaurant has a wide range of menus, and imaginative seafood dishes are a feature of the restaurant.

**Recommended in the area**

Walsall Art Gallery; Lichfield Cathedral; Cannock Chase Area of Outstanding Natural Beauty

# WILTSHIRE

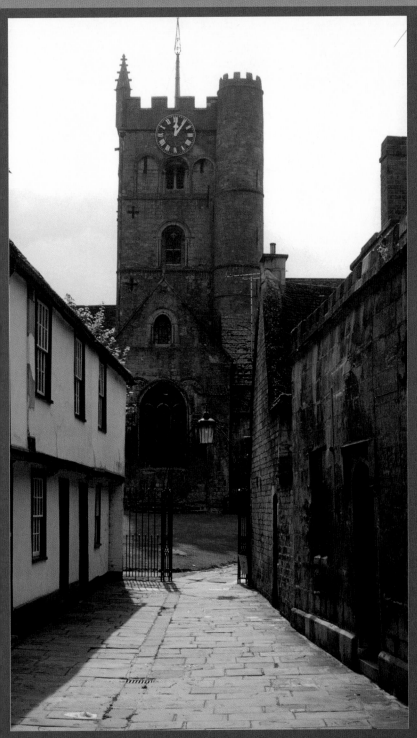

St John's Church, Devizes

Corsham

# Lucknam Park

★★★★★ ◎◎◎ CHH

| | |
|---|---|
| **Address:** | COLERNE, Chippenham SN14 8AZ |
| **Tel:** | 01225 742777 |
| **Fax:** | 01225 743536 |
| **Email:** | reservations@lucknampark.co.uk |
| **Website:** | www.lucknampark.co.uk |
| **Map ref:** | 2, ST87 |

**Directions:** M4 junct 17, A350 to Chippenham, then A420 to Bristol for 3m. At Ford village, left to Colerne, 3m right at x-rds, entrance on right

**Rooms:** 41, D £265–£925 **Facilities:** ⊗ Sauna Jacuzzi Tennis Gym STV Wi-Fi Conf Fac **Parking:** 70

Built in 1720 Lucknam park is set in 500 acres of parkland. Its 41 bedrooms include 13 suites, many with four-posters, and five with separate sitting rooms. The Park Restaurant (Head Chef Hywel Jones) has a Michelin star and 3 AA Rosettes. Only the best local ingredients, organic where possible, are used to produce seasonal dishes, old favourites and new ideas for the finest fine-dining. An equestrian centre and a health and beauty salon are available. A world class new spa will open in late summer 2008.

**Recommended in the area**

Thermae Bath Spa; Jane Austen Centre; Lacock Village (NT)

# WORCESTERSHIRE

Worcester

# Barceló The Lygon Arms

★★★★  78% ◉◉ HL

Address: High Street, BROADWAY  WR12 7DU
Tel:      01386 852255
Fax:     01386 854470
Email:   reservations@thelygonarms.co.uk
Website: www.barcelo-hotels.co.uk/lygonarms
Map ref: 3, SP03
Directions: From Evesham take A44 signed for
Oxford, 5m. Follow Broadway signs. Hotel  on left
Rooms: 77 Facilities: ⊗ Swimming Pool Sauna
Jacuzzi Solarium Tennis Gym STV Parking: 200

In the heart of one of the prettiest villages in the Cotswolds, this beautiful 16th-century former coaching inn has long been renowned as one of the country's finest hotels. Its honey-coloured stone walls, antiques and artefacts exude a sense of history that is matched by its associations with Charles I and Oliver Cromwell. A major project has expertly restored many of the original features, including the flagstone floors, wood panelling and stone mullions in addition to installing modern features. All of the Garden Wing rooms now have air conditioning and Bang and Olufsen flat-screen TVs and sound systems. The Great Hall Restaurant has also been returned to its original Elizabethan style, but with some chic contemporary features. Here guests can sample the creations of head chef Chris Lelliott, who has achieved two AA Rosettes here. Recent menus have featured such imaginative main course concoctions as a fricasse of braised pork cheeks and lobster, with coriander dumplings, lemon grass and ginger sauce. Good standards of service are paramount here, including valet parking and escorting guests to their historic or modern-style room on arrival (with porters to handle the luggage). Amenities include a superb spa, with a retractable glass roof over the indoor pool.

Recommended in the area

The Cotswold Way; Hidcote Manor (NT); Sudeley Castle

# Brockencote Hall Country House Hotel

★★★ ◉◉ HL

**Address:** CHADDESLEY CORBETT DY10 4PY
**Tel:** 01562 777876
**Fax:** 01562 777872
**Email:** info@brockencotehall.com
**Website:** www.brockencotehall.com
**Map ref:** 2, SO87
**Directions:** 0.5m W, off A448, opposite St Cassians Church
**Rooms:** 17, S £96–£140 D £120–£190 **Facilities:** Tennis Wi-Fi throughout **Parking:** 45
**Notes:** ⊗ in bedrooms

This fine mansion stands in 70 acres of landscaped grounds containing a lake and splendid trees, beyond which the Worcestershire countryside extends to the Malvern Hills. Sheep graze within sight of the residents taking tea in the conservatory. The high-ceilinged rooms are furnished in elegant fabrics and furnishings with many period features. Some bedrooms have a four-poster bed and a whirlpool bath. All rooms have en suite facilities, a restful view, satellite television, a telephone and wireless internet access. There are two conference rooms, able to accommodate 10 and 20 delegates respectively. The public rooms are light and airy, and warmed by log fires in the winter. In the elegant chandelier-lit restaurant the outstanding cuisine bears the stamp of the owner's and the head chef's French origins. The cooking also offers a choice of lighter dishes and is supported by an extensive wine cellar. The hotel is licensed for civil wedding ceremonies and is well equipped to host wedding receptions. Brockencote Hall is only 30 minutes from Birmingham, with its international airport.

.Recommended in the area

Ironbridge Gorge; Severn Valley Steam Railway; West Midlands Safari Park

# The Granary Hotel & Restaurant

★★★ 77% ◉ HL

Address: Heath Lane, Shenstone,
KIDDERMINSTER DY10 4BS
Tel: 01562 777535
Email: info@granary-hotel.co.uk
Website: www.granary-hotel.co.uk
Map ref: 2, SO87
Directions: On A450 between Stourbridge &
Worcester, 1m from Kidderminster
Rooms: 18, S £75–£90 D £90–£140 Parking: 96

Amid lovely Worcestershire countryside, with views of the Abberley Hills, this bright and modern hotel is a rural hideaway handy for exploring the Midlands' industrial heritage. Recent investment has given the place a chic contemporary décor, and refurbished the bedrooms and bathrooms (the power showers are terrific). Facilities include complimentary Wi-Fi, and an extra bed or cot can be provided for a small charge. The restaurant, renowned for carvery lunches, supports local produce wherever possible, and the à la carte dinner menu offers such dishes as local pheasant with Madeira and chestnut sauce.
Recommended in the area
Black Country Museum; Severn Valley Railway; West Midlands Safari Park

# The Cottage in the Wood Hotel

★★★ 83% ◉◉ HL

Address: Holywell Road, MALVERN WR14 4LG
Tel: 01684 588860
Email: reception@cottageinthewood.co.uk
Website: www.cottageinthewood.co.uk
Map ref: 2, SO74
Directions: 3m S of Great Malvern off A449, 500yds
N of B4209, on opposite side of road
Rooms: 30, S £79–£109 D £99–£179 Facilities:
STV Wi-Fi available Parking: 40

Spectacularly sited on a hillside with far-reaching views, this family-run hotel is a great base for enjoying the footpaths of the Malvern Hills. The hotel consists of three buildings: the main house has seven modest-sized bedrooms, the restaurant and the bar/lounge; Beech Cottage, more than 100 years older, has four cottage-style bedrooms; and The Pinnacles has 19 rooms, most of which share the best views of all. The restaurant, Outlook, is an ardent supporter of local suppliers and offers such dishes as pot-roasted pheasant with a parcel of confit leg and chestnuts, puréed roots and Anna potatoes.
Recommended in the area
Great Malvern Priory; Eastnor Castle; Worcester

Sign at Kidderminster station on the Severn Valley Railway

# Best Western Abbey Hotel

★★★★ 80% HL

| | |
|---|---|
| **Address:** | Hither Green Lane, Dagnell End Road, REDDITCH B98 9BE |
| **Tel:** | 01527 406600 |
| **Email:** | info@theabbeyhotel.co.uk |
| **Website:** | www.theabbeyhotel.co.uk |
| **Map ref:** | 3, SP06 |

**Directions:** M42 junct 2, A441 to Redditch. End of carriageway turn left (A441), Dagnell End Rd on left. Hotel 600yds on right

**Rooms:** 100, S £79–£129 D £99–£149 **Facilities:** ☒ Sauna Jacuzzi Solarium Gym STV Wi-Fi in bedrooms **Parking:** 200 **Notes:** ☒ in bedrooms

A £2 million investment programme has resulted in the creation of stylish and well-appointed bedrooms and two penthouses in this conveniently located hotel. Bramblings Restaurant offers a choice of freshly prepared dishes; Tawny's is more bistro style. Along with an 18-hole golf course with pro shop, there's a large indoor pool, beauty salon and health club.

**Recommended in the area**

Coughton Court (NT); Severn Valley Railway; Anne Hathaway's Cottage

Bolton Priory, Wharfedale

# Crathorne Hall Hotel

★★★★ ◎◎ HL

Address: CRATHORNE, Yarm TS15 0AR
Tel:      0845 072 7440
Fax:      01642 700814
Email:    crathornehall@handpicked.co.uk
Website:  www.handpicked.co.uk
Map ref:  8, NZ40
Directions: Off A19, take slip road signed
Teesside Airport and Kirklevington, then right
signed Crathorne to hotel
Rooms: 37, S £90–£160 D £120–£200 Facilities: STV Parking: 88

This stately Edwardian mansion, set in glorious grounds on the edge of the Yorkshire moors, was, until 1977, the home of the Dugdale family, one of whom was a minister in Churchill's post-war cabinet. Well connected, the family entertained royalty, politicians, socialites and performance artists amid the same elegance that today's guests can enjoy. One particular treat is to take afternoon tea in the stately Drawing Room, perhaps anticipating a bracing walk before enjoying further culinary treats in the sumptuous dining room. Here, the seasonal menus offer inspired use of the finest local produce, including Grand Reserve beef and Mount Grace Farm duck, olive oil from the hotel group's own groves in Italy and wines produced from their own vineyards. An à la carte meal might start with sweet-cured venison with marinated figs, parsnip and lentil vinaigrette, followed by saddle of Yorkshire hare pie and mash with bitter chocolate sauce, or roasted seabass with red wine risotto. The bedrooms at the hall, including family rooms and suites, have each been endowed with their own character, and have stylish furnishings and décor. They are all equipped with flat-screen TV, DVD and CD players, high-speed internet access and quality toiletries. The hotel is popular for weddings and team-building events.

**Recommended in the area**

North York Moors National Park; The Cleveland Way; Mount Grace Priory

# Rudding Park Hotel & Golf

★★★★ ◎◎ HL

Address: Rudding Park, Follifoot,
HARROGATE HG3 1JH
Tel: 01423 871350
Fax: 01423 872286
Email: reservations@ruddingpark.com
Website: www.ruddingpark.com
Map ref: 7, SE35
Directions: From A61 at rdbt with A658 take York exit and follow signs to Rudding Park
Rooms: 49, S £150–£350 D £180–£350 Facilities: STV Wi-Fi in bedrooms Parking: 150

Since opening as a hotel in 1997, Rudding Park has rapidly won widespread acclaim. Often called 'Yorkshire's Premier Hotel and Golf Resort', it certainly looks the part. Guests can unwind with a drink, a newspaper, or even a board game in the luxurious Mackaness Room. The menu in the AA Rosetted restaurant changes with the season and features as much local produce as possible in either the Clocktower restaurant, bar, conservatory or the terrace.

Recommended in the area

Harewood House; Castle Howard; Jorvik Viking Centre

# Pheasant Hotel

★★★ 78% SHL

Address: Harome, HELMSLEY YO62 5JG
Tel: 01439 771241 (771744 Fax)
Email: reservations@thepheasanthotel.com
Website: www.thepheasanthotel.com
Map ref: 6, SE68
Directions: 2.5m SE, leave A170 after 0.25m. Right signed Harome for further 2m. Hotel opposite church
Rooms: 14, S £85 D £170–£180 Facilities: ☺ STV
Parking: 20

The horse's loss is the modern visitor's gain at this country hotel, converted from two old blacksmith's cottages. Inside is a small oak-beamed bar with a log fire, and a large drawing room and conservatory dining room, both of which open on to the stone-flagged terrace and mill stream. Spacious, comfortable bedrooms, all en suite, face either the village pond, or overlook the courtyard and pretty walled garden. In her kitchen, Tricia Binks produces the best of English dishes, wherever possible using local produce, such as Whitby fish, Yorkshire lamb and Helmsley beef.

Recommended in the area

North Yorks Moors National Park; Rievaulx Abbey; North Yorkshire Moors Railway

# Hob Green Hotel

★★★  82%  CHH

Address: MARKINGTON  HG3 3PJ
Tel:        01423 770031
Fax:       01423 771589
Email:    info@hobgreen.com
Website: www.hobgreen.com
Map ref: 7, SE26
Directions: From A61, 4m N of Harrogate, left at
Wormald Green, follow hotel signs
Rooms: 12, S £98–£118 D £115–£135
Parking: 40

Hob Green is a late 18th-century property standing in beautiful award-winning gardens, surrounded
by rolling countryside. A small country-house hotel, it provides the ideal base for exploring the nearby
Yorkshire Dales and the North York Moors, and is located halfway between the attractive towns of
Harrogate and Ripon. The 12 en suite bedrooms are individually furnished in a traditional English style,
and are fully equipped with television, radio, facilities for making hot drinks, mini-bar, hairdryer, trouser
press and ironing board. One room features a four-poster bed and another has a separate sitting
room. The building retains much of its period character; public rooms are furnished with antiques and
offer lovely views over the valley below. A sun room, with an Oriental theme, leads out onto a terrace
furnished with wrought iron tables and comfortable garden seats. The restaurant makes much use of
seasonal local produce, including fruit and vegetables from the hotel's own Victorian kitchen garden.
Typical dishes include smoked mackerel pâté with warm toast; rolled venison wrapped in back bacon
with plum and port sauce; and white chocolate Bavarian cream with mango coulis. The Butler's Pantry,
adjoining the main dining room, is available for parties of eight to ten.

Recommended in the area

Ripon racecourse; Harrogate; Fountains Abbey; Studley Royal Water Garden

# Best Western Dean Court Hotel

★★★    85% ®® HL

Address: Duncombe Place, YORK  YO1 7EF
Tel:      01904 625082
Fax:      01904 620305
Email:    info@deancourt-york.co.uk
Website:  www.deancourt-york.co.uk
Map ref:  8, SE65
Directions: City centre opposite York Minster
Rooms: 37, S £99–£125 D £130–£220
Facilities: Wi-Fi in bedrooms Parking: 30
Notes: ⊗ in bedrooms

This hotel, located in the very centre of York next to the Minster, has been recently refurbished. The rooms are individually furnished in modern styles, with grades ranging from Single up to Deluxe Double and Four-Poster Deluxe, as well as suites. All rooms have en suite bathrooms, 20-channel television, clock radio/alarm, CD/DVD player, a writing-desk, direct-dial telephone, trouser press, hair dryer and facilities for making tea and coffee. The DCH Restaurant, looking out onto the Minster, offers fine dining, based on fresh local produce. The Court café-bistro and bar offers a more informal all day menu, including sandwiches and snacks, and a clotted-cream and champagne tea. The hotel offers a variety of imaginative add-ons to its normal service, such as "PS – I Love You!" (romantic additions to a night's stay) and "It's Show Time!" (meal, cocktail, etc, added when you book a visit to the nearby Theatre Royal). Other special offers include a two-night short break, a three-day Christmas in York package, and a New Year's Eve dinner-dance. From late November until early January there are disco-dinners and murder-mystery dinners. There are two  conference rooms, the larger able to accommodate up to 50 people in a theatre-style format, or 28 in boardroom format.

Recommended in the area

National Railway Museum; the Yorkshire Wheel; Jorvik Viking Centre; Castle Museum.

Fountains Abbey

# The Grange Hotel

★★★ ◉◉ HL

**Address:** 1 Clifton, YORK  YO30 6AA
**Tel:** 01904 644744
**Email:** info@grangehotel.co.uk
**Website:** www.grangehotel.co.uk
**Map ref:** 8, SE65
**Directions:** On A19 York/Thirsk road, approx 500yds from city centre
**Rooms:** 36, S £117–£270 D £140–£270
**Facilities:** STV Wi-Fi in bedrooms **Parking:** 24

This superbly restored Regency townhouse is in the city but feels just like a warm country house. Top priority is given to attention to detail and efficient room service in the luxuriously appointed en suite bedrooms, including three with four-posters. The award-winning Ivy Brasserie complements the hotel's stylish character, serving classic brasserie dishes, making good use of locally sourced produce wherever possible. The charming Cellar Bar serves lunches and snacks as well as dinner each evening. First class facilities for business meetings, private dining, weddings and receptions are available.

**Recommended in the area**

York Minster; National Railway Museum; Castle Howard

# SOUTH & WEST YORKSHIRE

Yorkshire Sculpture Park, West Bretton

# Best Western Mount Pleasant

★★★★   78% ◉ HL

Address: Great North Road, Rossington,
DONCASTER DN11 0HW
Tel:       01302 868696
Fax:      01302 865130
Email:    reception@mountpleasant.co.uk
Website: www.mountpleasant.co.uk
Map ref: 6, SK69
Directions: On A638 (Great North Road) between
Bawtry & Doncaster
Rooms: 56, S £79–£165 D £99–£190 Facilities: STV Wi-Fi in bedrooms Parking: 140

This charming 18th-century house stands in 100 acres of wooded parkland. Originally a farmhouse on the Rossington Hall Estate, in 1938 it was converted into a hotel by Alice Jenkinson and her husband, Thomas Stocks. Today it is owned and run by their four grandchildren, who make sure it continues to move with the times without compromising its special atmosphere and character. Spacious bedrooms are tastefully decorated and furnished, and offer luxury en suite bathrooms with bath and shower, a choice of bed – double, king, four- or five-poster, wireless internet, direct dial phone, tea- and coffee-making facilities, Sky TV, iron, ironing board and hairdryer. Eight self-catering cottages are popular with visitors staying for extended periods. Public rooms include the newer, but elegant, Garden Restaurant, built with mullioned windows to blend in with the rest of the house, hung with sylvan tapestries and lit by fine chandeliers from Crete. The restaurant was awarded an AA Rosette in 2004 for its seasonal menus prepared with local ingredients, delivered fresh daily. More informal lounges offer light snacks, bar meals and afternoon teas. There are six fully equipped conference rooms, and the hotel is licensed for civil weddings.

Recommended in the area

Doncaster Racecourse; Meadowhall Shopping Centre; Magna Science Adventure Centre

# Best Western Mosborough Hall

★★★  77%  HL

Address:  High Street, Mosborough,
SHEFFIELD  S20 5EA
Tel:  0114 248 4353
Fax:  0114 247 9759
Email:  hotel@mosboroughhall.co.uk
Website:  www.mosboroughhall.co.uk
Map ref:  8, SK49
Directions: M1 junct 30, A6135 towards Sheffield.
Follow Eckington/Mosborough signs 2m. Sharp bend
at top of hill, hotel on right
Rooms: 44, S £75–£100 D £75–£100 Facilities: Wi-Fi in bedrooms Parking: 100

It might be hard to believe that such a secluded spot could exist within such close proximity to Sheffield, but that city has always revelled in the glorious, sometimes wild countryside that lies on its doorstep. It is also very convenient for the renowned Meadowhall shopping centre too. Mosborough Hall is an imposing manor house that dates back to the 15th century, and has an interesting history (and, some say, a resident ghost). It is surrounded by four acres of lovely grounds and gardens. A £4 million refurbishment, to be completed in early spring 2008, will greatly enhance the already outstanding attractions. The bedrooms vary in size, but all are very distinctive. Those in the main building retain their historic character, while others have a very stylish modern design, with restful pastel shades and big, comfortable beds. Some of the rooms feature four-posters. All have en suite  bathrooms, a desk area, internet access, telephone, tea- and coffee-making facilities and cable or satellite TV. There is also a function room, featuring a wall of exposed brick dotted with windows, available for weddings or meetings.

Recommended in the area

Peak District National Park; Sheffield Arena; Meadowhall Shopping Centre;

# Sheffield Park Hotel

★★★★  74%  HL

**Address:** Chesterfield Rd South, SHEFFIELD S8 8BW
**Tel:** 0114 282 9988
**Email:** info.sheffield@pedersenhotels.com
**Website:** www.pedersenhotels.com/
sheffieldparkhotel
**Map ref:** 8, SK49
**Directions:** From N: M1 junct 33, A630 Sheffield.
A61 ring road Chesterfield. After Graves Tennis
Centre follow A61/Chesterfield/M1 South signs. Hotel
200yds on left. From S: M1 junct 29, A617 Chesterfield. Then follow A61/Sheffield signs
**Rooms:** 95, S £60–£135 D £60–£135 **Facilities:** ⊛ Sauna Jacuzzi Gym STV Wi-Fi available
**Parking:** 260 **Notes:** ⊗ in bedrooms

A large modern hotel on the city ring road, within 15 minutes of six, yes six, M1 junctions. The
spacious, individually designed, air-conditioned rooms, suites and executive bedrooms feature
comfortable beds, safe, mini-bar, complimentary mineral water, iron and ironing board, tea- and
coffee- making facilities, hairdryer and high-speed broadband access as standard. There is plenty of
desk area for those who have to work before, perhaps, succumbing to the urge for a drink in the light
and uncluttered Bar and Lounge, or out in the gardens at an umbrella-shaded wooden table. In the
Bar the culinary emphasis is on contemporary European cuisine, while in the Restaurant traditional
English cuisine and a selection of dishes from 'around the world' hold sway. Not sure which to choose
from the fine selection of wines? Ask to try before you buy – an excellent idea. The health and fitness
club, Revive, houses a 12m indoor pool, steam room, sauna, Jacuzzi, exercise studio and gymnasium
featuring the latest Technogym equipment. Conference and private dining facilities are available.

**Recommended in the area**

Peak District National Park; Chatsworth; Meadowhall Shopping Centre

Winnats Pass near Castleton

# Whitley Hall Hotel

★★★ 83% ⚙ HL

Address: Elliott Lane, Grenoside,
SHEFFIELD S35 8NR
Tel: 0114 245 4444
Email: reservations@whitleyhall.com
Website: www.whitleyhall.com
Map ref: 8, SK49
Directions: A61 past football ground, then 2m, r just
before Norfolk Arms, l at bottom of hill. Hotel on l
Rooms: 20, S £89–£110 D £105–£140
Facilities: STV Wi-Fi in bedrooms Parking: 100 Notes: ⊗ in bedrooms

Whitley Hall is an unexpected find just beyond the northern outskirts of Sheffield. Dispel any thoughts of the industrial north, because here is a splendid 16th-century mansion set in tranquil grounds that oozes history. Every modern comfort has been installed, the overall picture is of dark wood, big old fireplaces, leaded lights and oak-panelling, centred on a magnificent staircase. Bedrooms include two with magnificent four-poster beds, and extras include fluffy bath robes, luxury toiletries and a glass of port.

Recommended in the area

Sheffield; Peak District National Park; Magna Science Adventure Centre

# Holdsworth House Hotel

★★★  83% ◎◎ HL

Address: Holdsworth, HALIFAX  HX2 9TG
Tel:       01422 240024
Fax:       01422 245174
Email:    info@holdsworthhouse.co.uk
Website: www.holdsworthhouse.co.uk
Map ref:  7, SE02
Directions: From town centre take A629 Keighley Road. Right at garage up Shay Ln after 1.5m. Hotel on right after 1m
Rooms: 40, S £105–£155 D £120–£175 Facilities: STV Wi-Fi in bedrooms Parking: 60

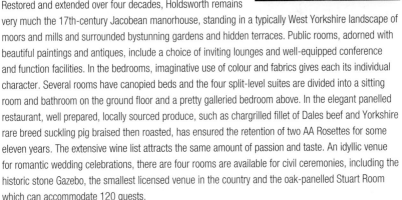

Restored and extended over four decades, Holdsworth remains very much the 17th-century Jacobean manorhouse, standing in a typically West Yorkshire landscape of moors and mills and surrounded by stunning gardens and hidden terraces. Public rooms, adorned with beautiful paintings and antiques, include a choice of inviting lounges and well-equipped conference and function facilities. In the bedrooms, imaginative use of colour and fabrics gives each its individual character. Several rooms have canopied beds and the four split-level suites are divided into a sitting room and bathroom on the ground floor and a pretty galleried bedroom above. In the elegant panelled restaurant, well prepared, locally sourced produce, such as chargrilled fillet of Dales beef and Yorkshire rare breed suckling pig braised then roasted, has ensured the retention of two AA Rosettes for some eleven years. The extensive wine list attracts the same amount of passion and taste. An idyllic venue for romantic wedding celebrations, there are four rooms are available for civil ceremonies, including the historic stone Gazebo, the smallest licensed venue in the country and the oak-panelled Stuart Room which can accommodate 120 guests.

Recommended in the area

National Media Museum; Hockney Gallery; Haworth and Bronte Country

# Best Western Rombalds Hotel & Restaurant

★★★　83%　◉　HL

**Address:** 11 West View, Wells Road,
1ILKLEY  LS29 9JG
**Tel:** 01943 603201
**Email:** reception@rombalds.demon.co.uk
**Website:** www.rombalds.co.uk
**Map ref:** 7, SE14
**Directions:** A65 from Leeds. Left at 3rd main lights,
follow Ilkley Moor signs. Right at HSBC Bank onto Wells Rd. Hotel 600yds on left
**Rooms:** 15, S £75–£109 D £95–£128 **Facilities:** STV Wi-Fi in bedrooms **Parking:** 28

Following Colin and Jo Clarkson's caring, extensive refurbishment Rombalds is a gracefully furnished, classic country house hotel. Day rooms include delightful lounges and a much commended restaurant, offering a pleasing selection of local and international cuisine, and wines from around the world. Ideal for a weekend country break. The hotel also has facilities for wedding receptions.

**Recommended in the area**

Ilkley Moor; Yorkshire Dales National Park; Harewood House

# Wentbridge House Hotel

★★★　79%　◉　HL

**Address:** Wentbridge, PONTEFRACT  WF8 3JJ
**Tel:** 01977 620444
**Fax:** 01977 620148
**Email:** info@wentbridgehouse.co.uk
**Website:** www.wentbridgehouse.co.uk
**Map ref:** 8, SE42
**Directions:** 0.5m off A1 & 4m S of M62 junct 33
onto A1 south
**Rooms:** 41, S £90–£190 D £120–£220
**Facilities:** Wi-Fi in bedrooms **Parking:** 100 **Notes:** ⊗ in bedrooms

This ivy-covered hotel dating from 1700 stands in 20 acres of landscaped gardens in the beautiful Went Valley. Bedrooms are individually designed, with sizes and styles to suit all, from standard doubles to some with traditional English four-posters. Classic and contemporary lunch and dinner dishes, prepared by an award-winning kitchen team, are served in the elegant Fleur de Lys Restaurant, or the more contemporary brasserie and bar. A popular venue for wedding receptions.

**Recommended in the area**

Noskell Priory; Brodsworth Hall and gardens; Leeds city centre

# Wood Hall Hotel and Spa

★★★★ ◉◉ CHH

Address: Trip Lane, Linton, WETHERBY  LS22 4JA
Tel:      01937 587271
Fax:      01937 584353
Email:    woodhall@handpicked.co.uk
Website:  www.handpicked.co.uk
Map ref:  8, SE94
Directions: From Wetherby take Harrogate road N
(A661) for 0.5m, left to Sicklinghall & Linton. Cross
bridge, left to Linton & Wood Hall. Turn right opposite
Windmill Inn, 1.25m to hotel

Rooms: 44 Facilities: ⊛ Jacuzzi Gym STV Wi-Fi available Parking: 200 Notes: ⊗ in bedrooms

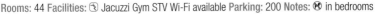

The anticipation that builds as you approach this hotel along its sweeping drive is more than satisfied on arrival at the stately creeper-clad country house. The setting alone is striking, with spectacular views across 100 acres of grounds to the surrounding countryside, which can be enjoyed on the many trails within the grounds. Many of the bedrooms enjoy the views too, and all are luxurious, with stunning elegant contemporary furniture and much use of leather, wood, marble and rich fabrics. Suites are available, and sofa beds in their living rooms make them suitable for family occupation – the 42-inch plasma TVs are also impressive. You will be pampered at the spa with its steam room, hot spa pool and beauty area with a range of luxurious treatments. The hotel restaurant provide a stunning formal setting with a relaxed and laid back atmosphere; here, the hotel is renowned for its traditional Sunday lunches and afternoon teas. The wine list which has evolved over a number of years and contains many familiar names as well as an impressive selection of little-known wines. You may also want to indulge in a glass of champagne or at the end of your meal retire to the drawing room with a fine cognac.

Recommended in the area

York; Royal Armouries at Leeds; Harewood House

# CHANNEL ISLANDS

St Peter Port. Guernsey

# La Barbarie Hotel

★★★  77% ◉ HL

**Address:** Saints Road, Saints Bay, ST MARTIN,
Guernsey GY4 6ES
**Tel:** 01481 235217
**Fax:** 01481 235208
**Email:** reservations@labarbariehotel.com
**Website:** www.labarbariehotel.com
**Map ref:** 13
**Directions:** Off road between St Peter Port and
airport; follow signs for Saints Bay
**Rooms:** 22, S £52–£70 D £64–£100 **Facilities:** ⚲ Wi-Fi **Parking:** 50 **Notes:** ⊗ in bedrooms

This fine hotel was named after Barbary Coast pirates who kidnapped and held to ransom the house's owner in the 17th century. A hotel since 1950, it lies in a quiet green valley close to some of the lovely bays, coves and cliffs in the south of the island, and retains all of its historic charm, not least in the lovely residents' lounge, with its old beams and open fireplace. Bedrooms have private bath or shower rooms, TV, radio, trouser press, iron, tea and coffee facilities and hair dryer. Two-room suites with inter-connecting doors are ideal for families with children. Some self-catering apartments are also available, most of which overlook the heated swimming pool and its surrounding patio. Dining at La Barbarie is serious but far from pretentious, and accolades include one from the producer of one of celebrity chef Rick Stein's TV series, who is quoted as saying that the lobster he had here was the best he had ever tasted in all his 15 years of travelling the world making food programmes. The fixed-price four-course dinner menu is very good value. There is also a bar and poolside menu, which includes 'old favourites', pastas, fish, salads and sandwiches. The patio is the ideal secluded spot for a lazy lunch or quiet aperitif before dinner. The hotel is ideally placed for walkers, cyclists, horse riders and joggers.

**Recommended in the area**

Saumarez Manor; Castle Cornet; South Coast Cliff Path

# Best Western Hotel de Havelet

★★★ 78% HL

**Address:** Havelet, ST PETER PORT, Guernsey GY1 1BA
**Tel:** 01481 722199
**Fax:** 01481 714057
**Email:** havelet@sarniahotels.com
**Website:** www.havelet.sarniahotels.com
**Map ref:** 13
**Directions:** From airport follow signs for St Peter Port through St. Martins. At bottom of 'Val de Terres' hill turn left into Havelet
**Rooms:** 34, S £50–£110 D £96–£150 **Facilities:** ⓧ Sauna Jacuzzi STV Wi-Fi in bedrooms
**Parking:** 40 **Notes:** ⊗ in bedrooms

A handsome Georgian house surrounded by sheltered gardens and flower-filled terraces on the outskirts of the island's capital. From its elevated position there are magnificent views over the harbour to Herm and other neighbouring islands. Many of the comfortable, well-equipped bedrooms are set around a pretty colonial-style courtyard. The elegant drawing room, one of several locations for afternoon tea, is always welcoming, but particularly so on chilly evenings and wintry days when warmed by a blazing log fire. Two of the island's most popular restaurants are within the hotel, in the converted coach house. The Wellington Boot offers an extensive four-course dinner menu featuring Guernsey fish, seafood and flambée dishes, while the Havelet Grill, where charcoal grills and fresh fish are served, has a more relaxed environment. The coach house is also home to the Saddle Room Bar, which offers hot and cold buffet lunches and afternoon tea. Hotel guests on half board terms may take advantage of a dinner exchange scheme with other Sarnia hotels in Guernsey.

**Recommended in the area**

Hauteville House; Castle Cornet; Sark; South Coast Cliff Path

# Somerville Hotel

★★★★  74% ◉◉ HL

**Address:** Mont du Boulevard, ST AUBIN,
Jersey JE3 8AD
**Tel:** 01534 741226
**Fax:** 01534 746621
**Email:** somerville@dolanhotels.com
**Website:** www.dolanhotels.com
**Map ref:** 13
**Directions:** From village, follow harbour then take Mont du
Boulevard and 2nd right bend
**Rooms:** 56, S £103.5–£126 D £138–£168 **Facilities:** ⤳ STV
Wi-Fi in bedrooms **Parking:** 26 **Notes:** ⊗ in bedrooms

Nestling on the hillside, overlooking the yachting harbour, the village of St Aubin and the bay beyond,
the views from the Somerville Hotel are breathtaking. As one of the island's finest hotels, it is well
known for its warm welcome and excellent reputation and most of the comfortable and tastefully
furnished bedrooms enjoy spectacular sea views. Jersey has earned a worldwide reputation for the
quality of its restaurants and Tides Restaurant at the Somerville Hotel is no exception. Recently awarded
two AA Rosettes for its food, coupled with the restaurant's panoramic views over the harbour, the
Somerville offers a memorable dining experience. Lunch on the terrace is a particular favourite. Before
and after a meal enjoy a drink in the cocktail bar, or simply relax and unwind with coffee in the lounge.
Following the completion of a two year refurbishment in 2007, including the addition of conference and
banqueting facilities, the hotel will offer a choice of three meeting rooms, two of which will benefit from
natural light and have spectacular views as a perfect backdrop. The hotel is just five minutes walk from
the sandy expanse of St. Aubin's Bay and the sheltered cove of Belcroute Beach.
**Recommended in the area**
Durrell Wildlife Conservation trust; Elizabeth Castle; Jersey War Tunnels

# The Club Hotel & Spa

★★★★ ◎◎◎◎ TH

Address: Green Street, ST HELIER, Jersey JE2 4UH
Tel: 01534 876500
Fax: 01534 720371
Email: reservations@theclubjersey.com
Website: www.theclubjersey.com
Map ref: 13
Directions: 5 mins walk from main shopping centre
Rooms: 46, S £195 D 195 Facilities: ⊗ ↗ Sauna STV Wi-Fi
throughout Parking: 30 Notes: ⊗ in bedrooms

This swish, town-house hotel in the centre of Jersey's capital features stylish, contemporary decor throughout. The fully air-conditioned bedrooms and suites have large, full-height windows opening on to a balustrade, while the beds are dressed with Frette Egyptian cotton sheets and duck-down duvets. All rooms are equipped with safes, flat screen TVs, DVD/CD players, Bang & Olufsen portable phones and private bars. Granite bathrooms include power showers, robes, slippers and aromatherapy products. Free Wi-Fi access is available throughout the hotel. The dining choice includes the Bohemia Bar and Restaurant, awarded four Rosettes by the AA in 2006/7, where a typical main course might be roast local turbot with braised frog's leg, minted peas, herb gnocchi and chicken emulsion. Overlooking the outdoor pool is The Club Café, a contemporary New York-style restaurant offering breakfast, light lunches and dinner. Several hours might easily be spent in The Spa, starting with a swim in the salt pool, followed by mud treatment in the rasul (a traditional Arabian ritual cleansing) room, and finally a spell on one of the luxurious loungers. Two luxury meeting rooms with oak tables and leather chairs can accommodate 50 theatre-style or up to 32 as a boardroom.

Recommended in the area

German Underground Hospital; Jersey Zoo; Mount Orgeuil

# Longueville Manor Hotel

★★★★ ◎◎◎ HL

Address: ST SAVIOUR, Jersey JE2 7WF
Tel:     01534 725501
Fax:     01534 731613
Email:   info@longuevillemanor.com
Website: www.longuevillemanor.com
Map ref: 13
Directions: A3 E from St Helier towards Gorey.
Hotel 1m on left
Rooms: 30, S £175–£225 D £200–£400
Facilities: ⚊ Tennis STV Wi-Fi in bedrooms Parking: 40

For more than fifty years this charming hotel has been run by the Lewis family, and is currently owned by Malcolm and Patricia Lewis. The recently refurbished 14th-century manor house is set in its own wooded valley, with 15 acres of grounds including vibrant flower gardens and a lake complete with black swans, yet is only five minutes' from St Helier. The hotel is stylishly presented, with warm colour schemes, fine antique furnishings and lavish floral displays. The tranquil location, historic setting and excellent food invite complete relaxation, with tennis courts and a heated swimming pool to enjoy, plus a poolside bar and barbecue. The 30 en suite bedrooms are each named after a type of rose and come with chaise longue, Egyptian cotton sheets, wide-screen TV and DVD/CD player, cordless phone, fruit, flowers and homemade biscuits. Additional in-room equipment includes a safe, hairdryer, iron and ironing board, and rooms on the ground floor have a private patio overlooking the garden. The hotel's restored Victorian kitchen garden provides abundantly for the dining room, including delicacies from the Victorian glass houses. The restaurant, awarded three AA Rosettes, offers a fine dining experience with a Master Sommelier to advise on wines.

Recommended in the area

Royal Jersey Golf Club; Mont Orgueil Castle; Durrell Wildlife Conservation Trust

# Water's Edge Hotel

★★★  78% ◉◉ HL

Address: Bouley Bay, TRINITY, Jersey JE3 5AS
Tel:     01534 862777
Email:   mail@watersedgehotel.co.je
Website: www.watersedgehotel.co.je
Map ref: 13
Directions: From St Helier, go N on A8, then follow signs for Bouley Bay
Rooms: 50, S £43–£69 D £86–£138
Facilities: ⌇ Parking: 20 Notes: ⊗ in bedrooms

Jersey's north coast can be hilly, but guests here need ascend only a few gently rising feet to reach the hotel after a day on the beach. As its name implies, Water's Edge could hardly be closer to the shoreline of pretty Bouley Bay, and many of the rooms and luxury suites face the ocean, while the rest have southward views over the garden. All the bedrooms are decorated in contemporary style and have en suite bathrooms, tea- and coffee-making facilities, telephone and TV. Through the huge picture windows of the Waterside Restaurant, the Cotentin Peninsula of France, about 11 miles distant, can usually be seen. The menu is modern British with hints of classical, and choices might include starters such as Royal Grouville Bay oysters or ham and foie gras terrine, followed by seafood and meat main courses, or a steak from the flambée trolley, the Waterside's signature dish. The well-balanced wine list guarantees something suitable as an accompaniment. On warm days, meals can also be enjoyed on the large deck overlooking the harbour, or in the Black Dog Bar, full of character and well known to locals for its delicious food, enjoyed in the cosy warmth of a real fire in winter. The heated outdoor kidney-shaped pool is on a delightful terrace overlooking the bay. There are spectacular cliffpath walks leading both east and west from the hotel, and a five-star dive centre not far away.

**Recommended in the area**

Durrell Wildlife Conservation Trust; Mont Orgueil Castle; Jersey Living Legend Village

# SCOTLAND

Kilchurn Castle, Loch Awe

# Aberdeen Patio Hotel

★★★★ 77% HL

**Address:** Beach Boulevard, ABERDEEN,
AB24 5EF
**Tel:** 01224 633339
**Fax:** 01224 638833
**Email:** info@patiohotels.com
**Website:** www.patiohotels.com
**Map ref:** 10, NJ90
**Directions:** From A90 follow signs for city, then for
sea. On Beach Blvd, turn l at lights, hotel on r

**Rooms:** 168, S £66–£285 D £76–£300 **Facilities:** ⓈSauna Jacuzzi Solarium  Gym STV Wi-Fi
available **Parking:** 172

Built in 1996, this splendid modern hotel is close to the beach and just a ten-minute walk from the
centre of the Granite City, an excellent location for either business or leisure trips. The main atrium is a
bright, informal space for meeting friends in the open bar area for a drink and a snack. From here you
can head for the Conservatory for a menu of simple dishes or to Footdees, a more traditional restaurant
where the menu changes monthly to make full use of the best fresh seasonal produce. There are three
types of room, all spacious and light and having king-size beds, satellite TV, trouser press and tea- and
coffee-making facilities. The Platinum Club rooms and suites form a hotel within the hotel grounds,
with separate reception and check-in, exclusive bar and dining in the Platinum Lounge, and its own
room service menu. These rooms offer a greater degree of luxury, with pillow-top beds, bath robes,
complimentary soft drinks minibar, chocolates and mineral water, broadband and a widescreen TV with
satellite channels and movies. All guests, of course, can make use of the superb leisure club, with pool,
spa bath, saunas, steamroom, solarium and Cybex gym, and the spa where treatments range from
massages to manicures.

Recommended in the area

# Banchory Lodge Hotel

★★★  81%  CHH

**Address:** BANCHORY, Aberdeenshire, AB31 5HS
**Tel:** 01330 822625
**Fax:** 01330 825019
**Email:** enquiries@banchorylodge.co.uk
**Website:** www.banchorylodge.co.uk
**Map ref:** 10, NO69
**Directions:** Off A93, 13m W of Aberdeen, hotel off Dee Street
**Rooms:** 22, S £90–£120 D £160–£160
**Parking:** 50

This privately-owned former coaching inn stands in richly wooded grounds alongside the Dee, one of Scotland's premier salmon rivers, and offers superior accommodation and high standards of service. Long ago, the old Deeside road passed this way and the mail coach would halt here for a change of horses. The hotel's homely atmosphere owes much to its traditional decor, fresh flowers, open fires and collection of original paintings. The 22 en suite bedrooms, among which are three with four-posters and several spacious family rooms, are all luxuriously furnished and comprehensively equipped. Many have river views. The hotel bar features an ornately carved oak counter and a selection of over 50 malt whiskies. Guests can choose one of the two public lounges in which to relax over morning coffee or afternoon tea with a newspaper, or watch anglers trying their skill. The Riverview Dining Room, overlooking the confluence of the Feugh and Dee, offers a daily menu of imaginative dishes including Scottish salmon, local lamb and Aberdeen Angus beef, all personally supervised by the owner. Breakfast is served in a smaller room, which is also available for private functions. Fishing (from 1st February to 30th September) and shooting can be arranged through the hotel.

**Recommended in the area**

Crathes Castle; Balmoral Castle; Lochnagar Whisky Distillery

# Falls of Lora Hotel

★★★ 75% HL

**Address:** CONNEL, Argyll & Bute, PA37 1PB
**Tel:** 01631 710483
**Fax:** 01631 710694
**Email:** enquiries@fallsoflora.com
**Website:** www.fallsoflora.com
**Map ref:** 9, NM93
**Directions:** Hotel set back from A85 from Glasgow, 0.5m past Connel sign, 5m before Oban
**Rooms:** 30, S £41.50–£59.50 D £49–£131
**Parking:** 40

This Victorian owner-run hotel enjoys views over the hotel gardens (across the road), Loch Etive and the Connel Bridge. The ground floor includes a comfortable traditional lounge and cocktail bar with open log fires, offering more than 100 whiskies. Well-equipped bedrooms come in a variety of styles, ranging from cosy standard doubles to high quality luxury suite-type rooms. Guests may eat in the comfortable and attractive Bistro and in the evening there is an exciting and varied menu.

**Recommended in the area**

Oban Distillery; Iona Abbey; Ben Nevis

# The Ardanaiseig Hotel

★★★ 85% ◉◉ CHH

**Address:** by Loch Awe, KILCHRENAN,
by Taynuilt, Argyll & Bute, PA35 1HE
**Tel:** 01866 833333
**Email:** ardanaiseig@clara.net
**Website:** www.ardanaiseig.com
**Map ref:** 9, NN02
**Directions:** Turn S off A85 at Taynuilt onto B845 to Kilchrenan. Left in front of pub (road very narrow) signed 'Ardanaiseig Hotel' & 'No Through Road'
**Rooms:** 16, S £95–£193 D £190–£386 **Facilities:** STV **Parking:** 20

Perfect for a refined West Highland experience, this romantic Scottish Baronial-style mansion, dating from 1834, sits amid 40 hectares of gardens and grounds, with spacious lawns abutting Loch Awe. The interior retains its original grandeur, and deep rich hues set off the architectural features. Each of the spacious bedrooms has its own style, some feature splendid four-poster beds and six overlook the Loch. The elegant dining room offers well cooked dishes and has two AA Rosettes.

**Recommended in the area**

Kilchurn Castle; Oban; Cruachan Power Station

# Taychreggan Hotel

★★★   81% ◉◉ CHH

**Address:** KILCHRENAN, Taynuilt,
          Argyll & Bute, PA35 1HQ
**Tel:**     01866 833211
**Fax:**     01866 833244
**Email:**   info@taychregganhotel.co.uk
**Website:** www.taychregganhotel.co.uk
**Map ref:** 2, NN02
**Directions:** W from Crianlarich on A85 to Taynuilt,
S for 7m on B845 to Kilchrenan & Taychreggan

**Rooms:** 20, S £99 D £127–£250 **Facilities:** Jacuzzi  bathtub in Sonachan suite **Parking:** 40

Surrounded by mountain grandeur, forest and abundant wildlife, Taychreggan makes a perfect venue for the walker, fisherman, cyclist or photographer. It stands in 40 acres on the shores of Loch Awe, Scotland's longest inland loch. Originally a humble cattle drover's inn, it's certainly humble no more. Beautifully furnished with antiques and original paintings, the public areas include a smart bar and adjacent Orangery, and two quiet lounges (one with an antique upright piano), with deep, luxurious sofas and views over the lawn to the loch. In the Snooker Room a full-size antique table comes complete with original rests, cues, scoreboard and rules. Some guest rooms, such as Inverinan and Walter Scott, have four-poster beds and a south-facing loch view, while the newly built Sonachan suite takes a sideways look at the loch and the hillsides beyond. The kitchen has earned a fine reputation, as well as two AA Rosettes, for the skilfully prepared contemporary and modern European menu that showcases seasonal local meat, fish, seafood, soft fruits and vegetables. A typical dish would be roast loin of Highland beef fillet with ratatouille, braised shallot and Madeira and thyme jus. Anglers will appreciate the fact that Taychreggan has its own fishing rights.

**Recommended in the area**

Inverary Castle; Arctic Penguins; Argyll Wildlife Park

# The Lodge on Loch Lomond Hotel

★★★★ 74% ◉◉ HL

**Address:** LUSS, Argyll & Bute, G83 8PA
**Tel:** 01436 860201
**Fax:** 01436 860203
**Email:** res@loch-lomond.co.uk
**Website:** www.loch-lomond.co.uk
**Map ref:** 9, NS39
**Directions:** Off A82, follow sign for hotel
**Rooms:** 47, S £131–£203 D £151–£223
**Facilities:** ◈ Sauna Jacuzzi STV **Parking:** 120

The Lodge on Loch Lomond Hotel stands on a quiet sandy cove amid some of Scotland's most stunning scenery. With panoramic views of the Loch and mountains it offers a warm, relaxing atmosphere, delicious modern cuisine from the award winning AA-Rosetted restaurant Colquhoun's, stunning accommodation and a luxury health suite with spa and swimming pool. The hotel has a superb range of accommodation, from rooms with en suite saunas and private balconies overlooking the Loch or towards the village of Luss, to the very contemporary accommodation in the Munro Lodge. The Cuillin Suites are two bedroom guest apartments, complete with 42" plasma television screens, surround sound Linn speakers and DVD players, living flame fires, temperature controlled baths and massaging showers. Colquhoun's innovative menu blends traditional and contemporary cuisine using the finest and freshest local produce. The uninterrupted views from the restaurant make this a very special place to dine. Guests can unwind in the health suite, amberspa, which features a 16m swimming pool, Jacuzzi, steam room, sauna and laconium, plus spa treatment rooms. The hotel is perfectly located to explore some of the most stunning parts of Scotland, from city to the Highlands, with easy access to Glasgow, Oban, Inveraray and the rugged west coast.

**Recommended in the area**

Loch Lomond Aquarium; Queen Elizabeth Forest Park; City of Glasgow

Ben Lomond from Loch Lomond

# Manor House Hotel

★★★  82% ◉ HL

**Address:** Gallanach Road, OBAN,
Argyll & Bute  PA34 4LS
**Tel:** 01631 562087
**Fax:** 01631 563053
**Email:** info@manorhouseoban.com
**Website:** www.manorhouseoban.com
**Map ref:** 9, NM93
**Directions:** Follow signs MacBrayne Ferries and pass
ferry entrance for hotel on right
**Rooms:** 11, S £80–£145 D £120–£170 **Facilities:** Wi-Fi in bedrooms **Parking:** 20

Built in 1780, the Manor House was the principal residence of the Duke of Argyll's Oban estate.
Featuring late Georgian architecture, great consideration has been given to preserving its elegance,
charm and atmosphere. All en suite rooms have been tastefully decorated in the period style and
include every modern amenity. The beautifully restored Dining Room is open both to residents and non-
residents each evening. This, and the Drawing Room have magnificent views over Oban Bay.
**Recommended in the area**
Morvern Mountains; Isle of Mull

# Airds Hotel

★★★★ ◉◉◉ HL

Address:  PORT APPIN,
          Appin, Argyll & Bute PA38 4DF
Tel:      01631 730236
Fax:      01631 730535
Email:    airds@airds-hotel.com
Website:  www.airds-hotel.com
Map ref:  9, NM94
Directions: From A828 Oban to Fort William road, turn at Appin signed Port Appin. Hotel 2.5m on left
Rooms: 11, S £180–£330 D £245–£415 **Facilities:** STV Wi-Fi in bedrooms **Parking:** 20

On a finger of land pointing southwest into the loch, this charming country house is surrounded by glorious Highland scenery. It has been offering hospitality since its days as a ferry inn during the 18th century, but these days it is renowned for the luxurious accommodation and exceptional standard of cooking. Remote it may be, but the journey is very well rewarded. Active guests can return from a day in the surrounding mountains in the knowledge that there are two cosy lounges and a satisfying meal awaiting, not to mention supremely comfortable beds. Each of the bedrooms is bright and stylishly decorated with quality fabrics and linens, and the en suite bathrooms are resplendent with marble and luxury fittings. The bedrooms also have flat-screen TVs with satellite channels and DVD players, but in six of them the view over the loch will be a compelling distraction. In the atmospheric restaurant, the dinner menu changes daily – recent offerings have included seared wild salmon and scallops with soft herb and parmesan risotto and a shellfish cappuccino – and the lunch menu is equally imaginative. There are also occasional gourmet events, providing seven courses with appropriate wines. It's all fairly informal, but check the dress code at dinner.

**Recommended in the area**

Scottish Sea Life Centre at Barcaldine; Island of Lismore; Oban; Isle of Mull

Edinburgh Castle

# An Lochan

★★★　◉◉ SHL

**Address:** Shore Road, TIGHNABRUAICH,
Argyll & Bute, PA21 2BE
**Tel:** 01700 811239
**Fax:** 01700 811300
**Email:** info@anlochan.co.uk
**Website:** www.anlochan.co.uk
**Map ref:** 9, NR97
**Directions:** From Strachur on A886 right onto A8003
to Tighnabruaich. Hotel on right at bottom of hill

**Rooms:** 11, S £120–£190 D £120–£190 **Facilities:** Wi-Fi available **Parking:** 20

In a remote, loch-side setting on the Kyles of Bute, this exceptional hotel has stunning views and offers the ultimate in peaceful relaxation, though the opportunity for hill-walking or stepping out along the coast are quite irrisistable too. Once you have worked up an appetite, it will be deliciously satisfied by the skilful preparation of fresh local seafood and game by head chef Louise McKie. After that, all that remains is to enjoy the sheer luxury of the individually furnished bedrooms

**Recommended in the area**

Isle of Bute; Kilmedan Sculptured Stones; Argyll Forest Park

# Highland Cottage

★★★ ◎◎ SHL

**Address:** Breadalbane Street, TOBERMORY,
Isle of Mull, Argyll & Bute, PA75 6PD
**Tel:** 01688 302030
**Email:** davidandjo@highlandcottage.co.uk
**Website:** www.highlandcottage.co.uk
**Map ref:** 9, NM55
**Directions:** A848 Craignure/Fishnish ferry terminal, pass Tobermory signs, straight on at mini rdbt across narrow bridge, turn r. Hotel on r opposite fire station
**Rooms:** 6, S £120 D £150–£185 **Facilities:** STV Wi-Fi available **Parking:** 6

David and Jo Currie designed and built this small hotel. Both are career hoteliers and bring to it many years of experience. The hotel stands above Tobermory, the Isle of Mull's pretty 'capital', in the town's quiet conservation area, yet only minutes from the hustle and bustle of Main Street and Fisherman's Pier. With just six individually-designed bedrooms, staff rarely need to ask guests for their room number. This relaxed policy continues in the rooms themselves, where the Curries have deliberately avoided decor that screams 'Hotel!' All are provided with a video TV, music centre, and an en suite bathroom with full-size bath and thermostatic shower, while some have four-posters. There are two inviting lounges – the Sitting Room upstairs, with an honesty bar and views across the bay to the mainland; and downstairs the Sun Lounge, an extension of the Dining Room and the ideal place for pre- or after-dinner drinks. Breakfasts are described as 'memorable', dinners as 'splendid'. Whenever feasible, the kitchen uses only the freshest of locally-sourced ingredients, such as scallops from Tobermory Bay, crabs from Croig on the island's west coast, mussels farmed at Inverlussa on Loch Spelve, and venison reared at Ardnamurchan.

**Recommended in the area**

Duart Castle; Fingal's Cave (Staffa); Whale-watching

# Balcary Bay Hotel

★★★   85% ◉◉ HL

**Address:** AUCHENCAIRN, Castle Douglas,
Dumfries & Galloway, DG7 1QZ
**Tel:** 01556 640217
**Fax:** 01556 640272
**Email:** reservations@balcary-bay-hotel.co.uk
**Website:** www.balcary-bay-hotel.co.uk
**Map ref:** 5, NX75
**Directions:** On A711 between Dalbeattie &
Kirkcudbright, hotel on Shore Rd, 2m from village
**Rooms:** 20, S £69 D £124–£154 **Parking:** 50

The hotel lawns run down to the edge of the beautiful bay from which it takes its name. Just offshore is Heston Isle, hideout of 17th-century smugglers who used to store contraband in the house's secret underground passages. Nowadays, while modernised and tastefully decorated, the hotel still retains much of its old character (without the smuggling, of course). Public rooms include the cocktail bar and log fire-warmed lounges. There are twenty well-appointed en suite bedrooms, all with TV, radio, phone, tea and coffee tray, and hairdryer. Other facilities at the Balcary are available on request. From many rooms there are magnificent views either across the Solway Firth to the beautiful peaks of the Lake District or over the gardens. Three superior ground floor rooms have their own patio overlooking the bay. In the restaurant award-winning cuisine is based on local Scottish fare, often given a Gallic twist. Local delicacies such as prime Galloway beef, lamb, lobsters, prawns and, of course, Balcary Bay salmon are likely to appear on the carte and fixed price menus. A bistro-style lunch menu is available seven days a week. The wine list is extensive and draws from both the Old and New Worlds, and even includes examples from Lebanon.

**Recommended in the area**

East Stewartry Coast; Threave Garden (NT); Loch Ken

# The Balmoral

★★★★★ 87% ◎◎◎ HL

**Address:** 1 Princes Street, EDINBURGH, EH2 2EQ
**Tel:** 0131 556 2414
**Fax:** 0131 557 8740
**Email:** reservations.balmoral@
roccofortecollection.com
**Website:** www.roccofortecollection.com
**Map ref:** 10, NT27
**Directions:** Follow city centre signs. Hotel at E end of
Princes St, adjacent to Waverley Station
**Rooms:** 188, S £305–£1650 D £360–£1650 **Facilities:** ⊗ Sauna  Solarium Gym STV Wi-Fi available
**Notes:** ⊗ in bedrooms

The Balmoral is more than a hotel, it's an Edinburgh landmark, thanks to the majestic clocktower that is a feature of the city skyline. Built as a traditional railway hotel, its public areas, conference and banqueting suites, and stylish bedrooms have been beautifully refurbished to designs by Rocco Forte's sister, Olga Polizzi. Each room is individually decorated in the muted hues of Scottish moors, mists and heathers. All are equipped with two phone lines, fax-modem, broadband, interactive national and satellite TV, in-room refreshments, air conditioning, and spacious marble and ceramic bathroom with fluffy towels, robes and other luxuries. Some look towards Edinburgh Castle, some the Old Town, and some over the courtyard. When it comes to fine dining, guests can choose between the attentive but non-intrusive service in Number One, with outstanding cuisine by chef, Jeff Bland; Hadrian's Brasserie for chic and informal dining; The Bollinger Bar at Palm Court for cocktails or afternoon tea, or The Balmoral Bar for a relaxing drink. Enjoy the facilities in the Spa - the Finnish sauna, Turkish steam room, 15-metre pool, air conditioned fully equipped gymnasium, and exercise room.

**Recommended in the area**

Palace of Holyroodhouse; St Giles Cathedral; Royal Mile

# Best Western Bruntsfield Hotel

★★★   85% @ HL

**Address:** 69 Bruntsfield Place, EDINBURGH
EH10 4HH
**Tel:**      0131 229 1393
**Fax:**     0131 229 5634
**Email:**   sales@thebruntsfield.co.uk
**Website:** www.thebruntsfieldhotel.co.uk
**Map ref:** 10, NT27
**Directions:** From S into Edinburgh on A702. Hotel
1m S of west end of Princes Street
**Rooms:** 67, S £70–£115 D £85–£210 **Facilities:** STV Wi-Fi in bedrooms
**Parking:** 25 **Notes:** ⊗ in bedrooms

Edinburgh hotels are known for their style, and this smart town house hotel overlooking leafy Bruntsfield Links park is no exception. In the 16th century Bruntsfield was a moor, home to outlaws and outcasts, but as the city expanded, first houses and then streets began to eat into this important green space. In 1827 a halt was called to encroachment and today these 30 acres are a real feature of Edinburgh. The city centre and all its main tourist attractions are within easy reach, either on foot or by buses which stop close by the hotel. Stylish public rooms include spacious lounges and a lively bar – perfect to relax in with a drink and *The Scotsman* after a busy day. En suite bedrooms come in a variety of sizes and styles, including executive, family and master rooms, some with four-poster beds, and offer all the usual facilities, including multi-channel TV, high speed internet access, tea and coffee tray, desk and chair, and voicemail. Imaginative dinner menus and hearty Scottish breakfasts are served in the bright, modern Bisque Bar and Restaurant – holder of an AA Rosette – with an outside terrace. Smart staff provide good levels of service and attention.

**Recommended in the area**

Edinburgh Castle; Royal Yacht Britannia; Scottish Parliament

# Prestonfield

★★★★★ ◎◎ TH

**Address:** Priestfield Road, EDINBURGH EH16 5UT
**Tel:** 0131 225 7800
**Fax:** 0131 220 4392
**Email:** reservations@prestonfield.com
**Website:** www.prestonfield.com
**Map ref:** 10, NT27
**Directions:** A7 towards Cameron Toll. 200mtrs beyond Royal Commonwealth Pool, into Priestfield Rd
**Rooms:** 22, S £225–£275 D £225–£275 **Facilities:** STV Wi-Fi in bedrooms **Parking:** 250

To the many AA and other awards this 17th-century mansion has gained should be added this plaudit from Tatler magazine: "Divine decadence. Rich, ripe and dangerously close to dissolute". Other commentators have sprinkled their reviews of this celebrated city centre hotel with words such as 'opulent', 'indulgent' and 'Baroque extravaganza'. So when James Thomson, the creative force behind Prestonfield and other prestigious Scottish restaurants, calls it the 'ultimate retort to minimalism', a picture begins to take shape. Interiors are gilded, brocaded and velvet-covered, and to the fine art and antique furnishings Thomson has added a quixotic assortment of finds from European auction rooms. Bedrooms and suites have discreet technology, including air conditioning, high-speed internet, Bose sound system and flat-screen TV. Bed linen is by Frette and there are luxurious bathrobes, fresh flowers and exclusive toiletries. The unusually named Rhubarb restaurant is split between a pair of grand oval Regency rooms. Here, exceptional cooking might include smoked salmon with Beluga caviar, fillet of Black gold beef, and Lindisfarne oysters, not to mention the famed rhubarb desserts, and a choice of wines from the much-praised cellars.

**Recommended in the area**

Museum of Scotland; Scottish Parliament (Palace of Holyroodhouse); Edinburgh Castle

# Best Western Keavil House Hotel

★★★ 79% ⊛ HL

**Address:** Crossford, DUNFERMLINE, Fife, KY12 8QW
**Tel:** 01383 736258
**Fax:** 01383 621600
**Email:** reservations@keavilhouse.co.uk
**Website:** www.keavilhouse.co.uk
**Map ref:** 10, NT08
**Directions:** 2m W of Dunfermline on A994
**Rooms:** 73, S £70–£95 D £80–£140 **Facilities:** ⊛
Sauna Jacuzzi Solarium  Gym STV Wi-Fi in bedrooms
**Parking:** 250 **Notes:** ⊗ in bedrooms

Dating from the 16th century, this old manor house turned country house hotel is set in secluded wooded grounds and gardens two miles west of Dunfermline, Scotland's ancient capital and burial place of its kings and queens. Bedrooms occupy the original house and a modern wing, and are available in different styles - classic, superior, family rooms and suites, master rooms with four-posters, and some with doors to the gardens. All have en suite bathroom and/or shower, multi-channel TV with Sky Sport, tea and coffee facilities, trouser press, ironing board and wired high speed internet access (it's wireless in public areas, by the way). There's a comfortable lounge and bar for light dining, while in the conservatory is the contemporary Cardoon Restaurant, awarded an AA Rosette for its locally sourced, quality food. Typical of the modern Scottish dishes on offer is canon of lamb with an Arran mustard and pine kernel crust. Cardoon overlooks the peaceful garden, which actually grows the globe artichoke-type vegetable after which the restaurant is named. The Picture of Health Club, with 15m and toddlers' pools, gym sauna and crèche is located within the grounds and is open to private members and residential hotel guests.

**Recommended in the area**

Deep Sea World; Falkland Palace; Edinburgh Castle

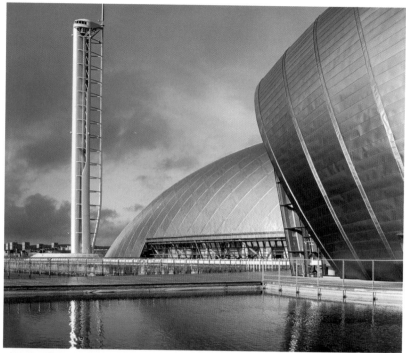

Glasgow Science Centre

# St Andrews Golf Hotel

★★★ ◉◉ HL

**Address:** 40 The Scores,
ST ANDREWS, Fife, KY16 9AS
**Tel:** 01334 472611
**Fax:** 01334 472188
**Email:** reception@standrews-golf.co.uk
**Website:** www.standrews-golf.co.uk
**Map ref:** 10, NO51
**Directions:** Follow signs 'Golf Course' into Golf Place
and in 200yds turn right into The Scores
**Rooms:** 22 **Facilities:** STV Wi-Fi in bedrooms **Parking:** 6

This chic and stylish boutique town house hotel has been recently restored and beautifully refurbished throughout. Featuring a variety of room types, most of which command spectacular views over St Andrews bay and links, the hotel is just a minute's walk from all golf courses and attractions. The AA-Rosetted and award winning 'Number Forty' restaurant serves the finest local produce and you can enjoy a drink in its bar or the famous Ma Bells Bar.

**Recommended in the area**

St Andrews Cathedral; Scotland's Secret Bunker; Falkland Palace

# ABode Hotel Glasgow

★★★★  73% ◉◉ HL

**Address:** 129 Bath Street, GLASGOW  G2 2SZ
**Tel:**  0141 221 6789
**Fax:**  0141 221 6777
**Email:**  reservationsglasgow@abodehotels.co.uk
**Website:** www.abodehotels.co.uk
**Map ref:** 9, NS66
**Directions:** From S M8 junct 19 onto Bothwell St,
turn left at Hope St, left onto Bath St. Hotel is 0.3m
on left
**Rooms:** 60, S  D £99–£225

No, it's not a mistake. The typographically quirky 'ABode' is an example of how this concept hotel seeks to stand out in a city generously endowed with chic establishments. The building, situated in Glasgow's historic art district, has been transformed from offices occupied by the Department of Education, which mercifully left untouched many of the original grand Edwardian features. Meticulous attention to detail is evident in the contemporarily designed rooms; each is decorated in subtle tones, and offers practicalities like a hand-built bed with cashmere throw, LCD TV, DVD player, comfort cooling, secondary glazing and a tuck box of regional produce. At street level is Michael Caines' hugely popular restaurant. Caines, one of Britain's most talented and respected chefs, and awarded an MBE in 2006 for services to the hospitality industry, works closely with local suppliers to ensure that all his menus showcase the best regional produce. The MC Grill serves breakfast, elevenses, lunch and full evening meals. ABode Glasgow is also home to the 1st Bar MC, a stylish and relaxed late-night lounge with funky lighting and furniture, and all the latest cocktails, and champagne by the glass or bottle. ABode Glasgow is also the perfect venue for weddings and business meetings.

**Recommended in the area**

Burrell Collection; Glasgow Cathedral; Museum of Transport

Urquhart Castle, Loch Ness

# Hotel du Vin at One Devonshire Gardens

★★★★ ◉◉ TH

**Address:** 1 Devonshire Gardens,
GLASGOW G12 0UX
**Tel:** 0141 339 2001
**Fax:** 0141 337 1663
**Email:** reservations.odg@hotelduvin.com
**Website:** www.hotelduvin.com
**Map ref:** 9, NS66

**Directions:** M8 junct 17, follow signs for A82, 1.5m turn left into Hyndland Rd, 1st right, right at mini rdbt, right at end **Rooms:** 49, S £140–£495 D £140–£950 **Facilities:** Gym STV Wi-Fi in bedrooms

This luxury boutique hotel, regarded as one of Scotland's finest, offers a relaxed style of hospitality. The rooms have superb beds with luxurious Egyptian linen and en suite bathrooms. In the Bistro you'll find great classic and modern dishes, cooked simply, with the freshest of local ingredients. The hotel has its own wine cellar, which guests can visit, a whisky snug and two terraced gardens.

**Recommended in the area**

Kelvingrove Art Gallery; Glasgow Botanical Gardens; House for an Art Lover

# Lovat Arms Hotel

★★★ 86% ◉ HL

**Address:** Loch Ness, FORT AUGUSTUS, Highland, PH32 4DU
**Tel:** 0845 450 1100
**Fax:** 01320 366677
**Email:** info@lovatarms-hotel.com
**Website:** www.lovatarms-hotel.com
**Map ref:** 12, NH30
**Directions:** In town centre on A82
**Rooms:** 29, S £65–£95 D £70–£270 **Facilities:** STV Wi-Fi in public rooms **Parking:** 30 **Notes:** ⊗ in bedrooms (except one Studio)

This charming, family-run hotel enjoys an elevated position overlooking the head of Loch Ness, the five-lock Caledonian Canal staircase and the surrounding mountains. Originally built to serve a long-vanished railway, it stands on the site of Kilwhimen Barracks, erected in 1718 for soldiers brought in to pacify the locals after the Jacobite uprisings. A wall of the old Hanoverian fort, complete with gun embrasures, still stands in the grounds. The hotel's innovative owners, who took over in 2005, have installed a central heating and water system that uses a biomass woodchip burner. Among many other eco-friendly initiatives are pencils made from recycled video cassettes and coasters fashioned from used car tyres. Impressively styled bedrooms are technologically advanced, with flat screen TVs and internet access, as well as the more utilitarian hospitality tray, iron and ironing board. The Studios also have underfloor heating. Three weeks after opening, the Bar Restaurant was awarded an AA Rosette but, but due to demand, the Hotel Restaurant will be having a makeover at the end of 2008. Outdoor activities abound – cycling along forest tracks, pony trekking, river fishing and golf at Fort Augustus.

**Recommended in the area**

Loch Ness; Isle of Skye; Urquhart Castle

# Inverlochy Castle Hotel

★★★★★ ◉◉◉ CHH

**Address:** Torlundy, FORT WILLIAM, Highland
PH33 6SN
**Tel:** 01397 702177
**Fax:** 01397 702953
**Email:** info@inverlochy.co.uk
**Website:** www.inverlochycastlehotel.com
**Map ref:** 12, NN17
**Directions:** Accessible from either A82 (Glasgow–
Fort William) or A9 (Edinburgh–Dalwhinnie). Hotel 3m
N of Fort William on A82, in Torlundy
**Rooms:** 17, S £250–£350 D £300–£490 **Facilities:** Tennis STV Wi-Fi in bedrooms **Parking:** 17

At the foot of mighty Ben Nevis, this imposing, mid-19th-century castle stands in 500 acres of landscaped gardens and grounds, incorporating its own small loch. After staying at the castle in 1873, when she dabbled at sketching and painting, Queen Victoria wrote in her diary 'I never saw a lovelier or more romantic spot'. Lavishly appointed in classic country-house style, the 17 spacious bedrooms are extremely comfortable and although each is individually designed, they all have large bathrooms, flat-screen TVs, laptops with internet access, an iron and ironing board and, it goes without saying, stunning views. Dinner is an experience to savour in any of its three dining rooms, each decorated with period and elaborate furniture presented as gifts by the King of Norway. The menu features modern British cuisine using the finest and freshest local ingredients. Watching the sun setting over the loch through the restaurant windows is one of those sights you will never forget. Cherubs at play adorn the painted ceiling of the sumptuous Great Hall and lounge, where afternoon tea or a pre-dinner cocktail is an essential part of this Scottish castle experience.
**Recommended in the area**
Loch Ness; Ben Nevis Distillery; Glenfinnan Monument

Glenfinnan Viaduct

# Moorings Hotel

★★★ 79% ◉ HL

| | |
|---|---|
| **Address:** | Banavie, FORT WILLIAM, |
| | Highland, PH33 7LY |
| **Tel:** | 01397 772797 |
| **Fax:** | 01397 772441 |
| **Email:** | reservations@moorings-fortwilliam.co.uk |
| **Website:** | www.moorings-fortwilliam.co.uk |
| **Map ref:** | 12, NN17 |

**Directions:** Take A380 (N from Fort William), cross
Caledonian Canal, 1st right

**Rooms:** 27, S £39–£122 D £78–£138 **Facilities:** STV Wi-Fi available **Parking:** 60

You will receive a true Highland welcome from the friendly staff at this extensively upgraded hotel
standing next to a famous series of canal locks known as Neptune's Staircase. In either the comfortable
Jacobean Restaurant, or the less formal Upper Deck Bar, dine in award-winning style on West
Coast seafood, salmon and game, as well as other Scottish fare. On summer evenings the pub-like
atmosphere of Mariners cellar bar is popular with both guests and locals.

**Recommended in the area**

Ben Nevis; Aonoch Mor; Caledonian Canal

# Kincraig House Hotel

★★★★ 77% ◉ CHH

**Address:** INVERGORDON, Highland
IV18 0LF
**Tel:** 01349 852587
**Fax:** 01349 852193
**Email:** info@kincraig-house-hotel.co.uk
**Website:** www.kincraig-house-hotel.co.uk
**Map ref:** 12, NH76
**Directions:** Off A9 past Alness towards Tain. Hotel on left 0.25m past Rosskeen Church
**Rooms:** 15, S £70–£80 D £120–£190 **Facilities:** Wi-Fi in bedrooms **Parking:** 30 **Notes:** ⊗ in bedrooms

Kincraig House Hotel is proud to be one of the most elegant country houses in the Highlands, set in the Ross-shire countryside with views of the Cromarty Firth. There is much to enjoy in the area, which boasts some of Scotland's finest golf courses, distilleries, castles and beaches. Special golf breaks are available at Kincraig, including two night's dinner, bed and breakfast with two rounds of golf at Tain and/or Fortrose and Rosemarkie. The hotel, which is just off the A9, is also within striking distance of Inverness, capital of the Highlands, and the world famous Loch Ness. Moulded ceilings, fireplaces and oak panelling create a warm, inviting atmosphere inside the hotel. Three styles of bedrooms are offered, Premier, Executive and Standard, the larger Premier rooms overlooking the gardens. A turreted room with a four-poster bed is the ideal choice for a special occasion; this has a fully tiled en suite bathroom with a corner bath and separate shower. The beautifully appointed restaurant, which has an AA Rosette, serves locally caught seafood, game dishes and other local produce, and from here there are views across the gardens to the Cromarty Firth.

**Recommended in the area**

Dunrobin Castle; Falls of Shin; Tain and Dornoch golf courses

Loch Linnhe

# Glenmoriston Town House Hotel

★★★ 85% ◉◉◉ HL

**Address:** 20 Ness Bank,
INVERNESS IV2 4SF
**Tel:** 01463 223777
**Email:** reception@glenmoristontownhouse.com
**Website:** www.glenmoristontownhouse.com
**Map ref:** 12, NH64
**Directions:** On riverside opposite theatre
**Rooms:** 30 **Facilities:** STV Wi-Fi in bedrooms
Conference facs **Parking:** 40 **Notes:** ⊗ in bedrooms

The Glenmoriston Town House is close to Inverness city centre and enjoys charming views of the River Ness. The hotel's bold contemporary designs blend seamlessly with its original classical architecture. The smart, well-proportioned bedrooms all have Wi-Fi access and any of the rooms look out over towards the river as does the Contract Brasserie. The refined French restaurant Abstract gives top priority to Scottish produce prepared by international award-winning chefs and attracts many tourists from across the world.

**Recommended in the area**

Culloden Battlefield; Loch Ness; Cawdor Castle

# The New Drumossie Hotel

★★★★   80% ◉◉ HL

**Address:** Old Perth Road,
INVERNESS, Highland, IV2 5BE
**Tel:** 01463 236451
**Fax:** 01463 712858
**Email:** stay@drumossiehotel.co.uk
**Website:** www.drumossiehotel.co.uk
**Map ref:** 12, NH64
**Directions:** From A9 follow signs for Culloden
Battlefield, hotel on left after 1m
**Rooms:** 44, S £95–£180 D £150–£200
**Facilities:** STV **Parking:** 200 **Notes:** ⊗ in bedrooms

The art deco-style Drumossie has undergone extensive refurbishment, hence its 'New' name. The impressive hotel stands in 9 acres of gardens and parkland overlooking the Moray Firth, yet it is only five minutes away from Inverness city centre and the head of Loch Ness. A welcoming complimentary drink awaits guests in their en suite room – there's a choice of single, double and family rooms. Other faciltes include a tea and coffee tray, a mini-bar, satellite TV, a telephone, Internet access, trouser press and an iron and ironing board. Concierge services include banking, currency exchange, laundry service and dry-cleaning. Only the best Scottish meats and the freshest fish and vegetables are allowed into the kitchen, so on the plate in the restaurant you might expect to find, for example, charred medallion of Angus beef tenderloin with turnip and haggis gâteau, or roasted fillet of salmon with asparagus risotto, and a selection of Celtic cheeses to follow. Wines, of course, are drawn from all over the world. The main conference suite can take up to 500 delegates theatre-style, and has all

the latest presentation and communications kit. Additional meeting rooms are ideal for smaller gatherings. An extensive range of outdoor pursuits and attractions awaits in the surrounding Highlands, including hiking and rambling, pony trekking; mountain biking; golf, mountaineering, skiing, traditional fishing and game shooting. The New Drumossie is also an ideal base for touring the Scottish Highlands. A magnificent new ballroom, with floor to ceiling windows with views over the lawns, is proving a popular venue with wedding parties.

**Recommended in the area**

Cawdor Castle; Culloden Battlefield and Visitor Centre (NTS); Loch Ness; Urquhart Castle; Caledonian Canal; Great Glen Way; Cairngorms National Park: Fort George Military Museum; Tomatin Whisky Distillery

# Toravaig House Hotel

★★★ 80% ◉ SHL

**Address:** Knock Bay, ISLEORNSAY, Isle of Skye,
Highland IV44 8RE
**Tel:** 0845 055 1117
**Fax:** 01471 833231
**Email:** info@skyehotel.co.uk
**Website:** www.skyehotel.co.uk
**Map ref:** 11, NG71
**Directions:** Cross Skye Bridge, turn left at Broadford onto
A851, hotel 11m on left. Ferry to Armadale, take A851, hotel 4m
on right **Rooms:** 9, DBB £160–£240 **Facilities:** STV
**Parking:** 20 **Notes:** ⊗ in bedrooms

This romantic Isle of Skye hideaway, set in 2 acres of grounds, has magnificent views over the Sound of Sleat and glorious sunsets are a frequent bonus. In addition, its proximity to the Skye Bridge and the Armadale ferry port means that seclusion need not mean remoteness from the mainland. There's plenty to explore on the island and in summer guests can take a trip on the hotel's own yacht, personally crewed by the owners. The bedrooms at the hotel are individually decorated, with beautiful fabrics and wall coverings, and have either brass or sleigh beds made up with crisp linens. The welcome includes a complimentary miniature of Toravaig malt whisky, a bowl of fruit, bottled water and nice toiletries, and the en suite bathrooms all have a power shower; some also have a bathtub. The chefs use only the finest and freshest local ingredients to create imaginative dishes that have earned Toravaig House an AA Rosette. The Skye seafood and Highland lamb, beef and game are succulent, and organic vegetables are prepared to perfection. Afternoon teas are another treat; in fact, food is available most of the day – ideal should you return hungry from an energetic hike over the hills of Skye.

**Recommended in the area**

Armadale Castle Gardens and Museum of the Isles; Cuillin Hills; Skye Serpentarium

# Scotland

Inverpolly National Nature Reserve

# Inver Lodge Hotel

★★★★ ◉◉ HL

**Address:** LOCHINVER, Highland, IV27 4LU
**Tel:** 01571 844496
**Fax:** 01571 844395
**Email:** info@inverlodge.com
**Website:** www.inverlodgehotel.com
**Map ref:** 12, NC02
**Directions:** A835 to Lochinver, through village, left after village hall, follow private road for 0.5m
**Rooms:** 20, S £155 D 200 **Facilities:** Sauna Solarium Wi-Fi in bedrooms **Parking:** 30

The Inver Lodge offers a tranquil retreat in spectacular surroundings. A blazing log fire warms the Residents' Lounge during afternoon tea, a card game, or the inevitable 'post mortem' following a day's fishing. The kitchen takes full advantage of abundant local produce, preparing such topographically named dishes as Kyle of Tongue scallops, Lochinver-landed sea bass or Stornoway black pudding. Head for bed in one of the comfortably equipped rooms, all named after local mountains and lochs.

**Recommended in the area**

Eas Caul Aulin Waterfall; Handa Island (RSPB); Knockan Cliff Nature Trail

# Pool House Hotel

★★★ ◉◉ SHL

**Address:** POOLEWE, Wester Ross,
Highland, IV22 2LD
**Tel:** 01445 781272
**Fax:** 01445 781403
**Email:** enquiries@poolhousehotel.com
**Website:** www.poolhousehotel.com
**Map ref:** 11, NG88
**Directions:** 6m N of Gairloch on A832. Village centre
**Rooms:** 7, D £255–£525 **Parking:** 12
**Notes:** ⊗ in bedrooms

Consistently listed among Britain's most romantic retreats, the Harrison Family's country house hotel has stood on the shores of Loch Ewe for some 300 years. It was from here, during the Second World War that the Royal Navy co-ordinated their North Atlantic convoys. Its understated façade gives little hint of its splendid public rooms, filled with antiques, paintings, porcelain and curiosities. Each individually designed guest suite has a lovely bathroom, and benefits from twice-daily maid service. The striking North by North West dining room has a nautical theme with a hand-painted starry ceiling, zodiac fresco and a large compass embellished with gold leaf. From it you can observe seals, otters, birds galore and, during the summer, glorious sunsets. Head Chef William Hay uses the finest Scottish produce and local ingredients. Meals available at the Pool House are of the highest quality and include poached fillet of Scottish beef with cannelonni of veal breast; osso bucco of monkfish with morels; red wine poached turbot with pomme mousseline and foie gras royal and cauliflower cream brûlée. Surrounding the hotel are the windswept beaches, glacial gorges and plunging waterfalls of the 'last great wilderness of Europe'.

**Recommended in the area**

Inverewe Garden; Eilean Donan Castle; Leckhelm Arboretum

# Bosville Hotel

★★★   80% ◉◉ HL

**Address:** Bosville Terrace, PORTREE,
Isle of Skye, Highland, IV51 9DG
**Tel:** 01478 612846
**Fax:** 01478 613434
**Email:** bosville@macleodhotels.co.uk
**Website:** www.macleodhotels.com
**Map ref:** 11, NG44
**Directions:** A87 signed Portree, then A855 into town.
Cross over zebra crossing, follow road to left
**Rooms:** 19, S £60–£118 D £98–£250 **Facilities:** Wi-Fi in bedrooms **Parking:** 10

Overlooking Portree's harbour and the Sound of Raasay, this elegant place blends the chic contemporary style of a boutique hotel with traditional Isle of Skye hospitality. Guests and locals mingle in the Merchant Bar, once the village bank, where you can sip a cappuccino, sample one of the malt whiskies, or enjoy the evening entertainment. The cuisine at the Bosville is Scottish with a French twist, featuring locally caught seafood, fresh game and meat, and organic Skye vegetables and berries. Chef John Kelly, author of *Flavours of Skye*, who trained at London's Savoy among other places, demonstrates his considerable flair in dishes such as pan-roast fillet of organic salmon, on a cauliflower and potato purée with tempura battered oyster and a little stew of mussels and clams, in a saffron, white wine and cream nage. Such creations have earned two AA Rosettes. As an alternative to the Chandlery Restaurant, there's simpler but no less interesting and accomplished fare on offer in the Bistro, and the Merchant Bar offers good-value lunches such as roasts, pasta, sandwiches and dishes such as cajun-spiced salmon with avocado salsa and roasted chilli sauce. The supremely comfortable bedrooms feature stylish modern décor and quality fabrics and furnishings.

**Recommended in the area**

Dunvegan Castle; Talisker Distillery; The Aros Experience

# Cuillin Hills Hotel

★★★★   73% ●● HL

**Address:** PORTREE, Isle of Skye,
Highland, IV51 9QU
**Tel:** 01478 612003
**Fax:** 01478 613092
**Email:** info@cuillinhills-hotel-skye.co.uk
**Website:** www.cuillinhills-hotel-skye.co.uk
**Map ref:** 11, NG44
**Directions:** Turn right 0.25m N of Portree off A855.
Follow hotel signs
**Rooms:** 27, S £70–£90 D £120–£240
**Facilities:** STV Wi-Fi available **Parking:** 56 **Notes:** ⊗ in bedrooms

The Cuillin Hills Hotel, on the famous Isle of Skye, enjoys some of the finest and most spectacular views from any hotel in Scotland and yet is just a short walk from the town of Portree. Built in the 1870s as a hunting lodge, it is set in 15 acres of mature private grounds overlooking Portree Bay with magnificent views to the Cuillin Mountain range. The bedrooms come in three categories, but all are spacious and luxurious, with fully tiled en suite bathrooms, satellite TV and complimentary fresh fruit. The Premier rooms at the front of the building enjoy the best of the outstanding views, while the two turret premier rooms include a large lounge area and have king-size beds. The hotel's stylish, split-level restaurant has been awarded two AA Rosettes for the quality of the food served, and the menu offers a good choice including highland game, locally caught seafood and home-made breads. Traditional desserts provide a very satisfying conclusion to the candlelit dinner experience, and there's a good range of malt whiskies and liqueurs, usually served in the residents' lounge (by a roaring log fire on cooler days). Guests can get a discount on green fees at the Isle of Skye Golf Club.

**Recommended in the area**

Dunvegan; Talisker Distillery; Bella Jane boat trips

Holy Island from the Isle of Arran

# Kilcamb Lodge Hotel

★★★ ◎◎ CHH

**Address:** STRONTIAN, Argyll, Highland, PH36 4HY
**Tel:** 01967 402257
**Fax:** 01967 402041
**Email:** enquiries@kilcamblodge.co.uk
**Website:** www.kilcamblodge.co.uk
**Map ref:** 11, NM86
**Directions:** Off A861, via Corran Ferry
**Rooms:** 10, S £95–£155 D £165–£245
**Facilities:** Wi-Fi available **Parking:** 18

Kilcamb Lodge is in a breathtaking location on the shores of Loch Sunart, where visitors will find a luxurious yet informal atmosphere coupled with very hospitable and professional service. Head Chef, Mark Greenaway, has achieved two AA Rosettes for his inventive twist on some classic dishes, which might include confit duck leg with hot orange jelly and beetroot carpaccio, sous-vide of organic Shetland salmon with pea puree, glazed snow peas and star annise foam. Desserts might include lemon meringue pie with honeycombe parfait, bubble wrap chocolate and lemon mousse.

**Recommended in the area**

Whale- and dolphin-watching boat trips; Ariundle Oakwood; Castle Tioram

# Best Western Kinloch Hotel

★★★   80% HL

**Address:** BLACKWATERFOOT,
Isle of Arran, North Ayrshire,
KA27 8ET
**Tel:** 01770 860444
**Fax:** 01770 860447
**Email:** reservations@kinlochhotel.eclipse.co.uk
**Website:** www.bw-kinlochhotel.co.uk
**Map ref:** 9, NR92
**Directions:** Ferry from Ardrossan to Brodick, follow
signs for Blackwaterfoot, hotel in centre of village
**Rooms:** 43, S £30–£55 D £60–£110 **Facilities:** 🛇 Sauna Gym STV Wi-Fi available Snooker Squash
**Parking:** 10 (public car park)

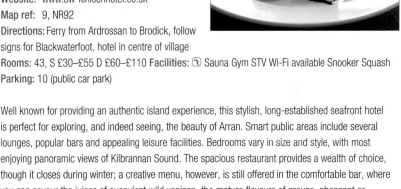

Well known for providing an authentic island experience, this stylish, long-established seafront hotel is perfect for exploring, and indeed seeing, the beauty of Arran. Smart public areas include several lounges, popular bars and appealing leisure facilities. Bedrooms vary in size and style, with most enjoying panoramic views of Kilbrannan Sound. The spacious restaurant provides a wealth of choice, though it closes during winter; a creative menu, however, is still offered in the comfortable bar, where you can savour the juices of succulent wild venison, the mature flavours of grouse, pheasant or partridge, and the tenderness of beef and lamb. Warm yourself with a good helping of peppery haggis, tatties and neeps, or a Scotch pie from the local bakery. In a region overflowing with seafood and fish, crack a crab or lobster shell, or slice open a salmon fresh from the loch, then finish with an Island cheese platter. Too much to eat? Never mind, there's an indoor pool, sauna, squash court, snooker room, gym, horse riding, quad biking and, a golf course nearby.

**Recommended in the area**

Machrie Moor Stone Circle; Balmichael Visitor Centre; Shiskine Golf Club

# The Glenmorangie Highland Home at Cadboll

★★ ◉◉ CHH

**Address:** Cadboll, Fearn, TAIN, Highland, IV20 1XP
**Tel:** 01862 871671
**Fax:** 01862 871625
**Email:** relax@glenmorangie.co.uk
**Website:** www.theglenmorangiehouse.com
**Map ref:** 12, NH88
**Directions:** From A9 onto B9175 towards Nigg.
Follow tourist signs **Rooms:** 9, S £165–£190 D £330–£390 **Parking:** 60

From the moment one is greeted, it's clear that guests are not in for a run-of-the-mill hotel experience. In fact, the Glenmorangie's owners have banished 'hotel' from their vocabulary. Evenings are dominated by the 'house party', where everyone socialises over malt whiskies in the drawing room, then dines together around one long table. Afterwards comes the big test – is your bedroom in the main house or in one of the cosy cottages in the grounds? Each room has its own character and all the expected en suite comforts. There is also an extra touch – a complimentary dram of (yet more) Glenmorangie. The daily changing menu is created with enthusiasm and to discover why the food here is so celebrated, start by wandering down to the centuries-old walled garden and look at the quality of the vegetables, herbs and soft fruit. Then remember that fresh seafood comes from two hundred yards away, world-renowned beef and lamb from the coastal grazing pastures, and ample supplies of game from neighbouring estates. Breakfast includes homemade porridge, fresh fruit, scrambled fresh farm eggs with smoked salmon, tea and home-made preserves. It's just the place too for discreet board meetings, conferences and seminars.

**Recommended in the area**

Dunrobin Castle; Falls of Shin; Dornoch Cathedral

# Kilmichael Country House Hotel

★★★ ◎◎ HL

**Address:** Glen Cloy, BRODICK, Isle of Arran,
North Ayrshire, KA27 8BY
**Tel:** 01770 302219
**Fax:** 01770 302068
**Email:** enquiries@kilmichael.com
**Website:** www.kilmichael.com
**Map ref:** 9, NS03
**Directions:** From Brodick ferry terminal towards
Lochranza for 1m. Left at golf course, inland between
sports field & church **Rooms:** 7, S £95 D £120–£195 **Facilities:** Jacuzzi STV **Parking:** 14

Believed to be the oldest house on the island of Arran, this place is special in many ways, not least in its blending of immaculate hotel-keeping with friendly informality. Each of the rooms here has been elegantly and individually decorated in keeping with the country house ambience and contains such welcoming extras as books of local interest, fresh flowers, fruit, and a dram of whisky. Some are within the main house and others occupy the 18th-century Stable Court.

**Recommended in the area**

Brodick Castle and Gardens; Lochranza Distillery; Machrie Prehistoric Standing Stones

# Ballathie House Hotel

★★★★ 76% ◎◎ CHH

**Address:** KINCLAVEN, Stanley,
Perth & Kinross, PH1 4QN
**Tel:** 01250 883268
**Fax:** 01250 883396
**Email:** email@ballathiehousehotel.com
**Website:** www.ballathiehousehotel.com
**Map ref:** 10, NO13
**Directions:** From A9 2m N of Perth, B9099 through
Stanley & signed, or off A93 at Beech Hedge follow
signs for Ballathie 2.5m
**Rooms:** 41, S £85–£98 D £170–£240 **Parking:** 50

Ballathie dates from the 17th century and great care has been taken to preserve its beauty, with many original features to give it an extremely classy air. Bedrooms range from well-proportioned master rooms to modern standards, many with antique furniture and art deco bathrooms. Menus change daily and use fresh local produce to create traditional Scottish cuisine with a modern twist.

**Recommended in the area**

Scone Palace; Pitlochry; Glamis Castle

# Pine Trees Hotel

★★★★  73% ◉ CHH

**Address:** Strathview Terrace,
PITLOCHRY, Perth & Kinross, PH16 5QR
**Tel:** 01796 472121
**Fax:** 01796 472460
**Email:** info@pinetreeshotel.co.uk
**Website:** www.pinetreeshotel.co.uk
**Map ref:** 10, NN95
**Directions:** Along main street (Atholl Rd), into
Larchwood Rd, follow hotel signs
**Rooms:** 20, S £60–£80 D £114–£170 **Facilities:** STV **Parking:** 40

A fine country house hotel within a classic Victorian mansion, set in 10 acres of elevated private grounds and woodland on the edge of this famous Highland resort. It has a tranquillity that belies its closeness to Pitlochry's busy, if admittedly hardly noisy, town centre. Many original features have been retained, including wood panelling, ornate ceilings and an impressive marble staircase. The public rooms look out over the well-kept lawns. Nineteen individually decorated bedrooms and one suite - the crimson-painted Molyneux (with a four-poster) – all have a private bathroom and feature the comprehensive range of useful extras that hotel guests expect. The Garden Restaurant, which benefits from plenty of natural daylight, has acquired a worthy reputation for sourcing and serving the best local fish, game and meat. Follow a delicious meal with a wee dram or two, ideally settled comfortably in an armchair or sofa in the Lounge Bar. The Fire Lounge, with an impressive fireplace that stretches to the ceiling, is another possibility. Loch and river fishing, hill walking, Munro-bagging (climbing Scottish mountains over 3000 feet), cycling and golf can all be arranged with the assistance of friendly hotel staff. There is ample private parking in the grounds.

**Recommended in the area**

Blair Castle; House and Falls of Bruar; Pitlochry Festival Theatre

# The Four Seasons Hotel

★★★ 83% ◉◉ HL

**Address:** Loch Earn, ST FILLANS, Perth & Kinross, PH6 2NF
**Tel:** 01764 685333
**Fax:** 01764 685444
**Email:** info@thefourseasonshotel.co.uk
**Website:** www.thefourseasonshotel.co.uk
**Map ref:** 9, NN62
**Directions:** on A85, towards W of village facing Loch
**Rooms:** 18, S £44–£94 D £88–£138 **Facilities:** Wi-Fi available
**Parking:** 40

Of countless highly desirable hotel settings in Scotland, this is unquestionably in the upper echelons. Looking south west down beautiful Loch Earn, the views are almost too good to be true – they include spectacular sunsets, morning mists and snow-covered mountains. Built in the 1800s for the manager of the local limekilns, the house has been extended over the years to become today's small but exceedingly comfortable hotel, with several individual sitting rooms, a choice of bedrooms and, out on the wooded hillside at the rear, six comfortable and well-equipped chalets. All bedrooms are spacious, most with bath and shower, and many have uninterrupted views down the loch. The chalets have a double or twin room and a bunk room making them ideal for family use. When eating, choose between the more formal Meall Reamhar Room or the Tarken Room. Both offer the same high standard of contemporary Scottish cuisine, with much, as you might expect, coming from local sources and suppliers – Loch Fyne mussels, Tweed Valley partridge, East Coast halibut, and Orkney scallops, for example. A large selection of malts is stocked in the bar. Dog owners will be gratified to know that resident canine Sham welcomes his cousins; he'll even tolerate cats, parrots and gerbils, depending on his current humour.

**Recommended in the area**

Tartans Museum; Stirling Castle; Doune Motor Museum

# Bowfield Hotel & Country Club

★★★ 80% ◉ HL

**Address:** HOWWOOD, Renfrewshire, PA9 1DZ
**Tel:** 01505 705225
**Fax:** 01505 705230
**Email:** enquiries@bowfieldhotel.co.uk
**Website:** www.bowfieldhotel.co.uk
**Map ref:** 9, NS36
**Directions:** M8 junct 28a/29, onto A737 for 6m, left onto B787, right after 2m, follow for 1m to hotel
**Rooms:** 23, S £90 D £140 **Facilities:** ⊗ Sauna Jacuzzi Solarium  Gym Wi-Fi in bedrooms **Parking:** 120

Just a short distance west of Glasgow, beyond Paisley and 15 minutes from the airport, this refreshingly different hotel can be a relaxing country retreat or an invigoratingly active destination, whichever you prefer. It is housed in a former 19th-century textile mill, and the exterior retains the sturdy, no-nonsense architecture of that time, albeit in a cleaned up and smartly painted way. The village location adds to the atmosphere, with locals in the bar, fellow guests relaxing in the informal lounges and an unhurried air about the place. For those who are up for a bit of exercise, the leisure club offers a comprehensive range of activities, from the pool and sauna to the 28-piece gym and squash courts. There are also billiards, pool and table tennis tables, basketball and short tennis and facilities. It's a great way to work up an appetite, and the restaurant will not let you down. Cooking, in modern and traditional styles, makes good use of local ingredients, including locally caught fish, Scotch beef and Highland venison, with at least some of the delicious desserts falling into the comfort food category. Food is also available in the bar and lounge from noon until 10pm. Bedrooms are very comfortable, and Bowfield is exceptionally child-friendly.

**Recommended in the area**

Glasgow; Clyde Muirshiel Regional Park; Kilbarchan Weaver's Cottage (NTS)

# Castle Venlaw Hotel

★★★ 82% ◉ CHH

**Address:** Edinburgh Road, PEEBLES,
Scottish Borders, EH45 8QG
**Tel:** 01721 720384
**Fax:** 01721 724066
**Email:** stay@venlaw.co.uk
**Website:** www.venlaw.co.uk
**Map ref:** 10, NT24
**Directions:** Off A703 Peebles/Edinburgh road, 0.75m
N of Peebles
**Rooms:** 12, S £80–£125 D £140–£270 **Facilities:** Wi-Fi available **Parking:** 17

This imposing 18th-century castle set on top of Venlaw Hill with panoramic views across Peebles and the surrounding countryside is situated in three acres of lawned and wooded grounds within the Royal Burgh of Peebles. The Castle comprises 12 bedrooms, most of which are particularly large with spectacular views across the town and the countryside beyond. Unusually, for a property of its size, Castle Venlaw offers four rooms with four poster beds including a Romantic Suite which is the ultimate in comfort and luxury. The AA-Rosetted restaurant, with its magnificent fireplace, elaborate plastered ceiling and cornices, seats 35 guests in comfort and the chef produces interesting and imaginative dishes using fresh local ingredients wherever possible. The cosy library bar is open to residents and non-residents on a daily basis, serving morning coffees, lunches and afternoon teas. In the winter, the library bar fire is lit to welcome back travellers after their day out. The hotel is fully licensed for civil partnerships, civil weddings and religious ceremonies and receptions can be catered for up to 35 people. For either business or pleasure, you can be sure of a relaxing visit along with a friendly and warm welcome.

**Recommended in the area**

City of Edinburgh; Traquair House; Abbotsford

Abbotsford House

# Peebles Hotel Hydro

★★★★  76% HL

**Address:** PEEBLES, Scottish Borders, EH45 8LX
**Tel:**  01721 720602
**Email:**  info@peebleshydro.co.uk
**Website:** www.peebleshydro.co.uk
**Map ref:** 10, NT24
**Directions:** On A702, 0.3m from town
**Rooms:** 129, S £125 D 214 **Facilities:** ⓢ  Sauna Tennis Gym
STV Wi-Fi available **Parking:** 200 **Notes:** ⊗ in bedrooms

A majestic resort hotel, dating from 1905, standing in 30 acres
of grounds on the edge of town. Surrounded by forest and
watched over by towering Dunslair Heights, its elevated position
affords beautiful views across the upper Tweed valley. With a huge range of indoor and outdoor leisure
activities, the hotel is a favourite with both families and conference delegates. The accommodation
comes in a range of styles, and is spacious, comfortable and well equipped. The richly decorated Dining
Room offers traditional and international dishes, while the bistro will appeal to the calorie conscious.
**Recommended in the area**
Edinburgh; Traquair House; Floors Castle (Kelso)

# Lochgreen House Hotel

★★★★ ◉◉◉ CHH

**Address:** Monktonhill Road, Southwood,
TROON, South Ayrshire, KA10 7EN
**Tel:** 01292 313343
**Fax:** 01292 318661
**Email:** lochgreen@costley-hotels.co.uk
**Website:** www.lochgreenhouse.co.uk
**Map ref:** 9, NS33
**Directions:** From A77 follow Prestwick Airport signs.
0.5m before airport take B749 to Troon. Hotel 1m
on left
**Rooms:** 38, S £99–£125 D £150–£170 **Facilities:** Tennis STV **Parking:** 50 **Notes:** ⊗ in bedrooms

As you drive through the hotel grounds you are likely to be surprised and delighted, by the astonishing precision of the manicured lawns and borders – a testament to the hard work of the maintenance team. Set in 30 acres of gardens and woodland, the hotel was built in 1905 by the Morton family, their exceptional light oak panelling still defining the hall, and cherrywood in the restaurant. Fine furnishings, paintings and blazing log fires enhance the two beautifully decorated lounges, one of which has a small bar. The well-proportioned en suite bedrooms are elegantly furnished with classy antiques. The highlight of a stay here has to be a gourmet meal in the magnificent Tapestry Restaurant, prepared by proprietor and master chef, Bill Costley. Bill was for many years a coach with the Scottish Culinary Team, a fact that speaks for itself. Extra hotel facilities include a coffee shop, gift shop and beauty treatments in The Retreat. Between the hotel and the sea are the fine fairways of Royal Troon Golf Club. Surely it is no accident then that Lochgreen is popular with golfers who, when not wielding a 5-iron, might consider playing tennis, or strolling through the gardens, instead.

**Recommended in the area**

Culzean Castle; Burns National Heritage Park; Scottish Maritime Museum

Scottish Maritime Museum, Irvine

# Shieldhill Castle

★★★★   73% ◉◉ CHH

**Address:** Quothquan, BIGGAR, South Lanarkshire, ML12 6NA
**Tel:**     01899 220035
**Email:**   enquiries@shieldhill.co.uk
**Website:** www.shieldhill.co.uk
**Map ref:** 10, NT03
**Directions:** A702 onto B7016 (Biggar to Carnwath road), after
2m  left into Shieldhill Road. Hotel 1.5m on right
**Rooms:** 16, S £90 D £100–£250 **Facilities:** Jacuzzi **Parking:** 50

Seat of the Chancellor family for more than 750 years, Shieldhill
Castle is steeped in history and atmosphere and is set in
beautiful gardens in the Upper Clyde Valley. The main building
contains 16 of the plush, individually styled bedrooms, and another 10 rooms are located in the
converted Victorian stables. The Chancellor's Restaurant, with two AA Rosettes, has a flexible menu
that offers any of the dishes as a starter or main course, or you can create your own tasting menu with
as many dishes as you wish. The variety of leisure pursuits includes game shooting, fishing and golf.
**Recommended in the area**
Dawyck Botanic Gardens; Lanark World Heritage Village; Falls of Clyde Visitor Centre & Wildlife Reserve

# Macdonald Crutherland House

★★★★ 77% ◉◉ HL

**Address:** Strathaven Road, EAST KILBRIDE,
South Lanarkshire, G75 0QZ
**Tel:** 0870 1942109
**Fax:** 01355 220855
**Email:** general.crutherland@
macdonald-hotels.co.uk
**Website:** www.macdonaldhotels.co.uk
**Map ref:** 9, NS65
**Directions:** Follow A726 signed Strathaven, straight
over Torrance rdbt, hotel on left after 250yds **Rooms:** 75, S £79–£167 D £98–£189 **Facilities:** ⊗
Sauna Solarium Gym STV Wi-Fi available **Parking:** 200 **Notes:** ⊗ in bedrooms

The original building, now the hub of the hotel, dates from 1700 and is set in 37 acres of landscaped
grounds. Behind its Georgian façade is a relaxing hotel with elegant public areas and extensive
banqueting and leisure facilities. The en suite bedrooms offer plenty of room to spread out and relax
or, if absolutely necessary, work. All have satellite TV, radio, direct-dial phone, hairdryer, trouser press,
iron and ironing board, tea- and coffee-making facilities and 24-hour room service. The Restaurant
was recently awarded two AA Rosettes for quality and service, making it one of the finest in Scotland's
central belt. Joe Queen's menu features innovative, often Scottish-influenced, food using the top quality
local ingredients, such as 21-day Scottish-bred beef, and fish from Loch Fyne Oysters smoked in
the traditional way. The wine list has a comprehensive selection of both traditional and contemporary
varieties. The cocktail bar serves tea and coffee with homemade shortbread, as well as light meals.
Enjoy a chilled Chardonnay on the patio, or sink into a sofa in the lounge with a decent malt. The Vital
Health beauty and fitness club has an 18m swimming pool, sauna, steam room and hi-tech gym.

**Recommended in the area**

Burrell Collection, David Livingstone Centre, Falls of Clyde

# WALES

Caernarfon Castle

# Park Plaza Cardiff

★★★★ 80% ⓐ HL

Address: Greyfriars Road, CARDIFF
CF10 3AL
Tel: 029 2011 1111
Fax: 029 2011 1112
Email: ppc_reception@parkplazahotels.co.uk
Website: www.parkplazacardiff.com
Map ref: 2, ST17
Directions: From M4 follow city centre (A470) signs.
Left into Boulevard de Nantes then immediately left
into Greyfriars Rd. Hotel on left by New Theatre
Rooms: 129, S £89–£280 D £99–£300 **Facilities:** ⓐ Jacuzzi Gym STV Wi-Fi in bedrooms

The Park Plaza is a modern building in the city centre, with impressive contemporary styling. The bedrooms are sumptuously furnished and have full facilities, including a mini-bar and safe. Free wireless internet access is available throughout the Hotel. There are facilities for wedding receptions and other functions. The Laguna Kitchen and Bar offers international and Welsh cuisine.
**Recommended in the area**
Cardiff Castle; Millennium Stadium; National Museum of Wales

# The St David's Hotel & Spa

★★★★★ 82% ⓐⓐ HL

Address: Havannah Street, CARDIFF CF10 5SD
Tel: 029 2045 4045
Fax: 029 2031 3075
Email: st.davids.reservations@principal-hotels.
com
Website: www.thestdavidshotel.com
Map ref: 2, ST17
Directions: M4 junct 33/A4232 for 9m, for
Techniquest, at top exit slip rd, 1st L at rdbt, 1st R
Rooms: 132, S D **Facilities:** ⓐ Sauna Jacuzzi Gym STV Wi-Fi available
Parking: 80 Notes: ⊗ in bedrooms

This striking hotel on the Cardiff Bay waterfront is next to Mermaid Quay, with its wide range of restaurants and bars. Inside, a dramatic glass-fronted atrium rises the full seven storeys of the building. All rooms and suites have private balconies, giving views across the bay while bathrooms feature stylish mosaic designs. The award-winning Tides Grill serves tempting and delicious dishes.
**Recommended in the area**
Cardiff Castle; Wales Millennium Centre; Techniquest; Millennium Stadium

# Wales

Millennium Stadium, Cardiff

# Ivy Bush Royal Hotel

★★★ 75% HL

**Address:** Spilman Street, CARMARTHEN,
Carmarthenshire, SA31 1LG

**Tel:** 01267 235111

**Fax:** 01267 234914

**Email:** reception@ivybushroyal.co.uk

**Website:** www.ivybushroyal.co.uk

**Map ref:** 1, SN24

**Directions:** M4 onto A48 W, over 1st rdbt, 2nd rdbt
turn right. Straight over next 2 rdbts. Left at lights.
Hotel on right at top of hill

**Rooms:** 70, S £55–£95 D £75–£130 **Facilities:** Sauna Gym STV Wi-Fi in bedrooms **Parking:** 80
**Notes:** ⊗ in bedrooms

This friendly, family-run hotel has been tastefully refurbished to offer spacious, well-equipped
bedrooms and bathrooms, including family and executive rooms, and private suites. In the restaurant
seasonal menus make extensive use of fresh local produce, such as Welsh Black beef.

**Recommended in the area**

National Botanic Garden of Wales; Aberglasney House and Gardens; Oakwood Theme Park

# Best Western Falcondale Mansion

★★★ 86% ◉◉ CHH

**Address:** LAMPETER,
Ceredigion, SA48 7RX
**Tel:** 01570 422910
**Fax:** 01570 423559
**Email:** info@falcondalehotel.com
**Website:** www.falcondalehotel.com
**Map ref:** 2, SN54
**Directions:** 800yds W of High St A475 or 1.5m NW of Lampeter A482
**Rooms:** 20, S £95–£120 D £130–£168
**Facilities:** Wi-Fi in bedrooms
**Parking:** 60

Falconale Mansion is set amongst breathtaking scenery in the heart of Wales surrounded by valleys of infinite shades of green. The Victorian mansion, built in the Italianate style, sits in 14 acres of glorious gardens that have been laid down over the centuries and contain many rare varieties of exotic and native trees and shrubs. The garden is particularly famous for its spectacular rhododendrons and azaleas, which provide vibrant colour in May and June. While certain luxuries have been added over the years Falcondale Mansion still today boasts a homely atmosphere and prides itself on a warm welcome. Bedrooms are generally spacious, well equipped and tastefully decorated, and in most there are delightful valley views. Bars and lounges are well appointed and diners have a choice of either the Valley restaurant or the less formal Peterwells brasserie. Fresh ingredients are sourced locally, the speciality being the Celtic Pride Welsh Beef and Welsh Salt Marsh Lamb.

**Recommended in the area**

Llanerchaeron House; National Botanic Garden of Wales; Aberaeon

# The Royal Oak Hotel

★★★ 83% ◉ HL

**Address:** Holyhead Road, BETWS-Y-COED,
Conwy, LL24 0AY
**Tel:** 01690 710219
**Fax:** 01690 710603
**Email:** royaloakmail@btopenworld.com
**Website:** www.royaloakhotel.net
**Map ref:** 5, SH75
**Directions:** On A5 in town centre, next to St Mary's
church

**Rooms:** 27, S £67.5–£87.5 D £85–£140 **Facilities:** STV Wi-Fi available **Parking:** 90

The wonders of Snowdonia National Park are right on the doorstep of this stately Victorian hotel,
nestling at the foot of a wooded hillside in one of the region's most picturesque villages. The age and
style of the building is reflected in the traditional comforts and quality of the interior. Bedrooms offer
a pleasing mix of period furnishings, stylish fabrics and contemporary facilities such as broadband
internet. They all have en suite bathrooms, and upgrade options include four-poster beds and whirlpool
baths. Guests also receive complimentary membership of the nearby Dukes Leisure Centre. There
are three dining choices at the hotel. The Llugwy Restaurant is the more formal, a splendid room with
a nice old fireplace and crisp table linens, where modern Welsh cooking is offered on a four-course
tasting menu. Dishes might include starters such as smoked local halibut, or pot-roasted belly pork on
crispy black pudding with apple Calvados cream. There'll be a soup to follow before main courses like
Conwy Valley lamb or Anglesey seabass. If the bara brith and butter pudding with Welsh whisky ice
cream is on the menu, try it. Simpler dishes are available in the Grill Bar and the Stables Bistro Bar,
the latter with regular live music.

**Recommended in the area**

Snowdon Mountain Railway (or a walk to the summit); Llechwedd Slate Caverns; Conwy Castle

# Castle Hotel Conwy

★★★    80% ◉◉ HL

**Address:**  High Street, CONWY  LL32 8DB
**Tel:**    01492 582800
**Fax:**    01492 582300
**Email:**   mail@castlewales.co.uk
**Website:** www.castlewales.co.uk
**Map ref:** 5, SH77
**Directions:** A55 junct 18, follow  town centre signs,
cross estuary (castle on left). Right then left at mini-
rdbts onto one-way system. Right at Town Wall Gate,
right onto Berry St then along High St on left
**Rooms:** 28, S £77–£89.50 D £110–£259 **Facilities:** STV Wi-Fi throughout **Parking:** 34

The distinctive building that houses the Castle Hotel hints at its long and fascinating history. Built on the
site of a Cistercian abbey, it has welcomed many famous people through its doors, including Thomas
Telford (who built the town's famous bridge), railway pioneer George Stephenson, William Wordsworth
and the Queen of Romania. The current owners, the Lavin family and partner/head chef Graham
Tinsley, have been very mindful of this important heritage while giving the place an attractive facelift. All
of the bedrooms have en suite bathrooms and modern facilities, and extra luxury in the superior rooms
includes spa baths. One of these rooms has an ornately carved four-poster bed, while another enjoys
a good view of the castle. Graham Tinsley MBE, and his award-winning kitchen team, have gained a
reputation for serving excellent Welsh produce. Food is served in both Shakespeare's and Dawson's
Rooms in a relaxed atmosphere, with the emphasis on locally sourced ingredients. As a result there is
a real seasonal feel to the menu. Conwy mussels feature in the winter months; Conwy valley lamb in
spring and early summer. There's also a good selection of vegetarian and organic food on the menu.
**Recommended in the area**

Conwy Castle; Caernarfon Castle; Snowdonia National Park

Afon Glaslyn, Beddgelert

# Quay Hotel & Spa

★★★★ 85% ◉◉ HL

**Address:** Deganwy Quay, DEGANWY, LL31 9DJ
**Tel:** 01492 564100
**Email:** info@quayhotel.com
**Website:** www.quayhotel.com
**Map ref:** 5, SH77
**Directions:** M56, A494, A55 junct 18, straight
across 2 rdbts. At lights bear L into The Quay.
**Rooms:** 74, S £120 D £175 **Facilities:** ⊗ Gym Wi-fi
in bedrooms Spa **Parking:** 96 **Notes:** ⊗ in bedrooms

Replacing an area of redundant railway sidings, it didn't take this newly opened boutique hotel long to become AA Hotel of the Year for Wales 2007–08. Occupying a marvellous position beside the Conwy estuary, its interior uses space, light and knife-sharp styling to create a refreshingly different style of hotel. Spacious bedrooms, many with balconies and wonderful views, are decorated in neutral colours and offer plenty of extras, including state-of-the-art communication systems. The first-floor restaurant, The Vue, combines contemporary fine dining with first-class service.

**Recommended in the area**

Conwy Castle, Great Orme Heritage Coast, Snowdonia National Park

# Dunoon Hotel

★★★  78%  HL

**Address:** Gloddaeth Street,
LLANDUDNO, Conwy, LL30 2DW
**Tel:** 01492 860787
**Fax:** 01492 860031
**Email:** reservations@dunoonhotel.co.uk
**Website:** www.dunoonhotel.co.uk
**Map ref:** 5, SH78
**Directions:** Exit Promenade at war memorial by pier onto wide avenue. 200yds on right
**Rooms:** 49, S £66.5–£72.5 D £105–£145 **Parking:** 24

Close to the promenade in this well preserved Victorian seaside resort, the Dunoon has a certain old world grace about it. Hushed and stuffy it isn't, though. In fact, the Williams family, who have been here a good while, make sure that it offers a happy antidote to what they regard as anodyne modern living. For example, they treat returning guests like old friends, and first-time customers as new ones. Their approach is evident too in the way they have styled the bedrooms, with no two alike, and in their attention to detail, with crisp Egyptian cotton bedlinen, and Molton Brown toiletries in every bathroom. It is evident too in the restaurant, where silver rings contain freshly pressed linen napkins, and white porcelain is used on the tables. Food and wine are their abiding passions. Cooking is unpretentious, using fresh ingredients sourced locally as far as the seasons allow, with specialities such as terrine of game, medley of local fish, ragout of Welsh lamb with mint dumplings and asparagus mousse. Their taste in wines is adventurous, with a wine list that, in their words, 'offers more than you would expect from a modest hotel in the sleepy outer reaches of Britain'.

**Recommended in the area**

Great Orme; Bodnant Gardens; Snowdonia National Park

# Empire Hotel & Spa

★★★★ 73% ◉ HL

**Address:** Church Walks, LLANDUDNO  LL30 2HE
**Tel:** 01492 860555
**Fax:** 01492 860791
**Email:** reservations@empirehotel.co.uk
**Website:** www.empirehotel.co.uk
**Map ref:** 5, SH78
**Directions:** From Chester, A55 junct 19 for Llandudno. Follow town centre signs. Hotel at end facing main street

**Rooms:** 53, S £70–£110 D £100–£140 **Facilities:** Spa, Sauna, Pool, Steam room, Whirlpool, Gym, Beauty Therapy suite Free broadband Wi-Fi **Parking:** 40 **Notes:** ⊗ in bedrooms

Location very centrally – close to the pier, promenade, shops and main attractions of Llandudno – the Empire Hotel is beautifully furnished with antiques and fine paintings. All rooms are en suite and have modern facilities. The award-winning Watkins & Co restaurant is elegant and traditional in style and offers an extensive menu. There is an all day lounge service for snacks and beverages.

**Recommended in the area**

Caernarfon Castle; Conwy Castle; Portmeirion Italianate village

---

# Osborne House

★★★★ ◉ TH

**Address:** 17 North House, LLANDUDNO  LL30 2LP
**Tel:** 01492 860330
**Fax:** 01492 860791
**Email:** sales@osbornehouse.com
**Website:** www.osbornehouse.com
**Map ref:** 5, SH78
**Directions:** Exit A55 junct 19. Follow signs for Llandudno then Promenade. Continue to junct, turn right. Hotel on left opposite pier entrance

**Rooms:** 6, S £145–£200 D £145–£200 **Facilities:** STV Wi-Fi in bedrooms **Parking:** 6

This intimate luxury town house has six spacious suites all with glorious views of the pier and promenade. Each room has a canopied large bed with down duvet, marble bathroom with walk in shower and a sitting room with fireplace. The award-winning Osborne's Cafe/Grill has stunning dècor, towering ornate ceilings and impressive crystal chandeliers. It is an all day venue featuring a diverse range of menus presented with an air of informality. Osborne House makes an ideal touring base.

**Recommended in the area**

Llandudno Great Orme Heritage Coast; Llandudno Pier; Snowdonia National Park; Portmeirion village

# St George's Hotel

★★★★  77% ◉ HL

**Address:** The Promenade, LLANDUDNO,
Conwy, LL30 2LG
**Tel:** 01492 877544
**Fax:** 01492 877788
**Email:** reservations@stgeorgeswales.co.uk
**Website:** www.stgeorgeswales.co.uk
**Map ref:** 5, SH78
**Directions:** A55–A470, follow to promenade,
0.25m, hotel on corner

**Rooms:** 75 **Facilities:** Sauna Jacuzzi Solarium Wi-Fi available **Parking:** 36 **Notes:** ⊗ in bedrooms

St George's Hotel is situated in a stunning position on the North Wales coast, overlooking the Llandudno seascape and the Great and Little Orme Mountains. Very close to the A55, Chester and Wrexham are less than 45 minutes' drive and Liverpool and Manchester are easily accessible. The hotel is proud to maintain many of its original architectural features, traditional quality service values and is just a five-minute walk from Venue Cymru, one of the largest theatres and conference centres in Wales. A £4 million refurbishment has enhanced the public areas and improved all 75 elegant bedrooms with air conditioning, sumptuous bathrooms and all the luxuries expected from a hotel of this quality. The restaurant, which has been awarded an AA Rosette, uses only the finest fresh, local Welsh produce – all traceable, and organic wherever possible, and is the perfect place to enjoy delicious home-cooked cuisine. Guests can also lunch in the Terrace Lounge, with its stunning seafront views and selection of light lunches and impeccable cappuccinos. During the evening the this room becomes a haven where guests congregate, perhaps to sample the range of malt whiskies or enjoy a gin and tonic before dinner.

**Recommended in the area**

Great Orme Mines; Alice in Wonderland; Bodnant Gardens

# St Tudno Hotel and Restaurant

★★★ ◉◉ HL

**Address:** The Promenade,
LLANDUDNO, Conwy, LL30 2LP
**Tel:** 01492 874411
**Fax:** 01492 860407
**Email:** sttudnohotel@btinternet.com
**Website:** www.st-tudno.co.uk
**Map ref:** 5, SH78
**Directions:** On Promenade towards pier, hotel
opposite pier entrance
**Rooms:** 18, S £75–£105 D £95 **Facilities:** ⓩ STV
**Parking:** 12

Right on the Llandudno seafront, this outstanding hotel is personally run by the owner, Martin Bland, who has put together a loyal and caring team to look after guests. There is a lovely sitting room with sea views as well as a leafy coffee lounge and Victorian style bar lounge, the latter renowned for its afternoon teas. The restaurant transports you to northern Italy with its vast murals depicting Lake Como, but it is the food that has the greatest impact of all. With its two AA Rosettes it is clear that you are in for a treat, and this might include slow-poached baby halibut with haricot blanc, fennel chardonnay and Pacific oysters, or roast fillet of Welsh beef with ox tongue ragout. The bedrooms are individually styled and only one does not have an en suite bathroom. All have fine linen, bathrobes and quality toiletries, a Villeroy and Boch tea service and home-made biscuits and facilities such as internet connection and television with VCR (video library available at no charge). Even more luxurious suites are also available. There is a heated indoor swimming pool in case the sea temperature is too bracing, and a delightful little garden.

**Recommended in the area**

Great Orme Tramway; Conwy Castle; Snowdonia National Park

Dwygydylchi from the Great Orme

# Palé Hall Country House Hotel

★★★★  84% ◉ CHH

**Address:** Palé Estate, Llandderfel,
BALA, Gwynedd, LL23 7PS
**Tel:** 01678 530285
**Fax:** 01678 530220
**Email:** enquiries@palehall.co.uk
**Website:** www.palehall.co.uk
**Map ref:** 5, SH93
**Directions:** Off B4401 (Corwen/Bala road) 4m from
Llandrillo
**Rooms:** 17, S £85–£150 D £115–£200 **Facilities:** Wi-Fi available **Parking:** 40
**Notes:** ⊗ in bedrooms

This enchanting mansion was built in 1870 and is surrounded by extensive grounds and beautiful woodland scenery. The spacious guest rooms contain an extraordinary selection of beds and bathing facilities, including the half-tester occupied by Queen Victoria in 1889. Dining is stylish and restful, with regularly changing menus bringing out the best of fresh, natural ingredients.
**Recommended in the area**
Snowdonia National Park; Llechwedd Slate Caverns; Penmachno Woollen Mill

# Seiont Manor Hotel

★★★ ◎◎ CHH

**Address:** Llanrug, CAERNARFON, Gwynedd, LL55 2AQ
**Tel:** 01286 673366
**Fax:** 01286 672840
**Email:** seiontmanor@handpicked.co.uk
**Website:** www.handpicked.co.uk
**Map ref:** 5, SH93
**Directions:** E on A4086, 2.5m from Caernarfon
**Rooms:** 28 **Facilities:** ℞ Sauna Gym STV
**Parking:** 60

Nestling in the foothills of Snowdonia, with views of the peak of
Snowdon on a clear day, this Georgian manor house was once at the heart of an agricultural estate. It is
hardly surprising, therefore, that the cuisine in the two Rosette restaurant is based on regional produce
(including Welsh whisky, wine and water), which is used to add a creative touch to traditional Welsh
dishes. In addition to the à la carte menu, there is also a 'comfort food' menu offering such dishes
as hearty stews and local venison sausages. After a busy day of exploring this fascinating part of the
country you can sit by the fire in the period lounge or relax with a book or a drink (or both) in the library.
The bedrooms, including spacious family rooms and executive rooms, all have a balcony or terrace from
which to enjoy the views, and all have an en suite bathroom with luxury toiletries. Many activities can be
enjoyed on the premises here, including fishing on the River Seiont, which flows through the grounds,
or swimming in the 40ft indoor swimming pool. The hotel has internet access (wired and wireless) and
business guests have a choice of three conference rooms.

**Recommended in the area**

Caernarfon Castle; Snowdonia National Park; Llechwedd Slate Caverns

# Maes y Neuadd Country House Hotel

★ ★ ★   80% ◉◉ CHH

Address: HARLECH, Gwynedd LL47 6YA
Tel:      01766 780200
Fax:      01766 780211
Email:   maes@neuadd.com
Website: www.neuadd.com
Map ref: 5, SH53
Directions: 3m NE of Harlech, signed on unclassified road, off B4573
Rooms: 15, D £98–£190 Facilities: Wi-Fi available Parking: 50

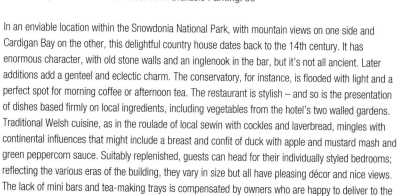

In an enviable location within the Snowdonia National Park, with mountain views on one side and Cardigan Bay on the other, this delightful country house dates back to the 14th century. It has enormous character, with old stone walls and an inglenook in the bar, but it's not all ancient. Later additions add a genteel and eclectic charm. The conservatory, for instance, is flooded with light and a perfect spot for morning coffee or afternoon tea. The restaurant is stylish – and so is the presentation of dishes based firmly on local ingredients, including vegetables from the hotel's two walled gardens. Traditional Welsh cuisine, as in the roulade of local sewin with cockles and laverbread, mingles with continental influences that might include a breast and confit of duck with apple and mustard mash and green peppercorn sauce. Suitably replenished, guests can head for their individually styled bedrooms; reflecting the various eras of the building, they vary in size but all have pleasing décor and nice views. The lack of mini bars and tea-making trays is compensated by owners who are happy to deliver to the room. Instead of rushing off after breakfast, take time to explore the 34 hectares of grounds.

**Recommended in the area**

Portmeirion; Harlech Castle; Ffestiniog Railway

# The Celtic Manor Resort

★★★★★  84% ®® HL

**Address:** Coldra Woods, NEWPORT  NP18 1HQ
**Tel:**  01633 413000
**Fax:**  01633 412910
**Email:**  postbox@celtic-manor.com
**Website:** www.celtic-manor.com
**Map ref:** 2, ST38
**Directions:** M4 junct 24, take B4237 towards
Newport. Hotel 1st on right
**Rooms:** 400, S £165–£1065 D £198–£1098
**Facilities:** ☢ Golf Spa Tennis Crèche Wi-Fi available **Parking:** 1000 **Notes:** ⊗ in bedrooms

The Celtic Manor Resort is two hotels, one old, one new, that stand together in 1400 acres of parkland
in the beautiful Usk Valley. The 19th-century Manor House was where the Resort's owner, Sir Terence
Matthews, was born when it was a maternity hospital. Original character is all around – admire, for
example, the leaded windows, wood-panelled walls and sweeping wooden staircase. Traditionally
styled bedrooms include three with four-posters. There's a choice of places to eat or drink: The Patio
Restaurant, serving Italian-style dishes, the Cellar Bar and the Manor Lounge. The five-star Resort
Hotel opened in 1999, with a soaring atrium and 330 individually decorated and beautifully appointed
bedrooms. One of the two Presidential Suites even has a baby grand piano. Guests in both hotels
may make complimentary phone calls to national landlines. Dining choices include a new fine dining
restaurant, The Crown; the informal Olive Tree offering contemporary Mediterranean cuisine; Merlins
piano bar serving afternoon teas; and the Forum Café providing light refreshments. The Resort also
offers a convention centre, 31 function rooms, three championship golf courses including The Twenty
Ten, a golf academy, two health clubs and two spas. Quite a venue for The 2010 Ryder Cup.

**Recommended in the area**

Caerleon Roman Town; Tintern Abbey; Raglan Castle

# Beggars Reach Hotel

★★★  80% HL

**Address:** PEMBROKE, Milford Haven,
Pembrokeshire, SA73 1PD
**Tel:** 01646 600700
**Fax:** 01646 600560
**Email:** stay@beggars-reach.com
**Website:** www.beggars-reach.com
**Map ref:** 1, SM90
**Directions:** 8m S of Haverfordwest, 6m N of
Pembroke, off A477 **Rooms:** 30, S £75–£95
D £100–£130 **Facilities:** STV Wi-Fi available **Parking:** 80 **Notes:** ⊗ in bedrooms

A privately owned hotel in a tranquil spot, run by experienced hoteliers, William and Gillian Smallman. "Beggars Reach is our long term future," they say, "and we intend to channel all our energies into fulfilling our dream". Formerly the village rectory, and retaining much of its Victorian character, it stands in three acres of grounds, surrounded by farmland. Comfortable, high-standard accommodation is provided in individually designed, en suite bedrooms with tea- and coffee-making facilities, phones and satellite TV; some have views over the garden and Pembrokeshire countryside. Guests can enjoy a morning coffee or pre-dinner drink in the cosy lounge before a typical meal of rack of Welsh lamb, perhaps, or pan-fried fresh marlin steak in the bright and airy Garden Restaurant, whose french windows open on to the terrace. The cuisine is traditional, with the menu written afresh daily, and food sourced largely from local suppliers. An alternative is to have a drink in Harry's Bar, followed by anything from a snack to a three-course meal in the smaller, less formal Anna's Restaurant. Wines from around the world may be enjoyed in both. Conference facilities cater for up to 80 delegates and wedding breakfasts for up to 140 guests.

**Recommended in the area**

Pembrokeshire Coast National Park; Pembroke Castle; Milford Haven Waterway

# Warpool Court Hotel

★★★   80% ◉◉ CHH

**Address:** ST DAVID'S, Pembrokeshire, SA62 6BN
**Tel:** 01437 720300
**Fax:** 01437 720676
**Email:** info@warpoolcourthotel.com
**Website:** www.warpoolcourthotel.com
**Map ref:** 1, SM72
**Directions:** At Cross Square left by Cartref Restaurant (Goat St). Pass Farmers Arms pub, after 400mtrs left, follow hotel signs, entrance on right
**Rooms:** 25, S £100–£115 D £150–£220 **Facilities:** ⊙ Tennis **Parking:** 100

A privately-owned hotel in large grounds on St David's peninsula, overlooking the gentle sweep of St Bride's Bay and the offshore islands. Bedrooms are well equipped and attractively furnished, and 14 of them have spectacular sea views. The spacious restaurant, overlooking the gardens and the sea, offers an extensive menu, with fish much in evidence, while the wine list offers a good choice. A heated swimming pool opens from Easter to the end of October and there is an all-weather tennis court.

**Recommended in the area**

Pembrokeshire Coast National Park; St David's Cathedral; Pembroke Castle

# Gliffaes Country House Hotel

★★★   80% ◉ CHH

**Address:** CRICKHOWELL, Powys, NP8 1RH
**Tel:** 01874 730371
**Fax:** 01874 730463
**Email:** calls@gliffaeshotel.com
**Website:** www.gliffaeshotel.com
**Map ref:** 2, SO21
**Directions:** 1m off A40, 2.5m W of Crickhowell
**Rooms:** 23, S £78.5–£99 D £143–£210
**Facilities:** Tennis Wi-Fi available **Parking:** 34
**Notes:** ⊗ in bedrooms

Off the beaten track between the Brecon Beacons and the Black Mountains, hidden among trees in 33 acres, and owned by the same family since 1948. The Gliffaes has a great view of the Usk, and actually owns 2.5 miles of this prime wild brown trout river. Elegant public rooms include a balcony and conservatory. The 23 individually decorated and furnished bedrooms, priced according to size and view, all have private bathrooms. The restaurant uses local produce and the freshest of ingredients.

**Recommended in the area**

Brecon Beacons National Park; The Big Pit; Tretower Court

# The Lake Country House & Spa

★★★ ◉◉ CHH

**Address:** LLANGAMMARCH WELLS,
Powys, LD4 4BS
**Tel:** 01591 620202
**Fax:** 01591 620457
**Email:** info@lakecountryhouse.co.uk
**Website:** www.lakecountryhouse.co.uk
**Map ref:** 2, SN94
**Directions:** W from Builth Wells on A483 to Garth
(approx 6m). L for Llangammarch Wells, follow hotel
signs **Rooms:** 30, S £115–£180 D £170–£250 **Facilities:** ⊗ Tennis STV Wi-Fi available **Parking:** 70

Standing serenely in 50 acres of parkland, with sweeping lawns, rhododendron-lined pathways and riverside walks, this magnificent former hunting and fishing lodge is the epitome of grandeur. Begun in 1840 and remodelled 60 years later, the house is an architectural mixture, with half-timbering declaring mock-Tudor, but with the verandas and french windows giving it a colonial air. From the turn of the 20th century until the Second World War it was the only barium spa resort outside Germany. Everywhere you look are beautiful paintings, fascinating features and fine furnishings. Bedrooms in the main house and the 12 suites in the Lodge overlooking the golf course, are individually styled and provide many extra comforts. Dining in the spacious and elegant restaurant is an experience to savour, with fresh local ingredients creatively combined to create an award-winning, modern Celtic style of cuisine. The owners are justifiably proud of their 350-bin wine list, one of the finest in Wales. A newly developed spa has an indoor pool, ground floor treatment rooms and a hot tub on the balcony overlooking the shoreline of the lake. Guests can fish the lake and river free of charge (angling tuition can be arranged) and use the 9-hole, par 3 golf course and tennis courts.

**Recommended in the area**

Dolaucothi Gold Mines; Brecon Beacons National Park; Black Mountains

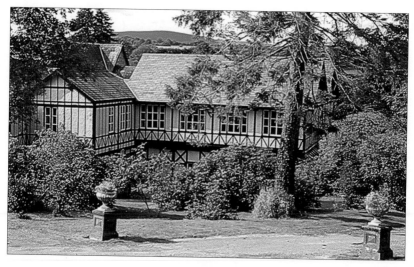

# Llangoed Hall

★★★★  85% ◉◉ CHH

| | |
|---|---|
| **Address:** | LLYSWEN, Nr Brecon, Powys, LD3 0YP |
| **Tel:** | 01874 754525 |
| **Fax:** | 01874 754545 |
| **Email:** | enquiries@llangoedhall.com |
| **Website:** | www.llangoedhall.com |

**Map ref:** 2, SO13
**Directions:** A470 through village for 2m. Hotel drive on right
**Rooms:** 23, S £150–£345 D £195–£385
**Facilities:**  STV **Parking:** 80 **Notes:** ⊗ in bedrooms

Formerly known as Llangoed Castle, the Hall is set in 17 acres of gardens and parkland in the Wye Valley. In the early 20th century, Sir Clough Williams Ellis, creator of Portmeirion, the Italianate village in North Wales, redesigned the 1632 mansion. By the early 1970s, however, it was in danger of demolition. Then, in 1987, Sir Bernard Ashley bought and restored it, opening it as a hotel in 1990. The impressive interior contains his noteworthy art collection, including works by Whistler, Sickert and Augustus John. Seventeenth century antique mirrors, cast-iron baths and fabrics from Elanbach, the Ashley family's textile design company, are just some of the features that make each of the 23 en suite bedrooms so welcoming. Indeed, everywhere you look are artefacts that reflect the Ashley family's interests, from Sir Bernard's models of boats and aircraft to Regine Ashley's rare wine labels. Head Chef, Sean Ballington, winner of two AA Rosettes, is a firm believer in fresh, local produce. From Welsh lamb, and Black beef to local salmon, his signature dishes are best described as classic with a twist. Regine, an acknowledged oenophile, chooses the wines. Llangoed Hall makes a stimulating setting for conferences and board meetings.

**Recommended in the area**

Elan Valley Dam and Reservoir; Brecon Beacons; Black Mountains

# West Arms Hotel

★★★  87% ◉◉ HL

**Address:** LLANARMON DYFFRYN CEIRIOG, Ceiriog
Valley, Nr Llangollen, Wrexham, LL20 7LD
**Tel:**  01691 600665
**Fax:**  01691 600622
**Email:**  gowestarms@aol.com
**Website:** www.thewestarms.co.uk
**Map ref:**  5, SJ13
**Directions:** Off A483/A5 at Chirk, take B4500 to
Ceiriog Valley. Llanarmon 11m at end of B4500
**Rooms:** 15, S £53.50–£118 D £87–£228 **Parking:** 20

In the beautiful Ceiriog Valley, this delightful old drovers' inn oozes warmth and character, with 17th-century timberwork, period furniture, undulating floors and blazing inglenook fires. Centuries ago, cattle drovers down from the hills rested and refreshed their cattle here on their slow journeys to Oswestry and Wrexham markets. Today, a comfortable lounge, a room for private dining and two bars, as well as an award-winning restaurant, await travellers. The hotel has seven 'character' bedrooms, plus a further eight, all with bath and hand shower facilities. Furnished in a mix of modern and period styles, many still feature their original exposed beams. The Howard Room has a four-poster bed, and overlooks the village. In the restaurant, chef Grant Williams has won many accolades for his set-price menus of freshly cooked dishes for which he makes extensive use of local produce. He has worked here for 14 years after travelling the kitchens of the world, and has even cooked for HRH Prince Charles. Lunch and dinner can also be taken round the log fire in the cosy bar. The hotel will arrange a range of activities for guests such as pony-trekking, quad-biking and even white water rafting. Alternatively, there are always the riverside gardens in which to wander and relax.

**Recommended in the area**

Chirk Castle; Llangollen Viaduct; Erddig Hall (NT)

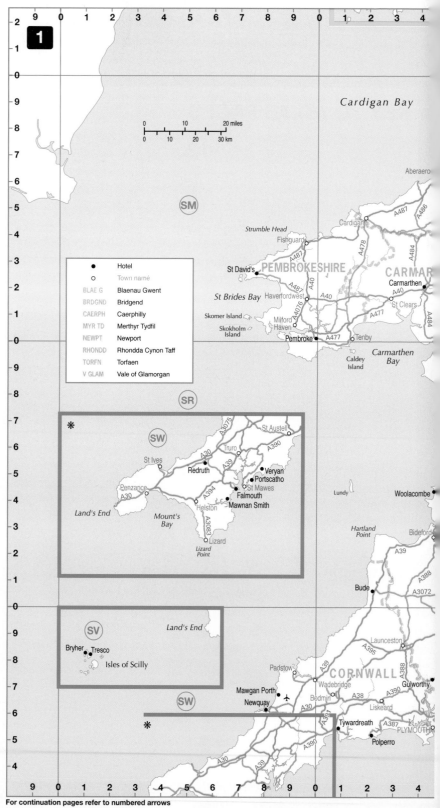

Cardigan Bay

For continuation pages refer to numbered arrows

332

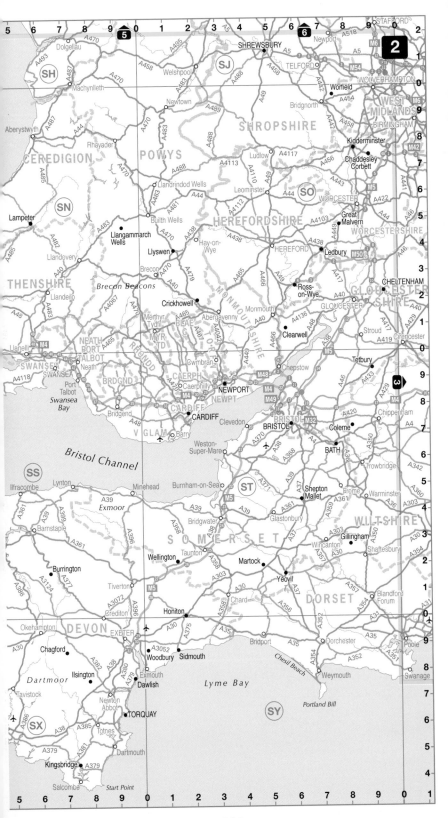

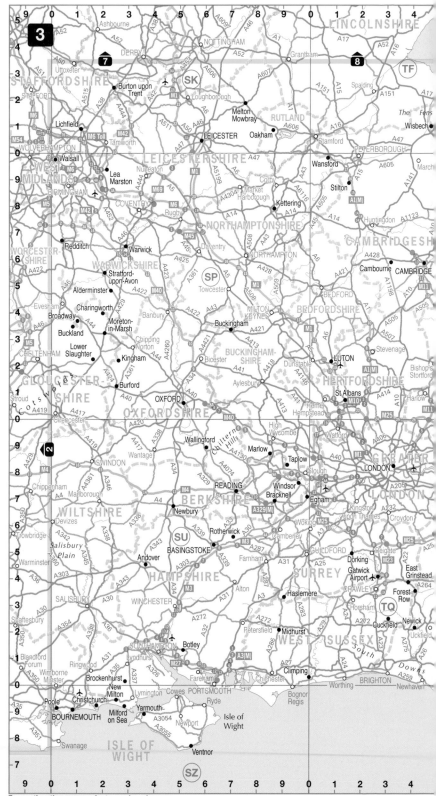

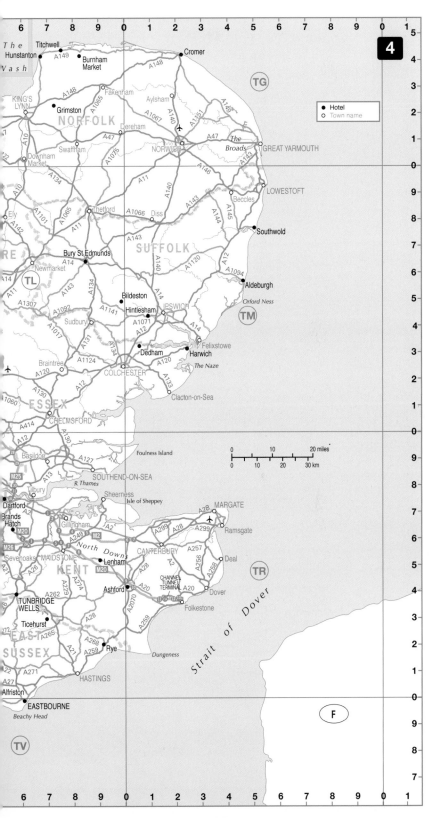

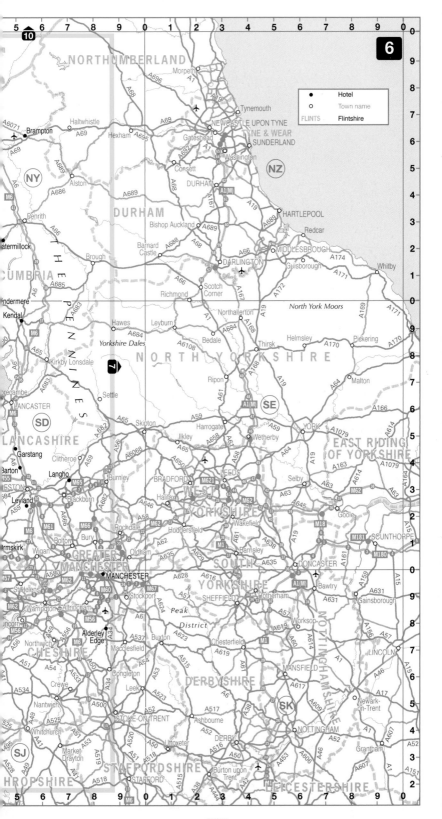

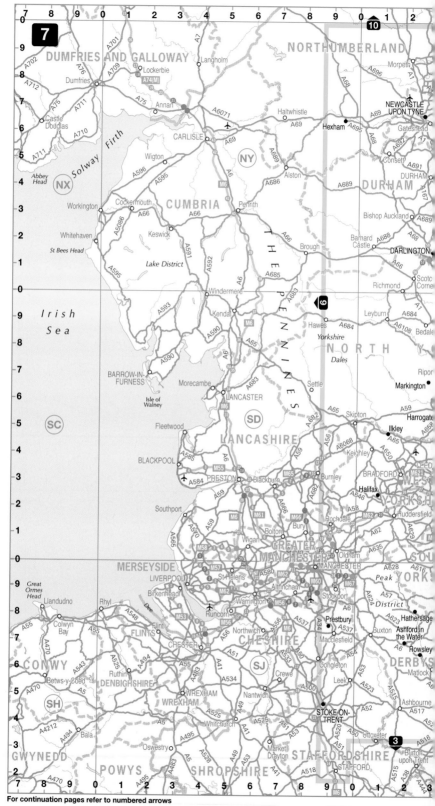

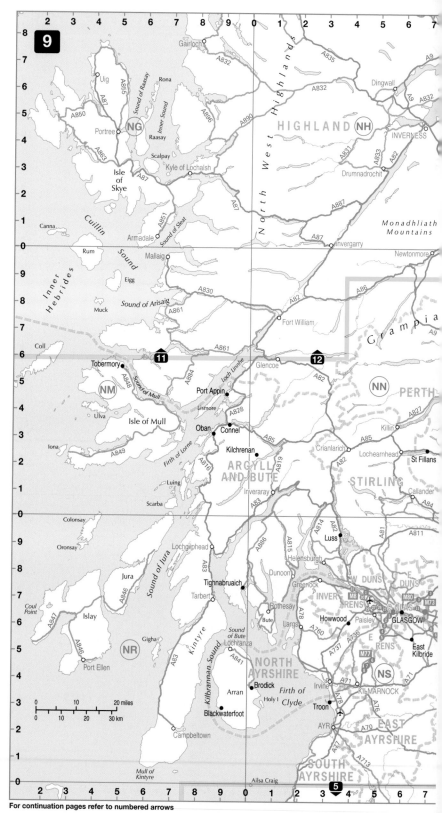

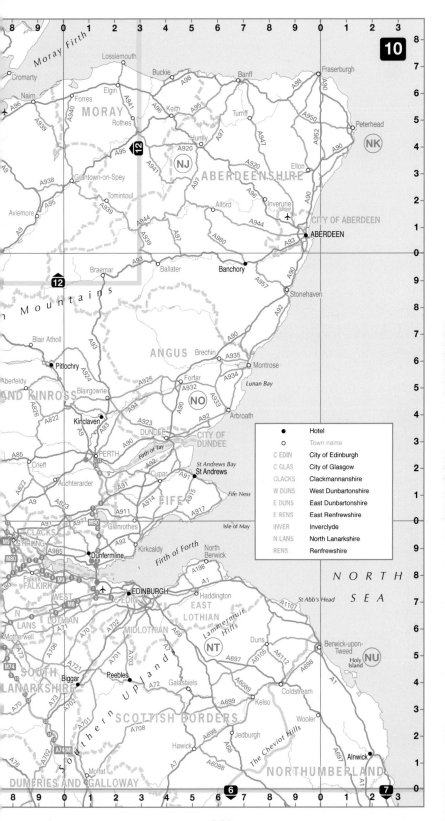

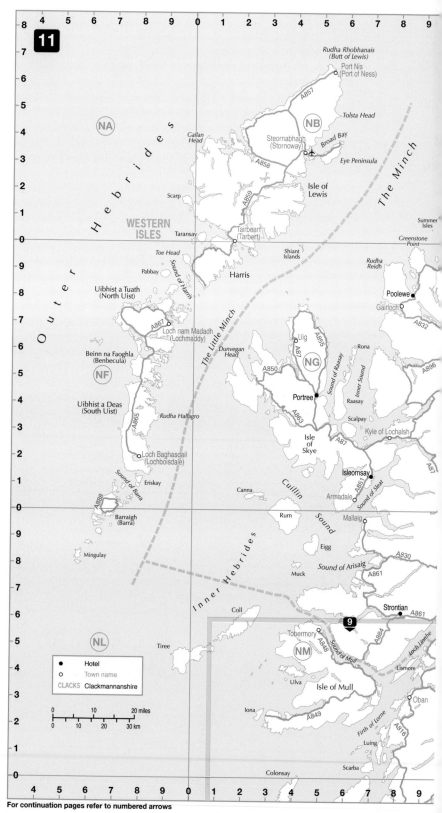

11

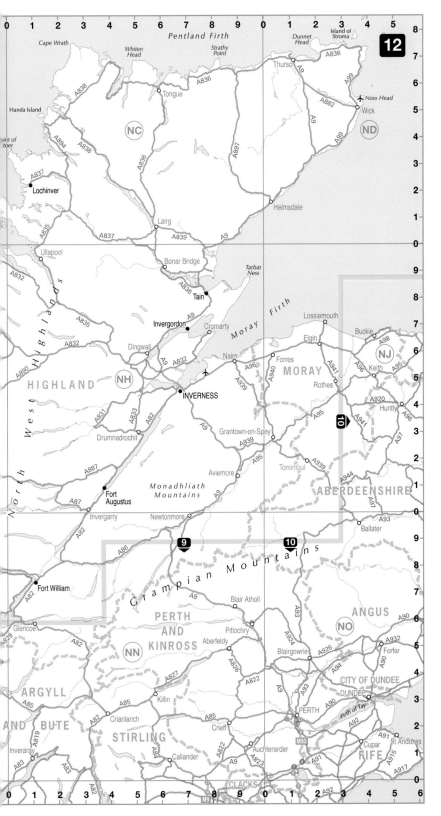

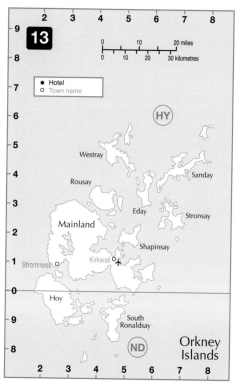

Hotel
Town name

HY

Westray

Rousay

Sanday

Eday

Mainland

Stronsay

Shapinsay

Stromness

Kirkwall

Hoy

South
Ronaldsay

ND

Orkney
Islands

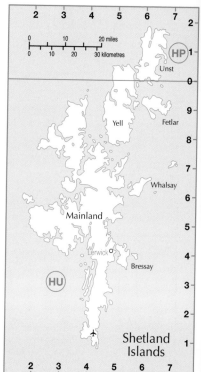

HP

Unst

Yell

Fetlar

Whalsay

Mainland

Lerwick

Bressay

HU

Shetland
Islands

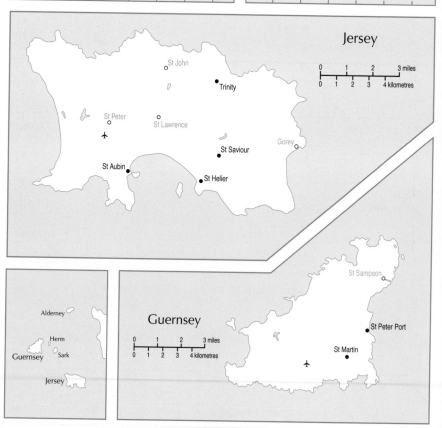

Jersey

St John

Trinity

St Peter

St Lawrence

St Saviour

Gorey

St Aubin

St Helier

Guernsey

Alderney

Herm

Guernsey

Sark

Jersey

St Sampson

St Peter Port

St Martin

# County Map

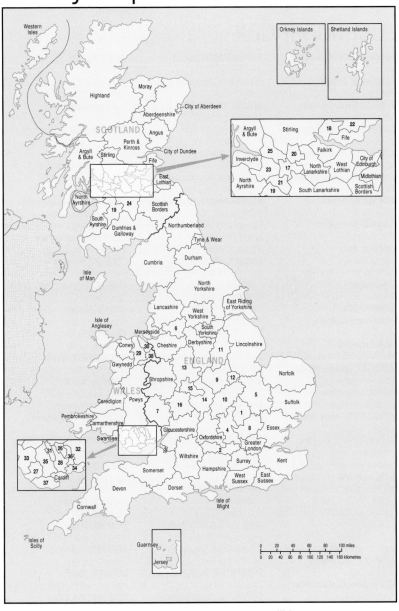

**England**

| | |
|---|---|
| 1 | Bedfordshire |
| 2 | Berkshire |
| 3 | Bristol |
| 4 | Buckinghamshire |
| 5 | Cambridgeshire |
| 6 | Greater Manchester |
| 7 | Herefordshire |
| 8 | Hertfordshire |
| 9 | Leicestershire |
| 10 | Northamptonshire |
| 11 | Nottinghamshire |
| 12 | Rutland |
| 13 | Staffordshire |
| 14 | Warwickshire |
| 15 | West Midlands |
| 16 | Worcestershire |

**Scotland**

| | |
|---|---|
| 17 | City of Glasgow |
| 18 | Clackmannanshire |
| 19 | East Ayrshire |
| 20 | East Dunbartonshire |
| 21 | East Renfrewshire |
| 22 | Perth & Kinross |
| 23 | Renfrewshire |
| 24 | South Lanarkshire |
| 25 | West Dunbartonshire |

**Wales**

| | |
|---|---|
| 26 | Blaenau Gwent |
| 27 | Bridgend |
| 28 | Caerphilly |
| 29 | Denbighshire |
| 30 | Flintshire |
| 31 | Merthyr Tydfil |
| 32 | Monmouthshire |
| 33 | Neath Port Talbot |
| 34 | Newport |
| 35 | Rhondda Cynon Taff |
| 36 | Torfaen |
| 37 | Vale of Glamorgan |
| 38 | Wrexham |

# Location Index

**ABERDEEN, City of Aberdeen**
Aberdeen Patio Hotel 270
**ALDEBURGH, Suffolk**
Wentworth Hotel 210
**ALDERLEY EDGE, Cheshire**
Alderley Edge Hotel 41
**ALDERMINSTER, Warwickshire**
Ettington Park Hotel 233
**ALFRISTON, East Sussex**
Deans Place 219
**ALNWICK, Northumberland**
White Swan Hotel 179
**AMBLESIDE, Cumbria**
Rothay Manor 56
**ANDOVER, Hampshire**
Esseborne Manor 112
**ASHFORD, Kent**
Eastwell Manor 131
**ASHFORD IN THE WATER, Derbyshire**
Riverside House Hotel 72
**AUCHENCAIRN, Dumfries & Galloway**
Balcary Bay Hotel 279
**BALA, Gwynedd**
Palé Hall Country House Hotel 322
**BANCHORY, Aberdeenshire**
Banchory Lodge Hotel 271
**BARTON, Lancashire**
Barton Grange Hotel 137
**BASINGSTOKE, Hampshire**
Audleys Wood 113
**BASSENTHWAITE, Cumbria**
Armathwaite Hall 57
Pheasant 58
**BATH, Somerset**
Bath Priory Hotel, Restaurant & Spa 197
Best Western The Cliffe Hotel 198
Dukes Hotel 199
Queensberry Hotel 200
Royal Crescent Hotel 201
**BETWS-Y-COED, Conwy**
Royal Oak Hotel 315
**BIGGAR, South Lanarkshire**
Shieldhill Castle 308
**BILDESTON, Suffolk**
Bildeston Crown 211
**BIRKENHEAD, Merseyside**
RiverHill Hotel 167
**BLACKWATERFOOT, North Ayrshire**
Best Western Kinloch Hotel 299
**BORROWDALE, Cumbria**
Borrowdale Gates Country House Hotel 59
**BOTLEY, Hampshire**
Macdonald Botley Park, Golf & Country Club 114

**BOURNEMOUTH, Dorset**
Best Western Chine Hotel 90
**BRACKNELL, Berkshire**
Coppid Beech 23
**BRAMPTON, Cumbria**
Farlam Hall Hotel 60
**BRANDS HATCH, Kent**
Thistle Brands Hatch 132
**BRISTOL, Bristol**
Mercure Brigstow Bristol 28
**BROADWAY, Worcestershire**
Barceló The Lygon Arms 242
**BROCKENHURST, Hampshire**
Balmer Lawn 115
Careys Manor Hotel 116
Whitley Ridge Hotel 117
Rhinefield House 118
**BRODICK, North Ayrshire**
Kilmichael Country House Hotel 301
**BRYHER, Cornwall & Isles of Scilly**
Hell Bay 44
**BUCKINGHAM, Buckinghamshire**
Villiers Hotel 30
**BUCKLAND, Gloucestershire**
Buckland Manor 101
**BUDE, Cornwall & Isles of Scilly**
Falcon Hotel 45
**BURFORD, Oxfordshire**
Bay Tree Hotel 186
Lamb Inn 186
**BURNHAM MARKET, Norfolk**
Hoste Arms Hotel 171
**BURRINGTON, Devon**
Northcote Manor 76
**BURTON UPON TRENT, Staffordshire**
Three Queens Hotel 206
**BURY ST EDMUNDS, Suffolk**
Best Western Priory Hotel 211
**CAERNARFON, Gwynedd**
Seiont Manor Hotel 323
**CAMBOURNE, Cambridgeshire**
Cambridge Belfry 34
**CAMBRIDGE, Cambridgeshire**
Arundel House Hotel 35
Best Western Gonville Hotel 37
Hotel Felix 37
**CARDIFF, Cardiff**
Park Plaza Cardiff 312
St David's Hotel & Spa 312
**CARMARTHEN, Carmarthenshire**
Ivy Bush Royal Hotel 313
**CHADDESLEY CORBETT, Worcestershire**
Brockencote Hall Country House Hotel 243

**CHAGFORD, Devon**
Gidleigh Park 77
Mill End Hotel 78
**CHARINGWORTH, Gloucestershire**
Charingworth Manor Hotel 102
**CHELTENHAM, Gloucestershire**
Charlton Kings Hotel 103
Greenway 104
**CHRISTCHURCH, Dorset**
Best Western Waterford Lodge Hotel 91
**CLEARWELL, Gloucestershire**
Tudor Farmhouse Hotel & Restaurant 105
**CLIMPING, West Sussex**
Bailiffscourt Hotel & Spa 225
**COLERNE, Wiltshire**
Lucknam Park 240
**CONNEL, Argyll & Bute**
Falls of Lora Hotel 272
**CONWY, Conwy**
Castle Hotel Conwy 316
**CRATHORNE, North Yorkshire**
Crathorne Hall Hotel 247
**CRICKHOWELL, Powys**
Gliffaes Country House Hotel 327
**CROMER, Norfolk**
Elderton Lodge Hotel & Langtry Restaurant 172
**CUCKFIELD, West Sussex**
Ockenden Manor 226
**DARLINGTON, Durham, County**
Headlam Hall 96
**DARTFORD, Kent**
Rowhill Grange Hotel & Utopia Spa 133
**DAWLISH, Devon**
Langstone Cliff Hotel 79
**DEDHAM, Essex**
Maison Talbooth 99
**DEGANWY, Conwy**
Quay Hotel & Spa 317
**DORKING, Surrey**
Mercure Burford Bridge Hotel 215
**DUNFERMLINE, Fife**
Best Western Keavil House Hotel 283
**EAST GRINSTEAD, West Sussex**
Gravetye Manor Hotel 227
**EAST KILBRIDE, South Lanarkshire**
Macdonald Crutherland House 309
**EASTBOURNE, East Sussex**
Grand Hotel 220
**EDINBURGH, City of Edinburgh**
Balmoral 280
Best Western Bruntsfield Hotel 281
Prestonfield 282

# Location Index

**EGHAM, Surrey**
Runnymede Hotel & Spa 216
**FALMOUTH, Cornwall & Isles of Scilly**
Falmouth Hotel 45
Green Lawns Hotel 46
Greenbank 47
**FOREST ROW, East Sussex**
Ashdown Park Hotel and Country Club 220
**FORT AUGUSTUS, Highland**
Lovat Arms Hotel 287
**FORT WILLIAM, Highland**
Inverlochy Castle Hotel 288
Moorings Hotel 289
**FRANKBY, Merseyside**
Hillbark 168
**GARSTANG, Lancashire**
Garstang Country Hotel & Golf Club 137
**GATWICK AIRPORT, West Sussex**
Langshott Manor 228
Sofitel London Gatwick 229
**GILLINGHAM, Dorset**
Stock Hill Country House Hotel & Restaurant 92
**GLASGOW, City of Glasgow**
ABode Hotel Glasgow 285
Hotel Du Vin at One Devonshire Gardens 286
**GRANGE-OVER-SANDS, Cumbria**
Clare House 61
**GRIMSTON, Norfolk**
Congham Hall Country House Hotel 173
**GULWORTHY, Devon**
Horn of Plenty 80
**HALIFAX, West Yorkshire**
Holdsworth House Hotel 257
**HARLECH, Gwynedd**
Maes y Neuadd Country House Hotel 324
**HARROGATE, North Yorkshire**
Rudding Park Hotel & Golf 248
**HARWICH, Essex**
Pier at Harwich 99
**HASLEMERE, Surrey**
Lythe Hill Hotel & Spa 217
**HATHERSAGE, Derbyshire**
Best Western George Hotel 73
**HELMSLEY, North Yorkshire**
Pheasant Hotel 248
**HEXHAM, Northumberland**
Langley Castle Hotel 180
**HINTLESHAM, Suffolk**
Hintlesham Hall Hotel 212
**HONITON, Devon**
Combe House Hotel & Restaurant 81
**HOWWOOD, Renfrewshire**
Bowfield Hotel & Country Club 304

**HUNSTANTON, Norfolk**
Caley Hall Hotel 174
**ILKLEY, West Yorkshire**
Best Western Rombalds Hotel & Restaurant 258
**ILSINGTON, Devon**
Ilsington Country House Hotel 81
**INVERGORDON, Highland**
Kincraig House Hotel 290
**INVERNESS, Highland**
Glenmoriston Town House Hotel 291
New Drumossie Hotel 292
**ISLEORNSAY, Highland**
Toravaig House Hotel 293
**KENDAL, Cumbria**
Best Western Castle Green Hotel in Kendal 62
**KESWICK, Cumbria**
Dale Head Hall Lakeside Hotel 63
Swinside Lodge 64
**KETTERING, Northamptonshire**
Rushton Hall 177
**KIDDERMINSTER, Worcestershire**
Granary Hotel & Restaurant 244
**KILCHRENAN, Argyll & Bute**
Ardanaiseig Hotel 272
Taychreggan Hotel 273
**KINCLAVEN, Perth & Kinross**
Ballathie House Hotel 301
**KINGHAM, Oxfordshire**
Mill House Hotel & Restaurant 187
**KINGSBRIDGE, Devon**
Buckland-Tout-Saints 82
**LAMPETER, Ceredigion**
Best Western Falcondale Mansion 314
**LANGAR, Nottinghamshire**
Langar Hall 182
**LANGHO, Lancashire**
Northcote Manor 138
**LEA MARSTON, Warwickshire**
Best Western Lea Marston Hotel & Leisure Complex 234
**LEDBURY, Herefordshire**
Feathers Hotel 123
**LEICESTER, Leicestershire**
Best Western Belmont House Hotel 142
**LENHAM, Kent**
Chilston Park Hotel 134
**LEYLAND, Lancashire**
Best Western Leyland Hotel 139
**LICHFIELD, Staffordshire**
Swinfen Hall Hotel 207
**LINCOLN, Lincolnshire**
Best Western Bentley Hotel & Leisure Club 145
**LLANARMON DYFFRYN CEIRIOG, Wrexham**
West Arms Hotel 330
**LLANDUDNO, Conwy**
Dunoon Hotel 318

Empire Hotel 319
Osborne House 319
St George's Hotel 320
St Tudno Hotel and Restaurant 321
**LLANGAMMARCH WELLS, Powys**
Lake Country House Hotel & Spa 328
**LLYSWEN, Powys**
Llangoed Hall 329
**LOCHINVER, Highland**
Inver Lodge Hotel 294
**LONDON NW1**
Landmark London 147
Melia White House 148
**LONDON NW2**
Crown Moran Hotel 149
**LONDON NW4**
Hendon Hall Hotel 150
**LONDON SE1**
London Bridge Hotel 151
London Marriott Hotel, County Hall 152
**LONDON SW1**
Cavendish London 152
Halkin Hotel 153
Mandarin Oriental Hyde Park 154
Sofitel St James London 155
**LONDON SW3**
Draycott Hotel 156
**LONDON SW7**
Bentley Kempinski Hotel 157
**LONDON W1**
Dorchester 158
Metropolitan 159
Millennium Hotel London Mayfair 160
Washington Mayfair Hotel 161
**LONDON W8**
Milestone Hotel & Apartments 162
Royal Garden Hotel 163
**LONDON WC1**
Jurys Great Russell Street 164
Renaissance Chancery Court 165
**LOWER SLAUGHTER, Gloucestershire**
Washbourne Court Hotel 106
**LUSS, Argyll & Bute**
Lodge on Loch Lomond Hotel 274
**LUTON, Bedfordshire**
Luton Hoo Hotel, Golf and Spa 21
**MALVERN, Worcestershire**
Cottage in the Wood Hotel 244
**MANCHESTER, Greater Manchester**
ABode Hotel Manchester 109
Midland Hotel 110
**MARKINGTON, North Yorkshire**
Hob Green Hotel 249
**MARLOW, Buckinghamshire**
Danesfield House Hotel & Spa 30
Macdonald Compleat Angler 31

# Location Index

**MARTOCK, Somerset**
Ash House Country Hotel 202
**MAWGAN PORTH,**
**Cornwall & Isles of Scilly**
Bedruthan Steps Hotel 47
**MAWNAN SMITH,**
**Cornwall & Isles of Scilly**
Meudon Hotel 48
**MELTON MOWBRAY,**
**Leicestershire**
Stapleford Park 143
**MIDHURST, West Sussex**
Spread Eagle Hotel and Spa 229
**MILFORD ON SEA, Hampshire**
Westover Hall Hotel 119
**MORETON-IN-MARSH,**
**Gloucestershire**
Manor House Hotel 107
**NEW MILTON, Hampshire**
Chewton Glen Hotel 120
**NEWARK-ON-TRENT,**
**Nottinghamshire**
Grange Hotel 183
**NEWBURY, Berkshire**
Donnington Valley Hotel & Spa 24
Vineyard at Stockcross 24
**NEWCASTLE UPON TYNE,**
**Tyne & Wear**
Vermont Hotel 231
**NEWICK, East Sussex**
Newick Park Hotel &
Country Estate 221
**NEWPORT, Newport**
Celtic Manor Resort 325
**NEWQUAY, Cornwall**
**& Isles of Scilly**
Headland Hotel 49
**NOTTINGHAM, Nottinghamshire**
Restaurant Sat Bains
with Rooms 184
**OAKHAM, Rutland**
Hambleton Hall 191
**OBAN, Argyll & Bute**
Manor House Hotel 275
**ORMSKIRK, Lancashire**
West Tower Country
House Hotel 140
**OSWESTRY, Shropshire**
Best Western Wynnstay Hotel 193
**OXFORD, Oxfordshire**
Westwood Country Hotel 188
**PEEBLES, Scottish Borders**
Castle Venlaw Hotel 305
Peebles Hotel Hydro 306
**PEMBROKE, Pembrokeshire**
Beggars Reach Hotel 326
**PITLOCHRY, Perth & Kinross**
Pine Trees Hotel 302
**POLPERRO, Cornwall**
**& Isles of Scilly**
Talland Bay Hotel 50

**PONTEFRACT, West Yorkshire**
Wentbridge House Hotel 258
**POOLE, Dorset**
Harbour Heights Hotel 93
Haven Hotel 93
Sandbanks Hotel 94
**POOLEWE, Highland**
Pool House Hotel 295
**PORT APPIN, Argyll & Bute**
Airds Hotel 276
**PORTREE, Highland**
Bosville Hotel 296
Cuillin Hills Hotel 297
**PORTSCATHO, Cornwall**
**& Isles of Scilly**
Driftwood 51
**PRESTBURY, Cheshire**
White House Manor Townhouse 42
**READING, Berkshire**
Novotel Reading Centre 25
**REDDITCH, Worcestershire**
Best Western Abbey Hotel 245
**REDRUTH, Cornwall**
**& Isles of Scilly**
Penventon Park Hotel 52
**ROSSINGTON, South Yorkshire**
Best Western Mount Pleasant 253
**ROSS-ON-WYE, Herefordshire**
Best Western Pengethley
Manor 123
**ROTHERWICK, Hampshire**
Tylney Hall Hotel 121
**ROWSLEY, Derbyshire**
Peacock at Rowsley 74
**ROYAL TUNBRIDGE WELLS, Kent**
Spa Hotel 135
**RYE, East Sussex**
George in Rye 222
**ST ALBANS, Hertfordshire**
Sopwell House 125
St Michael's Manor 126
**ST ANDREWS, Fife**
St Andrews Golf Hotel 284
**ST AUBIN, Jersey**
Somerville Hotel 264
**ST DAVID'S, Pembrokeshire**
Warpool Court Hotel 327
**ST FILLANS, Perth & Kinross**
Four Seasons Hotel 303
**ST HELIER, Jersey**
Club Hotel & Spa 265
**ST MARTIN, Guernsey**
La Barbarie Hotel 262
**ST PETER PORT, Guernsey**
Best Western Hotel de Havelet 263
**ST SAVIOUR, Jersey**
Longueville Manor Hotel 266
**SEAHAM, Durham, County**
Seaham Hall Hotel 97
**SHEFFIELD, South Yorkshire**
Best Western Mosborough Hall 254
Sheffield Park Hotel 255

Whitley Hall Hotel 256
**SHEPTON MALLET, Somerset**
Charlton House 202
**SHREWSBURY, Shropshire**
Prince Rupert Hotel 194
**SIDMOUTH, Devon**
Riviera Hotel 83
Westcliff Hotel 84
**SOUTHWOLD, Suffolk**
Swan Hotel 213
**STILTON, Cambridgeshire**
Bell Inn Hotel 38
**STOKE-ON-TRENT, Staffordshire**
Best Western Stoke-on-Trent
Moat House 208
**STRATFORD-UPON-AVON,**
**Warwickshire**
Menzies Welcombe Hotel Spa
and Golf Course 235
**STRONTIAN, Highland**
Kilcamb Lodge Hotel 298
**TAIN, Highland**
Glenmorangie Highland Home
at Cadboll 300
**TAPLOW, Buckinghamshire**
Cliveden 32
**TETBURY, Gloucestershire**
Calcot Manor 107
**TICEHURST, East Sussex**
Dale Hill Hotel & Golf Club 223
**TIGHNABRUAICH, Argyll & Bute**
An Lochan 277
**TITCHWELL, Norfolk**
Titchwell Manor Hotel 175
**TOBERMORY, Argyll & Bute**
Highland Cottage 278
**TORQUAY, Devon**
Corbyn Head Hotel &
Orchid Restaurant 85
Orestone Manor Hotel
& Restaurant 86
**TRESCO, Cornwall**
**& Isles of Scilly**
Island Hotel 53
**TRINITY, Jersey**
Water's Edge Hotel 267
**TROON, South Ayrshire**
Lochgreen House Hotel 307
**TYWARDREATH, Cornwall**
**& Isles of Scilly**
Trenython Manor Hotel and Spa 54
**VENTNOR, Isle of Wight**
Royal Hotel 128
**VERYAN, Cornwall**
**& Isles of Scilly**
Nare Hotel 54
**WALLASEY, Merseyside**
Grove House Hotel 169
**WALLINGFORD, Oxfordshire**
Springs Hotel & Golf Club 189
**WALSALL, West Midlands**
Fairlawns Hotel & Spa 238

# Location/Hotel Index

**WARWICK, Warwickshire**
Ardencote Manor Hotel, Country
    Club & Spa   236
**WATERMILLOCK, Cumbria**
Rampsbeck Country House Hotel  65
**WELLINGTON, Somerset**
Bindon Country House Hotel
    & Restaurant   203
**WETHERBY, West Yorkshire**
Wood Hall Hotel   259
**WINDERMERE, Cumbria**
Beech Hill Hotel   66
Gilpin Lodge Country House Hotel
    & Restaurant   67
Lindeth Howe Country House Hotel
    & Restaurant   68
Linthwaite House Hotel
    & Restaurant   68
Samling   69
**WINDSOR, Berkshire**
Sir Christopher Wren's House
    Hotel & Spa   26

**WISBECH, Cambridgeshire**
Crown Lodge Hotel   39
**WOODBURY, Devon**
Woodbury Park Hotel Golf
    & Country Club   87
**WOOLACOMBE, Devon**
Woolacombe Bay Hotel   88
**WORFIELD, Shropshire**
Old Vicarage Hotel   195
**WORKINGTON, Cumbria**
Washington Central Hotel   70
**YARMOUTH, Isle of Wight**
George Hotel   129
**YEOVIL, Somerset**
Lanes   204
**YORK, North Yorkshire**
Best Western Dean Court Hotel  250
Grange Hotel   251

# Hotel Index

**Aberdeen Patio Hotel**
ABERDEEN   270
**ABode Hotel Glasgow**
GLASGOW   285
**ABode Hotel Manchester**
MANCHESTER   109
**Airds Hotel**
PORT APPIN   276
**Alderley Edge Hotel**
ALDERLEY EDGE   41
**An Lochan**
TIGHNABRUAICH   277
**Ardanaiseig Hotel**
KILCHRENAN   272
**Ardencote Manor Hotel,**
  **Country Club & Spa**
WARWICK   236
**Armathwaite Hall**
BASSENTHWAITE   57
**Arundel House Hotel**
CAMBRIDGE   35
**Ash House Country Hotel**
MARTOCK   202
**Ashdown Park Hotel**
  **and Country Club**
FOREST ROW   220
**Audleys Wood**
BASINGSTOKE   113
**Bailiffscourt Hotel & Spa**
CLIMPING   225
**Balcary Bay Hotel**
AUCHENCAIRN   279
**Ballathie House Hotel**
KINCLAVEN   301
**Balmer Lawn**
BROCKENHURST   115
**Balmoral**
EDINBURGH   280

**Banchory Lodge Hotel**
BANCHORY   271
**Barceló The Lygon Arms**
BROADWAY   242
**Barton Grange Hotel** BARTON 137
**Bath Priory Hotel,**
  **Restaurant & Spa**
BATH   197
**Bay Tree Hotel**
BURFORD   186
**Bedruthan Steps Hotel**
MAWGAN PORTH   47
**Beech Hill Hotel**
WINDERMERE   66
**Beggars Reach Hotel**
PEMBROKE   326
**Bell Inn Hotel**
STILTON   38
**Bentley Kempinski Hotel**
LONDON SW7   157
**Best Western Abbey Hotel**
REDDITCH   245
**Best Western Belmont**
  **House Hotel**
LEICESTER   142
**Best Western Bentley Hotel**
  **& Leisure Club**
LINCOLN   145
**Best Western Bruntsfield Hotel**
EDINBURGH   281
**Best Western Castle Green**
  **Hotel in Kendal**
KENDAL   62
**Best Western Chine Hotel**
BOURNEMOUTH   90
**Best Western Dean Court H otel**
YORK   250

**Best Western Falcondale**
  **Mansion**
LAMPETER   314
**Best Western George Hotel**
HATHERSAGE   73
**Best Western Gonville Hotel**
CAMBRIDGE   37
**Best Western Hotel de Havelet**
ST PETER PORT   263
**Best Western Keavil**
  **House Hotel**
DUNFERMLINE   283
**Best Western Kinloch Hotel**
BLACKWATERFOOT   299
**Best Western Lea Marston**
  **Hotel & Leisure Complex**
LEA MARSTON   234
**Best Western Leyland Hotel**
LEYLAND   139
**Best Western Mosborough Hall**
SHEFFIELD   254
**Best Western Mount Pleasant**
ROSSINGTON   253
**Best Western Pengethley Manor**
ROSS-ON-WYE   123
**Best Western Priory Hotel** BURY
ST EDMUNDS   211
**Best Western Rombalds Hotel**
  **& Restaurant**
ILKLEY   258
**Best Western Stoke-on-Trent**
  **Moat House**
STOKE-ON-TRENT   208
**Best Western The Cliffe Hotel**
BATH   198
**Best Western Waterford**
  **Lodge Hotel**
CHRISTCHURCH   91

# Hotel Index

**Best Western Wynnstay Hotel**
OSWESTRY 193

**Bildeston Crown**
BILDESTON 211

**Bindon Country House Hotel & Restaurant**
WELLINGTON 203

**Borrowdale Gates Country House Hotel**
BORROWDALE 59

**Bosville Hotel**
PORTREE 296

**Bowfield Hotel & Country Club**
HOWWOOD 304

**Brockencote Hall Country House Hotel**
CHADDESLEY CORBETT 243

**Buckland Manor**
BUCKLAND 101

**Buckland-Tout-Saints**
KINGSBRIDGE 82

**Calcot Manor**
TETBURY 107

**Caley Hall Hotel**
HUNSTANTON 174

**Cambridge Belfry**
CAMBOURNE 34

**Careys Manor Hotel**
BROCKENHURST 116

**Castle Hotel Conwy**
CONWY 316

**Castle Venlaw Hotel**
PEEBLES 305

**Cavendish London**
LONDON SW1 152

**Celtic Manor Resort**
NEWPORT 325

**Charingworth Manor Hotel**
CHARINGWORTH 102

**Charlton House**
SHEPTON MALLET 202

**Charlton Kings Hotel**
CHELTENHAM 103

**Chewton Glen Hote**
NEW MILTON 120

**Chilston Park Hotel**
LENHAM 134

**Clare House**
GRANGE-OVER-SANDS 61

**Cliveden**
TAPLOW 32

**Club Hotel & Spa**
ST HELIER 265

**Combe House Hotel & Restaurant**
HONITON 81

**Congham Hall Country House Hotel**
GRIMSTON 173

**Coppid Beech**
BRACKNELL 23

**Corbyn Head Hotel & Orchid Restaurant**
TORQUAY 85

**Cottage in the Wood Hotel**
MALVERN 244

**Crathorne Hall Hotel**
CRATHORNE 247

**Crown Lodge Hotel**
WISBECH 39

**Crown Moran Hotel**
LONDON NW2 149

**Cuillin Hills Hotel**
PORTREE 297

**Dale Head Hall Lakeside Hotel**
KESWICK 63

**Dale Hill Hotel & Golf Club**
TICEHURST 223

**Danesfield House Hotel & Spa**
MARLOW 30

**Deans Place**
ALFRISTON 219

**Donnington Valley Hotel & Spa**
NEWBURY 24

**Dorchester**
LONDON W1 158

**Draycott Hotel**
LONDON SW3 156

**Driftwood**
PORTSCATHO 51

**Dukes Hotel**
BATH 199

**Dunoon Hotel**
LLANDUDNO 318

**Eastwell Manor**
ASHFORD 131

**Elderton Lodge Hotel & Langtry Restaurant**
CROMER 172

**Empire Hotel**
LLANDUDNO 319

**Esseborne Manor**
ANDOVER 112

**Ettington Park Hotel**
ALDERMINSTER 233

**Fairlawns Hotel & Spa**
WALSALL 238

**Falcon Hotel**
BUDE 45

**Falls of Lora Hotel**
CONNEL 272

**Falmouth Hotel**
FALMOUTH 45

**Farlam Hall Hotel**
BRAMPTON 60

**Feathers Hotel**
LEDBURY 123

**Four Seasons Hotel**
ST FILLANS 303

**Garstang Country Hotel & Golf Club**
GARSTANG 137

**George Hotel**
YARMOUTH 129

**George in Rye**
RYE 222

**Gidleigh Park**
CHAGFORD 77

**Gilpin Lodge Country House Hotel & Restaurant**
WINDERMERE 67

**Glenmorangie Highland Home at Cadboll**
TAIN 300

**Glenmoriston Town House Hotel**
INVERNESS 291

**Gliffaes Country House Hotel**
CRICKHOWELL 327

**Granary Hotel & Restaurant**
KIDDERMINSTER 244

**Grand Hotel**
EASTBOURNE 220

**Grange Hotel**
NEWARK-ON-TRENT 183

**Grange Hotel**
YORK 251

**Gravetye Manor Hotel**
EAST GRINSTEAD 227

**Green Lawns Hotel**
FALMOUTH 46

**Greenbank**
FALMOUTH 47

**Greenway**
CHELTENHAM 104

**Grove House Hotel**
WALLASEY 169

**Halkin Hotel**
LONDON SW1 153

**Hambleton Hall**
OAKHAM 191

**Harbour Heights Hotel**
POOLE 93

**Haven Hotel**
POOLE 93

**Headlam Hall**
DARLINGTON 96

**Headland Hotel**
NEWQUAY 49

**Hell Bay**
BRYHER 44

**Hendon Hall Hotel**
LONDON NW4 150

**Highland Cottage**
TOBERMORY 278

**Hillbark**
FRANKBY 168

**Hintlesham Hall Hotel**
HINTLESHAM 212

**Hob Green Hotel**
MARKINGTON 249

**Holdsworth House Hotel**
HALIFAX 257

**Horn of Plenty**
GULWORTHY 80

**Hoste Arms Hotel**
BURNHAM MARKET 171

**Hotel Du Vin at One Devonshire Gardens**
GLASGOW 286

**Hotel Felix**
CAMBRIDGE 37

**Ilsington Country House Hotel**
ILSINGTON 81

**Inver Lodge Hotel**
LOCHINVER 294

**Inverlochy Castle Hotel**
FORT WILLIAM 288

**Island Hotel**
TRESCO 53

**Ivy Bush Royal Hotel**
CARMARTHEN 313

**Jurys Great Russell Street**
LONDON WC1 164

**Kilcamb Lodge Hotel**
STRONTIAN 298

**Kilmichael Country House Hotel**
BRODICK 301

**Kincraig House Hotel**
INVERGORDON 290

# Hotel Index

La Barbarie Hotel
ST MARTIN 262
Lake Country House Hotel & Spa
LLANGAMMARCH WELLS 328
Lamb Inn
BURFORD 186
Landmark London
LONDON NW1 147
Lanes
YEOVIL 204
Langar Hall
LANGAR 182
Langley Castle Hotel
HEXHAM 180
Langshott Manor
GATWICK AIRPORT 228
Langstone Cliff Hotel
DAWLISH 79
Lindeth Howe Country
  House Hotel & Restaurant
WINDERMERE 68
Linthwaite House Hotel
  & Restaurant
WINDERMERE 68
Llangoed Hall
LLYSWEN 329
Lochgreen House Hotel
TROON 307
Lodge on Loch Lomond Hotel
LUSS 274
London Bridge Hotel
LONDON SE1 151
London Marriott Hotel,
  County Hall
LONDON SE1 152
Longueville Manor Hotel
ST SAVIOUR 266
Lovat Arms Hotel
FORT AUGUSTUS 287
Lucknam Park
COLERNE 240
Luton Hoo Hotel, Golf and Spa
LUTON 21
Lythe Hill Hotel & Spa
HASLEMERE 217
Macdonald Botley Park, Golf &
  Country Club
BOTLEY 114
Macdonald Compleat Angler
MARLOW 31
Macdonald Crutherland House
EAST KILBRIDE 309
Maes y Neuadd Country
  House Hotel
HARLECH 324
Maison Talbooth
DEDHAM 99
Mandarin Oriental Hyde Park
LONDON SW1 154
Manor House Hotel
MORETON-IN-MARSH 107
Manor House Hotel
OBAN 275
Melia White House
LONDON NW1 148
Menzies Welcombe Hotel Spa
  and Golf Course
STRATFORD-UPON-AVON 235
Mercure Brigstow Bristol
BRISTOL 28

Mercure Burford Bridge Hotel
DORKING 215
Metropolitan
LONDON W1 159
Meudon Hotel
MAWNAN SMITH 48
Midland Hotel
MANCHESTER 110
Milestone Hotel & Apartments
LONDON W8 162
Mill End Hotel CHAGFORD 78
Mill House Hotel & Restaurant
KINGHAM 187
Millennium Hotel London Mayfair
LONDON W1 160
Moorings Hotel
FORT WILLIAM 289
Nare Hotel
VERYAN 54
New Drumossie Hotel
INVERNESS 292
Newick Park Hotel &
  Country Estate
NEWICK 221
Northcote Manor
BURRINGTON 76
Northcote Manor
LANGHO 138
Novotel Reading Centre
READING 25
Ockenden Manor
CUCKFIELD 226
Old Vicarage Hotel
WORFIELD 195
Orestone Manor Hotel &
  Restaurant
TORQUAY 86
Osborne House
LLANDUDNO 319
Palé Hall Country House Hotel
BALA 322
Park Plaza Cardiff
CARDIFF 312
Peacock at Rowsley
ROWSLEY 74
Peebles Hotel Hydro
PEEBLES 306
Penventon Park Hotel
REDRUTH 52
Pheasant
BASSENTHWAITE 58
Pheasant Hotel
HELMSLEY 248
Pier at Harwich
HARWICH 99
Pine Trees Hotel
PITLOCHRY 302
Pool House Hotel
POOLEWE 295
Prestonfield
EDINBURGH 282
Prince Rupert Hotel
SHREWSBURY 194
Quay Hotel & Spa
DEGANWY 317
Queensberry Hotel
BATH 200
Rampsbeck Country House Hotel
WATERMILLOCK 65

Renaissance Chancery Court
LONDON WC1 165
Restaurant Sat Bains
  with Rooms
NOTTINGHAM 184
Rhinefield House
BROCKENHURST 118
RiverHill Hotel
BIRKENHEAD 167
Riverside House Hotel
ASHFORD IN THE WATER 72
Riviera Hotel
SIDMOUTH 83
Rothay Manor
AMBLESIDE 56
Rowhill Grange Hotel &
  Utopia Spa
DARTFORD 133
Royal Crescent Hotel
BATH 201
Royal Garden Hotel
LONDON W8 163
Royal Hotel
VENTNOR 128
Royal Oak Hotel
BETWS-Y-COED 315
Rudding Park Hotel & Golf
HARROGATE 248
Runnymede Hotel & Spa
EGHAM 216
Rushton Hall
KETTERING 177
St Andrews Golf Hotel ST
ANDREWS 284
St David's Hotel & Spa
CARDIFF 312
St George's Hotel
LLANDUDNO 320
St Michael's Manor
ST ALBANS 126
St Tudno Hotel and Restaurant
LLANDUDNO 321
Samling
WINDERMERE 69
Sandbanks Hotel
POOLE 94
Seaham Hall Hotel
SEAHAM 97
Seiont Manor Hotel
CAERNARFON 323
Sheffield Park Hotel
SHEFFIELD 255
Shieldhill Castle
BIGGAR 308
Sir Christopher Wren's House
  Hotel & Spa
WINDSOR 26
Sofitel London Gatwick
GATWICK AIRPORT 229
Sofitel St James London
LONDON SW1 155
Somerville Hotel
ST AUBIN 264
Sopwell House
ST ALBANS 125
Spa Hotel
ROYAL TUNBRIDGE WELLS 135
Spread Eagle Hotel and Spa
MIDHURST 229

# Hotel Index

**Springs Hotel & Golf Club**
WALLINGFORD 189
**Stapleford Park** MELTON
MOWBRAY 143
**Stock Hill Country House
Hotel & Restaurant**
GILLINGHAM 92
**Swan Hotel**
SOUTHWOLD 213
**Swinfen Hall Hotel**
LICHFIELD 207
**Swinside Lodge**
KESWICK 64
**Talland Bay Hotel**
POLPERRO 50
**Taychreggan Hotel**
KILCHRENAN 273
**Thistle Brands Hatch**
BRANDS HATCH 132
**Three Queens Hotel**
BURTON UPON TRENT 206
**Titchwell Manor Hotel**
TITCHWELL 175
**Toravaig House Hotel**
ISLE ORNSAY 293

**Trenython Manor Hotel
and Spa**
TYWARDREATH 54
**Tudor Farmhouse Hotel
& Restaurant**
CLEARWELL 105
**Tylney Hall Hotel**
ROTHERWICK 121
**Vermont Hotel**
NEWCASTLE UPON TYNE 231
**Villiers Hotel**
BUCKINGHAM 30
**Vineyard at Stockcross**
NEWBURY 24
**Warpool Court Hotel**
ST DAVID'S 327
**Washbourne Court Hotel**
LOWER SLAUGHTER 106
**Washington Central Hotel**
WORKINGTON 70
**Washington Mayfair Hotel**
LONDON W1 161
**Water's Edge Hotel**
TRINITY 267
**Wentbridge House Hotel**
PONTEFRACT 258

**Wentworth Hotel**
ALDEBURGH 210
**West Arms Hotel**
LLANARMON DYFFRYN CEIRIOG 330
**West Tower Country House Hotel**
ORMSKIRK 140
**Westcliff Hotel**
SIDMOUTH 84
**Westover Hall Hotel**
MILFORD ON SEA 119
**Westwood Country Hotel**
OXFORD 188
**White House Manor Townhouse**
PRESTBURY 42
**White Swan Hotel**
ALNWICK 179
**Whitley Hall Hotel**
SHEFFIELD 256
**Whitley Ridge Hotel**
BROCKENHURST 117
**Wood Hall Hotel**
WETHERBY 259
**Woodbury Park Hotel Golf
& Country Club**
WOODBURY 87
**Woolacombe Bay Hotel**
WOOLACOMBE 88

The Automobile Association would like to thank the following photographers, companies and picture libraries for their assistance in the preparation of this book.

Abbreviations for the picture credits are as follows: (t) top; (b) bottom; (l) left; (r) right; (AA) AA World Travel Library.

4 AA/L Dunmire; 5 AA/N Jenkins; 9 AA/J Smith; 10 AA/J Smith; 11 Imagestate; 17 Stockbyte; 18 AA/T Mackie; 20 AA/D Forss; 22 AA/M Birkitt; 27 AA/S L Day; 29 AA/C Jones; 32 AA/J A Tims; 33 AA/C Coe; 36 AA/C Coe; 39 AA/C Coe; 40 AA/A Tryner; 41 AA/A J Hopkins; 43 AA/J Wood; 55 AA/P Bennett; 56 AA/T Mackie; 59 AA/C Lees; 61 AA/E A Bowness; 69 AA/A Mockford & N Bonetti; 71 AA/P Baker; 75 AA/C Jones; 76 AA/N Hicks; 78 AA/A Lawson; 86 AA/N Hicks; 89 AA/C Jones; 90 AA/P Enticknap; 94 AA/A Burton; 95 AA/G Rowatt; 97 AA/L Whitwam; 98 AA/J Miller; 100 AA/D Hall; 101 AA/S L Day; 103 AA/H Palmer; 108 AA/C Molyneux; 109 AA/S L Day; 111 AA/A Burton; 113 AA/D Croucher; 119 AA/A J Hopkins; 121 AA/D Croucher; 122 AA/H Palmer; 125 AA/M Birkitt; 127 AA/D Forss; 128 AA/S McBride; 130 AA/J Miller; 132 AA/S & O Mathews; 136 AA/J Miller; 140 AA/S L Day; 141 AA/R Newton; 142 AA/P Baker; 144 AA/T Mackie; 146 AA/W Voysey; 147 AA/S McBride; 150 AA/S McBride; 164 AA/G Wrona; 166 AA/S L Day; 167 AA/S L Day; 169 AA/S L Day; 170 AA/T Mackie; 171 AA/T Mackie; 173 AA/L Whitwam; 176 AA/M Birkitt; 178 AA/C Lees; 181 AA/M Birkitt; 182 AA/R Newton; 185 AA; 190 AA/M Birkitt; 192 AA/M Hayward; 195 AA/C Jones; 196 AA/S L Day; 198 AA/S L Day; 203 AA/S L Day; 205 AA/P Baker; 206 AA/J Welsh; 208 AA/R Surman; 209 AA/T Mackie; 213 AA/T Mackie; 214 AA/D Forss; 218 AA/J Miller; 224 AA; 227 AA/D Forss; 230 AA/R Coulam; 232 AA/P Baker; 234 AA/F Stephenson; 237 AA/J Welsh; 238 AA/P Baker; 239 AA/S & O Mathews; 240 AA/S L Day; 241 AA/M Moody; 245 AA/F Stephenson; 246 AA; 251 AA/L Whitwam; 255 AA/A J Hopkins; 256 AA/P Wilson; 260 AA/W Voysey; 268 AA/J Carnie; 275 AA/P Sharpe; 277 AA/D Corrance; 284 AA/S J Whitehorne; 286 AA/J Smith; 289 AA/J Carnie; 291 AA/S L Day; 294 AA/J Henderson; 298 AA/K Paterson; 306 AA/J Beazley; 308 AA/S Anderson; 310 AA/P Aithie; 313 AA/N Jenkins; 317 AA/I Burgum; 322 AA.

Every effort has been made to trace the copyright holders, and we apologise in advance for any accidental errors. We would be happy to apply the corrections in the following edition of this publication.